Property is arguably the foundational issue in legal and political philosophy. Billy Christmas insightfully illuminates this foundational issue by elaborating a radical liberal – libertarian – theory of property. This provocative book will surely spur controversy and deepen understanding by showing how a libertarian account of property rights can address the perennial concerns of libertarianism's critics while grounding robust safeguards for autonomy and flourishing.

– *Gary Chartier, La Sierra University, USA*

This book is the first serious attempt to combine a right-libertarian theory of individual private property with a solid theory of other forms of property, such as collective, public, and common property. It makes for a much more plausible and humane theory of property.

– *Karl Widerquist, Georgetown University-Qatar*

Property and Justice

This book gives an account of a full spectrum of property rights and their relationship to individual liberty. It shows that a purely deontological approach to justice can deal with the most complex questions regarding the property system. Moreover, the author considers the economic, ecological, and technological complexities of our real-world property systems. The result is a more conceptually sound account of natural rights and the property system they demand.

If we think that liberty should be at the centre of justice, what does that mean for the property system? Economists and lawyers widely agree that a property system must be composed of many different types of property: the kind of private ownership one has over one's person and immediate possessions, as well as the kinds of common ownership we each have in our local streets, as well as many more. However, theories of property and justice have not given anything approaching an adequate account of the relationship between liberty and any other form of property other than private ownership. It is often thought that a basic commitment to liberty cannot really tell us how to arrange the major complexities of the property system, which diverge from simple private ownership.

Property and Justice demonstrates how philosophical rigour coupled with interdisciplinary engagement enables us to think clearly about how to deal with real-world problems. It will be of interest to political philosophers, political theorists, and legal theorists working on property rights and justice.

Billy Christmas is Lecturer in Political Theory at King's College London in the Department of Political Economy, where he is also PPE Programme Director. As a philosopher, his research interests lie in Rights, Property, and Political Authority. He has previously published articles in journals such as *The Journal of Politics*, *Economics and Philosophy*, and *The Philosophical Quarterly*.

Political Philosophy for the Real World
Edited by Jason F. Brennan
Georgetown University

Unequivocal Justice
Christopher Freiman

Justice and the Meritocratic State
Thomas Mulligan

Unjust Borders
Individuals and the Ethics of Immigration
Javier S. Hidalgo

Economic Liberties and Human Rights
Edited by Jahel Queralt and Bas van der Vossen

Commutative Justice
A Liberal Theory of Just Exchange
Carl David Mildenberger

Property and Justice
A Liberal Theory of Natural Rights
Billy Christmas

For more information about this series, please visit: www.routledge.com/Political-Philosophy-for-the-Real-World/book-series/PPRW

Property and Justice

A Liberal Theory of Natural Rights

Billy Christmas

Routledge
Taylor & Francis Group
NEW YORK AND LONDON

First published 2021
by Routledge
52 Vanderbilt Avenue, New York, NY 10017

and by Routledge
2 Park Square, Milton Park, Abingdon, Oxon, OX14 4RN

Routledge is an imprint of the Taylor & Francis Group, an informa business

Library of Congress Cataloging-in-Publication Data
A catalog record for this book has been requested

ISBN: 978-0-367-27516-7 (hbk)
ISBN: 978-0-367-75266-8 (pbk)
ISBN: 978-0-429-29725-0 (ebk)

Typeset in Sabon
by Apex CoVantage, LLC

Contents

Epigraph

The keys lay on his desk
The wallet lay beside
Framed by all the other things
He'd slowly cast aside
I can't remember seeing it
And I don't remember when
He lost his sense of ownership
I write now with his pen
Abandoned on his desk
Where the wallet lay beside
Never given nor possessed
Just orphaned by his demise

Tom Mayman

Acknowledgements

This book is the culmination of work that I began as an undergraduate in philosophy at the University of Manchester when I decided to write my dissertation on the left-libertarianism of Hillel Steiner and Michael Otsuka. At the time, I liked the idea of making natural rights libertarianism more left-wing, but I did not like the idea of marrying it with distributive egalitarianism. The work I did on that dissertation, continued during the early stages of my Ph.D. (also at Manchester), eventually led me to the conclusion that if libertarianism is a left-wing creed, its leftism is not born directly out of clarifying the conceptual content and structure of our rights, but rather in what comes before and after our rights. Namely, the kinds of commitments that lead us to believe we each have the same right to be free and the kinds of socio-economic patterning we can empirically expect from the institutionalisation of these rights. The work to be done, I came to believe, on the rights themselves was not to show that they were somehow left-wing rather than right-wing but to show that they were actually coherent at all. My dissatisfaction with the left-libertarian account of property acquisition soon led me to realise that, problematic though it is, it is a symptom of a prior problem – that putative "right"-libertarians have not persuasively demonstrated the relationship between our original right to be free and the kinds of property they think are justified in virtue thereof. I took this problem to be the one that held back liberal approaches to natural rights generally, and therefore it was something to give my attention to. What I found was that the preoccupation with private property was a mistaken one, but not one which should lead us into distributive egalitarianism.

Although this book is something that I undertook to create, the ideas in it more meaningfully represent something I discovered. It is what I regard as the kernel of truth in all the previous attempts to understand natural rights and property. That journey of discovery was a long one, so there are many people to thank.

First, there are those who supported me in one way or another in pursuing and ultimately completing my Ph.D. Graham Stevens gave me tremendous encouragement to carry on when the application process had set me back, and Christian Schemmel and John O'Neill provided masses of ongoing help and support throughout the Ph.D. as my supervisors, as well as Miriam Ronzoni while John was on sabbatical in my first year. Liam Shields and James Pattison provided invaluable annual reviews of my progressing thesis. Hillel Steiner and Eric Mack graciously agreed to examine my Ph.D. and both provided a steady stream of incredibly helpful advice and argument. My fellow Ph.D. students during my time at Manchester were a great support, as well as all the members and participants of MANCEPT. I'm very thankful to the University of Manchester's School of Social Sciences for awarding be a Studentship for the duration of my Ph.D. I am also eternally grateful to the Institute for Humane Studies for providing financial support and an extended global network of scholars to develop my ideas with. I also thank the Charles Koch Foundation for the grant they awarded me to support the completion of my Ph.D.

Gary Chartier, Jason Lee Byas, and Cory Massimino all strongly encouraged me to transform the work I had done for my thesis into a monograph back when I was quite ambivalent about the idea. David Schmidtz, Adam Tebble, and Carmen Pavel all provided detailed advice and encouragement in the process of turning a thesis into a monograph. I am also very grateful to Ralf Bader and Bas van der Vossen for helpful discussions of property and rights over the years. Work on the book began during my Fellowship at the New York University School of Law under the mentorship of Richard Epstein and Mario Rizzo. My fellow Classical Liberal Institute post-docs were a constant sounding wall, as were members of the Colloquium on Market Institutions and Economic Processes. Nick Cowen in particular must have heard me present umpteen different articulations of the core positions defended in this book. The book represents a total restatement and partial revision of the view developed in my thesis; none of the original material is reused. Indeed, one part of the thesis was scrapped altogether from the book project due to Eric Mack's generously long, written rebuttal of my account of property abandonment.

I thank the journals that published my work and the reviewers who reviewed it during the period between my Ph.D. and this book's publication, all of which represent very round-about rehearsals of this statement of my view of property and justice. Those journals are *Environmental Politics, Moral Philosophy and Politics, Raisons Politiques, The Philosophy Quarterly, Economics and Philosophy, Res Publica*, and *The Journal of Politics*. Though no material from any of those articles was used in the book, they all represent fragmentary attempts to shine light at certain angles upon the overarching thesis. I therefore also thank the audiences at too many conferences, workshops, and seminars to mention by name at which versions of these works were presented. I thank my colleagues in the Department of Political Economy at King's College London for their comments on my most recent (and final) presentation of this view at the departmental seminar at the end of 2019. I am very grateful for a grant from the Templeton Foundation in relation the Ideal of Self-Governance project headed by Mark Pennington with Sam De Canio, to which Chapter 4 of this book contributes.

Although I have mentioned their names already, special thanks are due to Hillel Steiner, Mark Pennington, David Schmidtz, Richard Epstein, and Mario Rizzo for the general support they have given me in my academic career hitherto. I would have been truly lucky to have had only one such inspiring and supportive mentor.

For topical inspiration I thank John Salter, without whom I may have never read and understood the work of Hugo Grotius, and also Hillel Steiner and Eric Mack (again) whose bodies of work were consumed many times over as I meandered towards my own conclusions. I can imagine how different this book would be without any one of the people who inspired and helped it along the way. But I cannot imagine that I would have written it all if I had not made the acquaintance of Roderick Long and his vast and deeply generative writings on rights, and all things adjacent.

Finally, I thank my family and friends.

Thank you, all.

Introduction

Property and Justice

This book develops and defends an account of justice as property. The elementary particles of justice are individual rights, and those rights, in turn, pertain to particular uses of external objects or spaces at particular times. Importantly, those rights are *natural* rights, meaning that they exist in virtue of our humanity, which is a natural fact rather than an artificial construction or human contrivance. Property rights are simply particularisations of one's right to be free. When one respects the property rights of a person, one respects her freedom. As such, this account reflects a tradition that has grown out of the proto-liberal early modern protestant natural law tradition identifiable with Hugo Grotius (1583–1645), John Locke (1632–1704), and Immanuel Kant (1724–1804). Contemporary defenders of this view are typically referred to as *libertarian*,[1] most prominent among whom are Murray Rothbard, Robert Nozick, Hillel Steiner, and Eric Mack. This is not a historical enquiry into the development of those theories. Rather, the view will be conceptually built from the ground up with considerable help from these and many other scholars. In many ways, the view is a significant departure from those theories; nonetheless, I take myself to be making a contribution to, rather than merely be a critique of, that tradition.

The first significant departure – at least, from those early modern thinkers – is that the account of rights that I develop is not taken to be, in a discursive sense, the building blocks of a theory of *government*. The end-goal in sight is not the defence of any particular kind of political regime. The rights that I defend are claims about the moral status of social relations that bear directly between persons.[2] I do believe that these normative claims should be used, inter alia, to build any plausible theory of just or legitimate government or ideal of political society. But I do not have any such ideal in mind as I make the arguments. The claims made in these pages should not be imagined to be susceptible to straightforward invocation in the defence of any public policy platform. In this book, I remain agnostic[3] as to how these rights should be institutionally created, enforced, or interpreted. However, I will of course have much to say about the their status as original or acquired, their enforceability, and the ontology of their interpretation.

The second departure is in explicitly pivoting away from taking *private property* to be the fundamental explanandum in a theory of property and justice. The presupposition – albeit, not *totally* without support – that private ownership is the most basic notion of property rights has created problems internal to theories of property and justice, as well as problems in the reception of its theories. The internal problems revolve around the fact that there is not always a robust connection between an individual's right to be free and a right to private property. Though I argue that freedom must sometimes be particularised as something akin to private ownership, there is by no means any a priori assumption of such always or even typically being the case.

This dovetails with the third significant departure. The theory of original acquisition – how objects not specifically included in any person's property rights can come to be so – has a very different structure. In the typical view, one not only has some right to freedom, but one also has a partially distinct right to acquire property. This right is then checked by another principle, invariably referred to as the *proviso*, which places a limit to how much one can acquire, the circumstances under which one can acquire, etc. The view developed here is more austere. And in its parsimony I think lies its plausibility. Acquisition only ever takes place as an application of one's basic right to be free. One's acquired rights are therefore automatically compatible with everyone else's rights, and there is no need (nor space) for a proviso. What this means is that there is an inbuilt guarantee that one's property rights – whatever they are – are truly a particularisation of one's right to freedom. This makes for a more plausible theory of original acquisition, where the leap from freedom to private ownership is typically very flimsy.

My hope is that I present a plausible alternative to the most prominent views in the property and justice literature: left-libertarianism, right-libertarianism, Kantian statism, contractualism, and rule-consequentialism. Left-libertarianism follows Nozick in ignoring the need for a robust principle of original acquisition and instead understands all the action to take place within the proviso. Private property is justified so long as we all have an equal share. Right-libertarians believe that all property must be private property, yet make no sufficiently strong connection between individual freedom and that form of property. Kantian statism argues that there is no natural right to property; we must establish political institutions before property rights have any normative force, and natural justice therefore cannot make as strong or as direct normative demands of the "actually existing" legal system, as it can according to libertarians. Contractualists (as I perhaps clumsily refer to them) implicitly not only believe something similar to Kantian statists regarding the existential dependence of justice on the state, but also invoke contractualist procedures for establishing the just distribution of property. The most pre-eminent example of this is John Rawls's "original position" device.[4] Rule-consequentialists deny that any deontological principle such as a right to freedom can handle the difficult work of fine-tuning a property system, and for that we need cost–benefit analysis and some impersonal measure of human welfare as our yardstick. While the view defended here countenances a natural right to property and denies that a state or equality of outcome is required to justify private property, the view is not an example of right-libertarianism, since on that view, all property must be private. However, it is similar to both versions of libertarianism in that it supports natural property rights that are historically vindicated by human actions and constitute a standard against which the justice of proposed or actually existing regulative conventions are judged. In this sense, they are pre-political in that no actual or hypothetical political deliberation is necessary to make their normative demands true.

Original Acquisition: Connecting Property to Personhood

Robert Nozick analyses this view of justice as a *historical entitlement* theory which he presents in contradistinction to the view of Rawls which he parses as an *end-result* theory.[5] Nozick's purpose was to present an internal critique to prominent notions of distributive justice. Rawls believed that justice could demand a particular arrangement of resource holdings without consequence to liberty. Namely, that liberty was consistent with government legally (and therefore, coercively) structuring the economy so that inequality in access to resources was only permitted to the extent that it generated benefits for those with least access to resources.[6] Nozick's contribution was not to reject the concept of distributive justice tout court but rather to argue that any conception of distributive justice that did not permit alterations to the pattern of holdings made between consenting adults was not a conception that was consistent with liberty. Individuals may choose to transfer their property to others in ways which upsets the overall pattern demanded by Rawls's principle, but respecting their liberty to do so requires not intervening to either stop, reverse, or otherwise alter the transaction.[7]

At the heart of this view is the idea that consent is the ultimate engine that powers and generates normative change in society and the economy.[8] Historical entitlement theory says that the justice of any given socio-economic arrangement, including but not limited to the distribution of income, is strictly determined by whether or not it came about through *just steps* or, in other words, consensual transactions (contracts, agreements, exchanges, etc.)[9]

But how do we know whose consent is required to determine the disposition of any given holding? What connects a person to a holding in such a way that renders *her* the agent whose consent needs to be acquired?

It is intuitively plausible that transfers be made consensually and that those that have occurred non-consensually be rectified, but a principle is needed to show who "starts out" with which holdings, so as to determine which departures from which must be consensual.[10] Nozick was aware of this, which is why alongside his principles of justice in transfer and rectification he also supported a principle of justice in acquisition. The question of original acquisition is also one that Grotius, Locke, and Kant considered carefully.

The question of original acquisition is often cast as one with little, if any, relevance to us today. Katharina Nieswandt argues that it cannot help us understand justice in property in a developed capitalist economy and is only of relevance in the heuristic of "frontier town."[11] In most societies there are few, if any, resources that are legally treated as unowned. Everything that anyone might want to use is already subsumed within someone's property rights, most importantly in the means of production. Terms of access to means of production, that is natural resources that have already been transformed into capital through human action within a system of legal constraints, is the fundamental question of property and justice that we face. In a similar vein, Dan Moller argues that since almost all value creation today occurs through the exchange of *services* rather than through the discovery of natural resources, any story about how tangible objects come to be anyone's property bears little import for how we ought to structure property relations, since they only negligibly determine the distribution of "value" that is created in the economy.[12]

I think that such views misconstrue what a theory of original acquisition is for. The normative role of a theory of original acquisition need not be to find out how everything could have started off justly to try to work out the extent to which we have converged with or diverged from that over time. Rather, it is to establish a relationship between personhood and property. If we are bound by justice to respect each person's right to freedom, a plausible theory of original acquisition will tell us that respecting legitimately acquired property is how we do that. It provides a connection between freedom and property that we need if we are to understand freedom or justice through the lens of property whatsoever.

An essential question then is whether the principle of original acquisition is plausible – does it present good reason to think that respect for a person's putative property right constitutes respect for that person in the way demanded by justice? Within a broadly liberal understanding, an affirmative answer will need to show how a person's right to freedom entails that they have this particular property right.

Nozick's critics often argue that his treatment of liberty here just presupposes a set of rights that includes property.[13] Rothbard has received similar criticism for putatively presupposing that the violation of property rights is straightforwardly a type of aggression against persons.[14] Connecting property rights to personal freedom is something which has not been plausibly done and widely agreed to be the weak link that breaks down such theories.[15]

Beyond Private Property

"Property" tends to have an equivocal meaning. Sometimes we use it broadly to refer to the social relations regarding access to and use of physical objects; as Henry Smith calls it "the law of things."[16] Other times, however, we have a very particular notion in mind: what Tony Honoré called the "full, liberal" sense of private ownership.[17] This is when the fullest set of juridical incidents that could pertain to an object or a space is held by a single individual. William Blackstone parsed property as "that sole and despotic dominion which one man claims and exercises over the external things of the world, in total exclusion of the right of any other individual in the universe."[18] This is often referred to as a right of exclusive possession, where exclusive possession pertains, according to Steiner, when "inasmuch as what happens to that thing – allowing for the operation of physical laws – is determined by no person other than oneself."[19] Though it is always admitted that there are less "full" conceptions of property, not least that exist in actual legal systems of property, for some reason it is this totalising conception of property which is problematised in the property and justice literature. Too often it is this notion (that I will simply refer to as private property or private ownership) that is taken to be the necessary explanandum of a theory of property and justice – by both defenders and critics. If freedom demands property, then it must demand private property; if freedom fails to ground private property, then it has failed to ground property.

Implicit in this discourse – and explicit in right-libertarianism – is a cluster of empirical beliefs about private property. In Garrett Hardin's landmark article, he argues that the only way to avoid the tragedy of the commons is through parcelling resources out into exclusive private holdings to respective individuals, for a coercive authority to directly impose rules that optimise resource usage.[20] The "tragedy of the commons" is a situation in which relatively self-interested actors use as much of a resource as they can, while contributing to its upkeep as little as they can (through investment or conservation), in the knowledge that if they do not, others will, and the resource will dwindle without them getting any benefit at all. Private property or command-and-control is the institutional choice societies face at the most fundamental level, according to his analysis. Hardin's was a more systematic account of an observation that has been made in print at least as far back as Aristotle.[21] The presumptive desirability of avoiding the socio-economic ruin of the tragedy of the commons and obvious liberty-based aversion to the authority of a centralised agency that controls everything have contributed to the sometimes implicit assumption that if we are concerned with the relationship between freedom and property, it must be private property that we bear in mind, since, after all, we all "know" what happens when resources are held in common.

Nozick explicitly raises this idea in his discussion of original acquisition. He considers Locke's account; that we come to own that which we mix out labour with, but raises objections to it:

> Why does mixing one's labor with something make one the owner of it? Perhaps because one owns one's labor, and so one comes to own a previously unowned thing that becomes permeated with what one owns. Ownership seeps over into the rest. But why isn't mixing what I own with what I don't own a way of losing what I own rather than a way of gaining what I don't? If I own a can of tomato juice and spill it in the sea so that its molecules (made radioactive, so I can check this) mingle evenly throughout the sea, do I thereby come to own the sea, or have I foolishly dissipated my tomato juice?[22]

Without offering any qualifications to the labour-mixing account, or his own alternative that might connect our rights to be free to private ownership of objects, he swiftly moves onto a cluster of "considerations" that favour the institutions of private property:

> Here enter the various familiar social considerations favouring private property: it increases the social product by putting means of production in the hands of those who can use them most efficiently (profitably); experimentation is encouraged, because with separate persons controlling resources, there is no one person or small group whom someone with a new idea must convince to try it out; private property enables people to decide on the pattern and types of risks to bear, leading to specialized types of risk bearing; private property protects future persons by leading some to hold back resources from current consumption for future markets; it provides alternate sources of employment for unpopular persons who don't have to convince any one person or small group to hire them, and so on.[23]

Given what he takes to be the prima facie case for permitting individuals to unilaterally acquire private property, he then says that the ultimate question is simply whether or not permitting acquisition makes anyone else worse off. The only reason to not permit any given acquisition is if it makes any affected parties worse off in terms of welfare. Nozick's version of the proviso therefore ends up doing all the justificatory work in his theory of acquisition. It lacks a positive principle that connects freedom to private property, affirming when and why acquisitions *should* be justified, and instead has only a negative principle that says when and why acquisitions *should not* be justified.[24] Aside from the insulation this creates between liberty and private property, it shifts all the moral content onto the proviso, since the power or right of acquisition itself is entirely "bare."[25] It is simply something one can do at will, so long as one respects the proviso.

Fixation on a single model of property has been addressed by treating the symptoms but not the sickness. Rather than modify and seek to enrich the theory of acquisition so that it is shaped in a way that concretises each person's freedom in a way that makes it compatible with all others, a second-order principle is invoked to check the power to acquire that kind of property. Locke famously qualified his account of acquisition with the proviso that "enough, and as good [be] left in common for others."[26] In contemporary views, this proviso has become the site of debates over reconciling property and freedom. For example left-libertarians mount a variety of argumentative strategies for the conclusion that the proviso demands that one cannot acquire more private property than is compatible with an *equal* share for all.[27] Sufficientarian libertarians argue that one may not acquire where it would be incompatible with a *sufficient* share of private property for all.[28] Others still argue that the proviso ought to demand that acquisition of private property do not stop persons from being able to exercise their rights without leave from others,[29] and that the proviso places restrictions on how one uses one's private property, namely, that one may not exercise those rights in ways that are disabling of other person's world-interactive powers,[30] or that one may acquire at will so long as you compensate anyone who is made worse off in terms of welfare by the acquisition.[31]

Relaxing any implicit or explicit assumptions about the necessity of private property to human sociality enables us to build a more plausible theory of property and justice in both substantive and superficial ways. First, when one does not have some conception of property in mind, it is possible to build a theory of acquisition that is far more flexible and therefore more capable of robustly connecting freedom to property. Second, it allows views such as this to step away from the image it often portrays as being only superficially interested in human liberty as such, and more concerned with justifying a particular kind of political economy: the capitalist state. Locke and libertarian property theorists have come under fire for privileging the establishment of European-style fee-simple property in land for those that engaged in sedentary agriculture which protects the interests of European settlers at the direct expense of those of the less sedentary indigenous Americans who are deemed not to use the land in a way that ought to engender the protection of a property system.[32] In even stronger terms, the project has been construed as one that seeks the privatisation of political power, akin to the English feudal system, albeit with freedom of occupation for the serfs.[33]

What has historically been called property has indeed often been simply a political office that grants one the privilege of extracting rents from those who work on that property and who, on any natural rights view, ought to be regarded as the rightholders to the land and the revenue derived therefrom.[34]

The inclusion from the ground up of property rights such as those that serfs rightly had to their village common, or that displaced indigenous peoples had to their hunting territories, means that these historical forms of *political* property rights were clear violations of *natural* property rights.[35]

Moreover, there are good independent grounds for rejecting the idea that private property is essential to human sociality. As Elinor Ostrom has shown, empirical reality seldom fits the model that Hardin uses. Resource users can communicate with each other, have knowledge of one another as well as the resource so that they can converge upon robust rules for ongoing prosperous use thereof, either through the endogenous formation of social norms accompanied by social sanction or through the nomination of third-party enforcers. In both cases, neither parcelled-out private holdings nor a centralised coercive authority are necessary to responsibly administer resource usage.[36] Rights of use and access can be known and enforced even when those rights and resources overlap in a way that does not give rise to the need for a single authoritative decision-maker over each discrete area of space.[37] So, moving away from making private property the ultimate explanandum of a theory of property and justice is not at odds with the empirical facts about what is necessary to sustain human society.[38]

My account connects myriad property forms to the natural right to freedom; most importantly, property forms form beyond private property. What I refer to as collective and public property, respectively, are not collective or public in the sense of being state-owned, managed, nor regulated. Nor are they commons in the sense used by Hardin as spaces devoid of rules of use. Rather they are confluences of specific property rights held by several different people such that no one has any final authority over the disposition of the resource.

Natural Rights and Social Conventions

I articulate the natural right to freedom as a claim-right to non-interference in one's non-interfering activities. This invocation of "activities" in the content of our natural rights means that the specific actions we take are of significant moral import to the content of our acquired property rights. The property right one acquires through incorporating external objects into one's activities is a claim-right against interference in those specified activities. What constitutes this or that activity therefore becomes hugely important in knowing what our rights amount to in any concrete circumstance. I argue that it is the constitutive rules for whatever activity one is ostensibly engaged in that determine the actions' content for the purposes of acquiring rights. Therefore, the shape of acquired rights will vary across time, place, and culture. It is not the private psychological state of the actor that determines what they are doing, and therefore the content of their rights against interference in it, but rather the socially constructed constitutive rules that govern and define that activity within the social practice it occurs in.

An explicit account of how natural property rights interact with positive social conventions pre-empts other grounds for scepticism that a theory of natural rights cannot give us many of the finer details of how to structure property relations. Some argue that natural rights can only stipulate very broad ranges of kinds of property conventions that are demanded by justice, while we must look to those conventions themselves and evaluate them distinctly in order to know ultimately how our institutions should look. On this view, our natural rights are rather indeterminate. However, in my theory, natural rights are singularly realisable at the level of regulative conventions, even if they are subject to diverse realisation at the level of constitutive conventions. In any given case, our natural right to non-interference combined with a complete account of what constitutes all salient activities through which rights are acquired, gives determinacy to our acquired rights.

The Not-So-Minimum Content of Natural *Rights*

There are two views broadly within the property and justice literature that my own account provides tools to resist. Both could be regarded as a form of minimalism with regard to the content of natural rights.

On the one hand, there are those who are favourable to a property system in which there is a preponderance of private property, and at the margins where private property appears to be inappropriate, a pivot away from deontological first principles and toward a rule-consequentialism familiar in the law-and-economics field. Some resources need to be common property and subject to particular governance rules as opposed to privately owned and governed exclusively at the will of the owner. Private property sometimes comes in different forms in different circumstances, so we must engage in a little cost–benefit analysis to work out its finer contours.

Richard Epstein has argued that individual liberty has intrinsic value, but that it ought not to be overstated.[39] Deontological principles regarding the value of individual liberty cannot do all the work; a complete account of our enforceable obligations to one another must also be informed by welfarist cost–benefit analysis.[40] Indeed, he does not doubt that a right to property is an appropriate application of the ideal of individual liberty, but takes natural rights approaches to be too hamfisted to provide the finer contours. For example the idea that individuals can come to own rivers through first possession is obviously *not* an appropriate application, and therefore we need to consider efficiency of different alternatives through the lens of welfarist approaches to law-and-economics.[41] When one person's use of their property interferes with another's, the appropriate fine-tuning of their property rights in order to determine their respective limits must take into account the social benefits (including the social benefits to the owners) of restricting their prima facie property rights. Indeed, he argues that if natural law can do all the work, then natural law must be, to a significant extent, utilitarian in its content.[42]

Similarly, David Schmidtz signals scepticism that natural rights theories on their own can tell us how to structure property relations ahead of time. Rather, we need to start out with some system of property, and learn through trial and error what works and what does not. The ultimate yardstick of what counts and that which works is something like Pareto optimality: if a system of property relations makes at least someone better off and nobody worse off, then it is justified.[43]

I think views such as these can be seen as varieties of deontic minimalism. That is the view that deontic principles tell us something – that freedom and property are conceptually intertwined, but they cannot tell us all that much more. Some kind of consequentialist analysis will tell us ultimately what precise shape property rights should take. In other words, we know that liberty demands property, but we need some kind of cost–benefit analysis to get us the rest of the way.

On the other hand, there are those that argue that we have a natural right to make use of external resources, but this natural right cannot extend to private property or any kind of property deemed "fully fledged." In order to justify private property and arrive at a determinate and complete system of property, political institutions are required. Rawlsian contractualism or democratic procedures take us to the rest of the way. Again, the notion of freedom itself tells us we need a system that allocates some kind of property rights to individuals, but it cannot get us all the way. Anna Stilz has developed such a view extensively.[44] She argues that the right to freedom clearly entails a right to make *use* of external objects, but as is the norm in property scholarship generally, she places a strong dichotomy between a right of use and a right of possession. The former cannot permit one to exclude others from property when one is not directly using the objects or spaces in question, nor can it include a power to transfer the right, or bequeath it, and so forth, all of which are taken to be *essential* features of property as such. Beyond the physical use of an object, property is stipulated not directly by natural justice, but by conventions. And given that these conventions allocate authorisations to use force (in the defence of the relevant rights), only a political organisation can determine their shape. No individual could unilaterally acquire a right to use force against another beyond that which is necessary to protect their bodily integrity and their primitive use of external objects. Although freedom demands *some* fully fledged system of property beyond mere use-rights, only a state could authorise it. The state therefore becomes essential to specifying the contours of our right to freedom through property, whereas in the former minimalist view, it is whatever turns out to secure mutual benefit.

The former position takes the ham-fistedness of theories of original acquisition to be the weak point in the theory connecting individual liberty and property rights. In the latter, it is similar, but hinges on the indeterminacy of the relationship between individual liberty and anything beyond mere use of the external world. I believe that both theories would have more significant hurdles to mount were there a robust theory that connected individual liberty to property in a way which did not presume that all property must be privately owned, and that demonstrated how liberty demands a particular type of property right in a particular case. Liberty does demand rights to external objects that go beyond the primitive use-right described by Stilz, but it does not always and everywhere demand that private ownership be acquired. Freedom can give us all the information we need to structure a fully fledged set of property relations that protects the reciprocal freedom of rightholders.

The Theory

The book proceeds by analysing what justice, rights, and property are. It is out of consideration of these concepts that an account of freedom is drawn – freedom as a claim-right to non-interference in one's non-interfering activities. I do not begin with a set of intuitions about what freedom is, and then define justice as freedom – rather, the reverse. Therefore, I do not support any particular theory about what "freedom" does or ought to refer to; I only argue that the freedom we have an enforceable right to is freedom from interference so long as we ourselves are non-interfering. It is this right that I argue is natural, original, and the only basis for any further rights. Further rights can only be acquired insofar as they are an application of original rights. That is to say that all of our rights are rights to non-interference in particular activities. Those activities, insofar as they ground our enforceable rights and give shape to justice, are defined in terms of their spatial components – spatio-temporal objects both internal and external to the human body. But they are not merely rights *to* or *over* such objects *tout court*, but only insofar as they serve as a means to the relevant activities. These rights, in order to be mutually consistent – or *compossible* – must be differentiable from one another. One person's activities to which they have a right to cannot conflict with the activities anyone else has a right to. Yet, this does not mean that the same objects cannot appear with the rights of more than one person – not all simultaneous uses of the same object are incompatible or mutually frustrating.

Why should such rights be regarded as *property* rights? It is not merely that they are rights to physical things, but that they are *in rem* and hence exclusive. No two or more people can simultaneously have the same right to the same object. Property rights are universally regarded to have this general structure.[45] This exclusivity ought not to be conflated with another kind of exclusivity often but mistakenly attributed to property rights. This exclusivity means that content of one person's right cannot also feature in another person's right. Much hangs on how we construe "content" here. It is often argued that property rights give one exclusive possession over some defined space or set of objects at some particular time. It means that one has a sole authority over all human-caused changes that occur within that spatio-temporal sphere. No one else may have an effect on that sphere, at least not without acquiring one's consent first. On this view, exclusivity applies directly to time-indexed physical objects. One's property right is taken to be more complete the closer to this ideal one's right reaches. If there are restrictions over whom one may transfer it to, how long one holds it for, the uses one can put it to, one's property right is diluted. William Blackstone is often quoted in support of this view:

> There is nothing which so generally strikes the imagination, and engages the affectations of mankind as the right of property; or that sole and despotic dominion which one man claims and exercises over the external things of the world, in total exclusion of the right of any other individual in the universe.[46]

The invocation of "dominion" in such accounts of property right reveal it to be the analogue of the absolutis conception of political sovereignty. Just as the seat of sovereignty has complete authority over its territorial jurisdiction, in the same way the individual has complete authority over her property. The *property* one has a right to is taken to be a set of objects.

However, the rights that I argue we have here – and claim are the limit of what can be legitimately claimed as one's property – are exclusive in a related but weaker sense. Since the content of a right is not *merely* a set of time-indexed objects but, rather, their deployment within a particular kind of activity, one's authority within one's "sphere" does not saturate the physical space. One does not have a claim correlative with duties of total abstention by others, only that they abstain from interference in some range of activities – activities that, in part, define the content of the right. So, while the content of one's rights must be exclusive, this does not mean that one's right to physical objects is exclusive, because it is more than a list of objects that constitute the content of our rights, and it is also a list of *uses* of those objects that limits the requirements of others to exclude themselves from them.

The metaphorical sphere, over which one has rightful jurisdiction in which what happens is subject strictly to one's own choices, is therefore not merely a physically defined space. It is also an *intentionally* defined space inasmuch as it is a conjunction of time-indexed objects and intentional activities that partially subsume those objects that one has a right that others abstain from. This seemingly pedantic alteration to the typical articulation of property rights has significant implications: it makes our right to private property *more robust* when it can in fact be justified. However, it also means that other "lesser" property rights are also very often justified, opening up a vast spectrum of property rights that are required by freedom in different circumstances. The intentional content of our natural rights also helps fill in the finer details of the property system, details which *must* be found somewhere once one faces the incoherence of a purely physicalistic account of property rights, in which there would be no space for innocuous nuisances, daylight easements, or even use-rights of any kind.

Without any ex-post invocation of anything like a proviso, there are therefore significant limits to the individual's ability to acquire private property – it can only be justified for certain uses of external objects; namely, where the use is so broad the duty not to interfere becomes functionally equivalent with a duty to abstain from use (almost) altogether. One cannot acquire private ownership of vast swathes of natural resources or land simply by "discovering" them, attempting to enclose them, or simply by being the first to privately intend to make them one's own. Nor can one ever maintain property rights to that which becomes necessary for other person's subsistence. The right to non-interference includes not being interfered with in the ongoing subsistence of one's body. Nor is it possible for anyone to acquire so-called "intellectual property rights." Neither exclusive rights to use immaterial ideas or ideal objects, nor exclusive rights to *profit* from particular uses of tangible objects can be justified within this theory. Actually existing intellectual property rights therefore turn out to constitute unjust interferences with persons attempting to sell the products of their labour (as well as their would-be customers) for the benefit of those already established within those markets, like any other straightforward form of protectionism. Even if intellectual property rights were necessary to some degree to incentivise bringing new products to market which contribute to welfare in a more generalised way, the natural right to freedom gives us rights not to be used for the public benefit.

Notes

1. Libertarianism is typically taken to be the species of the genus of modern liberalism that understands liberty, at least in large part, through the lens of property rights. Often the term *classical liberalism* is preferred to emphasise

the parity with those proto-liberal theorists of property and justice. However, classical liberalism is often taken to include theories of liberalism that are not grounded in this discourse of property rights, but more generally around economic and civil liberty and/or limited government, perhaps in more consequentialist terms (Tomasi and Zwolinski 2012; Forthcoming). However, many take issue with what they regard as an anachronistic use of "classical" in that label (Freeman 2001; Rosenblatt 2018, chap. 7).

2. I, therefore, resist the idea that thinking about property both as a right and as a custom are mutually exclusive (contra Wilson 2020). To make assertions about natural property rights is to make normative propositions about property customs, actual or imagined.
3. This agnosticism with regard to the means by which (any theory of) justice is to be implemented is defended in Byas and Christmas (2021).
4. Rawls (1999).
5. Nozick (1974, chap. 7).
6. Rawls (1999, secs 11–13).
7. Long (2002; Brennan and van der Vossen 2018).
8. Attas (2006, 147 fn 35).
9. In this, Nozick buttresses F. A. Hayek's claim that justice is about compliance with just rules of *conduct*, rather than about compliance with what is required to achieve a certain, purportedly just outcome or state of affairs (Hayek 1982, chaps 8–9). Some argue that Nozick's is not really a theory of *distributive* justice at all, but a critique of the entire concept thereof, because it is purely about just procedures and not just distributions of wealth (Schmidtz 2005). However, if one considers a thinner concept of distributive justice, like that invoked by Kant, which is concerned with a settled system of rights – without reference to any pattern of the wealth that those rights give persons access to, Nozick could be seeing to vindicate a more classical notion of distributive justice, rather than attempting to do away with it whatsoever (Kant 1991, sec. 6:297, 6:306).
10. Nozick (1974, 151).
11. Nieswandt (2019).
12. Moller (2017).
13. For example see Nagel (1975).
14. Zwolinski (2016).
15. For example see O'Neill (1976, 320); Bader (2013, 85–86).
16. Smith (2012).
17. Honoré (1961, 109, 111).
18. Blackstone (1893, vol. 1, sec. II.I).
19. Steiner (1994, 39 fn 44).
20. Hardin (1968).
21. For example see Aristotle (1981, sec. II.III); Aquinas (1947, sec. II.II. Q66.2); Hobbes (1983, sec. 1, 2012, sec. XIII – XIV); Lloyd (1833); Gordon (1954, 124); Olsen (1965).
22. Nozick (1974, 174–75).
23. Nozick (1974, 177).
24. Attas (2003).
25. Gibbard (1976, 83).
26. Locke (1764, sec. II.27).
27. Steiner (1994; Otsuka 1998; Vallentyne 2000).
28. Wendt (2018).
29. van der Vossen (2020).
30. Mack 1995, (2002).

31. Nozick (1974, 178–82); De Jasay (1997, 171–80).
32. Arneil (1996); Argenton and Rossi (2021); McCall and Widerquist (2021); cf. Mills (1997, 31–40, 62–81).
33. Freeman (2001); Carson (2006), I do not think this is an accurate picture of what libertarianism is, with one exception. However, it does contain the discursive tools that can be used to construct such a project. Evidence of this is that exception: Hans-Hermann Hoppe's articulation of an anarcho–fascist utopia which he defends in the language of natural property rights (Hoppe 2018).
34. I have learned a great deal about the institutional origins of political property rights and how they function, as well how far they diverge from my own natural rights account of property rights, from North, Wallis, and Weingast (2009, chaps 1–3); Cox, North, and Weingast (Unpublished manuscript); Salter (2015a, 2015b, 2016a, 2016b); Salter and Young (2019); Piano and Salter (2020); Salter (Forthcoming). It is for the reasons of this divergence that I resist the idea that ownership should be regarded as an *office*, rather than a social relation bearing directly between natural persons, proposed by Christopher Essert (Essert 2013). Indeed, if David Seipp is correct, before 1490, English common lawyers did not regard land as *property*, unlike chattels (Seipp 1994).
35. This theory therefore presents a counter case to James Tully's thesis that "Western theory" must be at odds with "Aboriginal property"(Tully 1994).
36. Ostrom (1990); McKean and Ostrom (1995); cf. Rose (1986); Levine (1986).
37. Bradshaw and Lueck (2015); Bradshaw, Christmas, and Lueck (2020).
38. The right-libertarian embrace of a folk version of the Hardin account is evidenced by Walter Block's review of Ostrom's *Governing the Commons* in which he opens by saying that it is "an evil book."(Block 2011).
39. Epstein (1985).
40. Epstein (1998, 23–31, 2015).
41. Epstein (1994).
42. Epstein (2005b).
43. Schmidtz (1990, 1994, 2009, 2010, 2011).
44. Stilz (2009, chap. 2, 2012, 2018, 2019, chaps 2–3) Elsewhere I have referred to this – and its broader family of views – as *Kantian statism* (Christmas 2021).
45. Stern (2017).
46. Blackstone (1893, vol. 1, sec. II.I emphasis added).

1 The Form of Justice

Introduction

Justice has a unique place in morality inasmuch as it addresses itself to a specifically socio-economic domain: that is the conditions of scarcity and uncertainty in a social context. In this chapter, I develop the view that justice gives us guidance in how to deal with a moral problem that arises in such a context: interpersonal practical conflict over scarce resources among those with whom we may not spontaneously coordinate. These circumstances of justice are, however, not incidental to our moral condition but essential to it. So, the rules of justice are not merely prudential or artificial. Our obligation to comply with them is one of natural morality.

The circumstances of justice, as I will argue, determine the form that it takes. Given that justice is the moral virtue that deals with the coordination of potentially mutually disinterested persons in a shared physical world, justice must lay down rules of priority determining who gets to act in what way with regard to which parts of the world. Mitigation of conflict between physically embodied agents is what gives justice its propertarian structure.

This chapter will argue for that structure from the formal standpoint of the moral functionality of justice. In the following chapter, I will develop the substance of justice further. Here, I will only argue that justice deals with the moral problems that arise for agents under conditions of scarcity and sociality, and that this means that justice provides reciprocal constraints on individual behaviour, such that each agent has an enumeration of actions in conjunction with external physical objects that they are permitted, prohibited, and required to take. The pattern of permissions, prohibitions, and requirements across the total set of agents must be mutually consistent. Hence, justice can be understood as a set of compossible rights. Moreover, those rights authorise agents to use force. In order to give final pronouncement on what actions may prevail over which others, this must be the case. Hence, justice constitutes a set of legitimately enforceable claims.

Regarding justice as being constituted by a set of compossible rights to physical objects is often associated with the view that all rights are private property rights, as that is the overarching view developed by Hillel Steiner[1] and less directly by Robert Nozick.[2] However, as I will show here, the criteria for compossibility of a set of rights do not demand that they be private property rights. All sets of private property rights are compossible; however, not all sets of compossible rights include or are limited to private property rights. This account of compossibility is the formal framework upon which the account of the commons will be built.

The Circumstances of Justice and Deontology

David Hume famously said that human society finds itself afflicted with two conditions: scarcity and limited benevolence.[3] He referred to these conditions as comprising the circumstances of justice, because it is in virtue thereof that we should have need for justice as a set of interpersonal constraints on our action.

Scarcity refers to the fact that the physical world that we find ourselves in is one of certain kinds of limits. The resources that we might want to use, occupy, or need to consume are often rivalrous and always finite. Resources are rivalrous when one person's use of them is mutually exclusive of another person's use of them. For example for me to build a house on a particular plot of land, no one else can use that land to farm wheat. If I want to hunt in a particular valley, no one else is able to flood that valley to build a hydroelectric dam. For any given time-indexed object, if two person's use of it are incompatible, then that object is rivalrous with regard to those two persons' ends.

Resources are finite inasmuch as they are quantitatively limited. Land, for example, is not a boundless plane. There is only so much activity with regard to land that can take place at any given time before there is no more space for additional activities to occur. Many resources are *used up* in their use. While I could abandon my use of a plot of land, and that land would then become available for other uses or other persons; if I pick an apple from a tree and eat it, this apple may never be eaten again. That particular apple, as a resource, is consumed and hence used up. Of course, one could plant another apple tree, but that requires time, energy, and space to do so, which comes at the expense of all the other things society could do with that time, energy, and space. The economist's notions of scarcity and opportunity cost presuppose these essential truisms about that nature of space–time and human action.[4] Hume contrasts the reality of the scarce world with an imaginary world in which everything anyone could possibly want was freely available in as large a quantity as they desired, at no expense to anyone else, if they but reached out their hand and took it. "Justice, in that case being totally useless, would be an idle ceremonial, and could never possibly have place in the catalogue of virtues."[5] Finitude and scarcity are two ways of describing the same fact: given that there are a plurality of persons sharing the same physical space and time, their different desires and needs with regard to the use of resources mean not all of their ends can be satisfied. The finite nature of resources means that rivalry in the uses of resources generates scarcity.

Limited benevolence refers to the fact that spontaneous affection of persons does not extend to humanity generally, but only those close to us: those we have a history of intimate sociality with (family, friends, etc.) or those who, though we do not interact with, we identify with as sharing common identity and hence membership of our in-group, rather than the out-group (members of the same religion, tribe, community, etc.). We naturally have deeper care for those we have some sort of concrete tie with, not simply anyone who happens to be a human, and therefore is part of "our" society in the abstract.[6] The practical conflicts that arise with regard to how to make use of the scarce world take on a new form among persons who not only have different desires, needs, goals, and values, but who also lack much care for one another.

If the only other persons we share the world with were people we have strong concrete ties with, people might predictably and reliably be happy to defer to the needs and wants of others and abstain from that which they might want for themselves; and others would be happy to reciprocally do the same. Given the fact that our benevolence is truncated, however, we do not all care for one another in this way; hence, the possibility – or *inevitability* – of interpersonal practical conflict. Given that many of the ends that we set for ourselves as individuals and in groups will overlap with the same external resources that other individuals and groups need for the ends they set themselves, some sort of allocation of those resources must be made between the respective individuals and groups, since both cannot simultaneously pursue their ends as they are originally set, nor can they be expected to spontaneously adjust to one another in ways that are mutually deemed agreeable. This inevitably results in the frustration of the ends persons set. Given that such frustration cannot be expected to come from the spontaneous deferment of any one individual or group to the other, it must come from a set of rules.[7]

Hume in fact understates the problem. As Adam Tebble has argued, there is also a fundamental knowledge problem that afflicts human society that gives rise to the need for rules to adjudicate inevitable interpersonal practical conflict.[8] There is not only a physical and motivational problem with regard to human sociality, but also an epistemic one. Even if we were in a world in which we shared spontaneous benevolence for one another, we would not know how best to coordinate our actions as to actually achieve the other-regarding ends we seek. We can only ever have very limited information about what others are doing elsewhere, and how these affect the success conditions of our own actions – regardless of what motivates them. The primary problem is perhaps then not that we do not all love each other, but that we do not all *know* each other.[9]

Rules can act as a surrogate that enables persons to act on dispersed and fragmented information that they do not possess. If we can be confident that other people elsewhere are, whatever else they are doing, following a particular set of known rules, we can adjust our conduct accordingly.[10] Even if we all loved each other, we would nonetheless need rules to fill the gaps left by our limited capacity for knowledge of one another's actions and circumstances.

It is compliance with rules that prevent generalised conflict and interpersonal chaos that Hume says the virtue of justice consists in. Such rules evolve over a long period of time and are in part responsive to the particular socio-economic circumstances of the society in which they emerge; for example the types of resources that are widely depended upon and the modes of cooperation that there is a need for. Hume argued that since these circumstances were socio-economically determined and highly contingent, that justice itself must simply be a set of conventional norms[11] that humanity developed to deal with these circumstances, rather than something that comes naturally to us psychologically, or as something that we can identify through pure reason.[12] It is for this reason that Hume says that justice is an "artificial" virtue rather than a natural one.[13] While it is undeniably true that the rules that adjudicate in cases of interpersonal practical conflict with regard to scarce resources emerge over time through conventional means, we ought not to mistake this descriptive account as being exhaustive of any prescriptive account of justice. The conventionalised rules of justice and the benefits they bring to society can be explained anthropologically, but that need not mean they cannot also be derived and understood purely morally.[14]

In the picture painted by Hume, justice presents as morally optional for the individual. Due to the limitations presented by human society, our social shortcomings, and the vices of others,[15] we ought to comply with rules of justice in order to achieve our ends under such conditions. But this "ought" is purely instrumental; justice is simply the means by which we successfully pursue ends within a socio-economic context. Perhaps for social leaders or political rulers, it is good for *them*[16] to inculcate justice among the people given their social or political role.[17] But the only moral reason the individual has is strictly subordinate to their other moral obligations. It happens to be the case that in order to achieve their ends (including the fulfilment of their moral obligations) in a social context, they must obey these rules that either have emerged or are being imposed upon them by a virtuous leader.

However, the circumstances of justice are not contingent nor are they an external limitation upon our moral action. They are the context which defines the very constitution of our socio-economic action and hence part of the goodness of our action in the first place. Again, Hume understates the problem somewhat.

That fact that persons have a capacity and hence a potentiality to set and pursue their own ends and that they do so in the context of scarcity and of other persons they may not know is not a limitation upon our activities, such that we must prudentially or merely instrumentally adopt rules of justice in order to get by as best we can. As Arthur Ripstein argues, our capacity for action and the context which defines it "is not a limitation; it is our humanity itself."[18]

Even if we imagine away external scarcity in a world of unbridled abundance with regard to resources, our persons would still be scarce. That is our spatio-temporally embodied selves cannot simultaneously engage in an infinite number of different actions, even if there were infinite opportunities for the pursuit of all and every end imaginable.[19] In order to make use of anything in the world in pursuit of an end, we must make use of ourselves as a matter of priority. It is not a contingent inconvenience that as persons we find ourselves to be physically embodied and temporally subjected. Such is part of what it means to be a person. Our existence as persons presupposes our purposiveness,[20] and our purposiveness cannot be conceptually disentangled from its spatio-temporal boundedness. Indeed, to speak of "boundedness" is perhaps misleading: our purposiveness *just is* spatio-temporal. Acting within a world of non-scarce things would always require us to make use of at one least one scarce thing: ourselves.[21] This gives rise to the potentiality of practical interpersonal conflict because other persons are also scarce. In order to cooperate with us, they must forgo some other end that is mutually exclusive with cooperation with us. The need for cooperation, whether it is with those we love or those we do not, is also essential to our humanity.[22] We must live both with and among others who can potentially have different ideas about how their time is best spent and their bodies are best used. Note that this is the case regardless of whether such persons feel spontaneous benevolence. Even if we assume that everyone acts on the same benevolent and other-regarding motivations, we cannot assume that they all also have the same knowledge and act on it in the same way. To assume that everyone has identical knowledge and applies it in the exact same way is to deny that persons are meaningfully distinct.

We would still need rules of justice in a materially abundant world with regard to how and when we may use both ourselves and each other; that is, we would still need just terms of cooperation. It is because of the fact that the conditions which give rise to the need for rules of justice are unavoidable for humans that Immanuel Kant believed we are *naturally* obligated to justice, rather than artificially.[23] In this respect, at least, he was right.

The inherent nature of space is that it is made of locations that can be physically occupied over time by physical objects such as human bodies.

And it is inherent to our nature that we act in such an environment among other similarly situated but distinct persons. Like Hume, Kant also believed that we "cannot avoid living side by side" with others, even (or especially) those we are likely to come into conflict with.[24] We must, however, understand this "cannot" to be one of mere modal impossibility but one of moral impermissibility. It is not morally optional to live in society any more than it is morally optional to make choices for oneself.[25] We are not only naturally rational beings but also naturally social beings. We need, morally speaking, to include others in our lives in a variety of ways. We may not avoid considering how we should engage with others by simply avoiding others altogether.[26]

The value of justice therefore consists in respecting and adhering to the rules laid down therein. The circumstances that give rise to justice are simply our shared yet distinct human natures. It is in our nature that we ought to be just.[27] It is not that justice achieves certain ends, and that if we value these ends then we ought to be just (though this may also be case); it is that compliance with justice is partially constitutive of what we ought to do. It places constraints on how our pursuit of our ends can count as being moral, because both the ends we seek and the way we seek them must, in some way, reflect our nature as rational, social beings.

Douglas Den Uyl and Douglas Rasmussen argue that compliance with justice renders our moral action compossible with the moral action of others, as if justice exerted constraints on our otherwise moral action. They therefore argue that justice is not merely normative but rather *meta*normative.[28] It facilitates a framework in which everyone can pursue moral action without impeding one another's ability to do so. However, if this is truly possible and moral activity can be constrained in a pro-social way without impeding it normatively, then those actions which justice then rules out were not really moral in the first place.[29] Justice illuminates one particular normative aspect of our interpersonal morality. But for it to facilitate moral conduct in a socio-economic context without itself cannibalising any of that moral conduct, then truly moral conduct – in the final analysis – must already be internally adjusted to such a context.

This does not mean that what is just and what is good can never come apart in specific situations when viewed myopically. What it means is that what is just is not determined *independently* of the good, therefore considerations of justice count toward considerations of the good and vice versa, and justice must be a moral norm like any other.

This is in line with at least one version of deontology.[30] For justice to be a deontological value is for the rules prescribed therein to be intrinsically valuable for what they are in and of themselves, rather than only because of their promotion or causation of some further good. Deontology might determine the rules of justice *irrespective* of the consequences it brings about. However, it need not be non-consequentialist in this manner if it does not determine the good in a manner that makes it independent of justice.[31] Given that justice is grounded in human nature, as is the human good more generally, it conforms to this version of deontology. This is how I understand the idea of natural justice, which I take to be in keeping with the spirit of the natural law tradition.

Individual Rights

Justice, as a moral response to the circumstances thereof, needs to adjudicate which actions may override or "trump" others.[32] The potentiality for our chosen actions to clash with those of other agents vis-à-vis the rivalrous external world means some choices may *not* be made, and that persons will, in certain circumstances, have to yield to the choices of others.

Justice makes prescriptions of individuals, not of society as a whole or any subgroup therein. If the prescriptions of justice were issued to society as a whole or various subgroups within it, it would open the question of who within the group has the relevant permission on behalf of the group. Of course, it may assign power to determine who in the group has such a permission, but in order to exercise that power, the group as a whole would need to exercise it. There may be disagreement within the group over whether or not the group should so exercise it in any particular way. In cases of such disagreement, a moral question necessarily arises as to whose choice ought to prevail. There must be some individual identified who has the power to determine which coalition or individual in the group ultimately gets to decide how to delegate the permission. Since disagreement between individuals is always in principle possible, ultimately, it is only those loci of agency that are not subject to internal disagreement and impasse that must be assigned final permissions – individuals. Justice must therefore assign permissions to engage in certain actions to particular individuals.

However, it must do more than merely assign permissions.[33] It must assign an *exclusive* permission. A merely having the permission to φ only entails that she is not prohibited from φ-ing; it does not mean that she alone is assigned authority as to whether or not she gets to φ. What is needed in addition to the permission is the *right* to φ.[34] A right, unlike a mere permission, necessarily correlates with certain duties in all third parties; namely, duties not to engage in actions which are incompatible with A's exercise of her right to φ. Without a right to φ and the correlative duties in third parties to not interfere with her φ-ing, those third parties would each themselves have permissions to engage in actions that might render A's φ-ing impossible. This, again, raises the potentiality of interpersonal practical conflict – that which justice is supposed to tell us how we ought to overcome.[35]

Let us stipulate that any instance of ψ-ing by a third party is incompatible with A's φ-ing. In order for A to be assigned final decision-making power – as is required by justice – as to whether or not φ takes place at a certain time or not, all third parties must have a duty not to ψ. A system of mere permissions or liberties is therefore insufficient to furnish the structural content of justice. Justice demands rights as well as liberties. Whatever actions justice gives us the natural liberty to engage in, it also assigns a right to do so.[36]

H. L. A. Hart distinguishes between "naked" and "vested" liberties. Acting on a naked liberty is not protected by a mesh of duties among third parties to abstain from interfering in that action, whereas the latter is. A right is the name given to the vest, as this is what can be ascribed to the liberty-holder, which correlates with third parties' duties.[37] However, the two need not always be assigned to one and the same person. If A has the right to φ then she may give permission to B to ψ. Since A has ultimate decision-making power as to whether or not her act of φ-ing gets to prevail in any given case, she may choose *not* to φ, and allow B to ψ. In this instance, B has a permission to ψ, and not a right; since A has the right to φ and therefore has ultimate decision-making power as to whether φ takes place or not, and for φ to take place, ψ may not.[38]

The structure of justice is such that if anyone has a permission to ψ, that permission itself must be permitted by another person; namely, the person with the right to φ. In all cases where the potential for interpersonal practical conflict arises, there must be an individual who has ultimate decision-making power as to what happens. This is what I mean by a "right of justice."

Whatever actions justice assigns permissions and rights to engage in, it must at least assign individuals a right to use force to override the choices of others, where those choices are incompatible with the action the performance of which the right protects. If justice did not authorise the use of force, it could not solve the moral problem that agents face.

If justice simply prescribed that certain actions be taken, but *not* tell us when we may take actions constitutive of force, it would leave open the possibility of morally unguided interpersonal practical conflict. Imagine that justice requires that all agents are required to perform action φ in circumstances c. Imagine further that when c arises, one agent engages in an action ψ which renders another agent's performance of φ impossible, because it involves the use of space or object that the latter needs in order to perform φ. The latter could use force against the former in order get her to stop ψ-ing and so that φ-ing may take place without interference. If justice does not tell us when and how we may use force, then justice has run out of instructions to give the latter agent, given that the former agent has made it impossible for her to φ without the use of force. We could suppose that the unjust agent just gets away with ψ-ing, or we could suppose that the agents have to fight it out to see whose application of force against the actions of the other prevails.[39] This situation of interpersonal practical conflict that has arisen is *precisely* the fact about human social life that justice is supposed to tell us how to deal with. It must, then, at least tell us when we may resort to the use of force against others[40] or, as Jeremy Waldron puts it, "who must give way when bodies collide."[41]

Justice therefore (at least) describes morally permissible uses of force. Such permissions must necessarily be assigned to particular persons in the final analysis. In order to provide moral guidance as to which actions may override others, justice must give prescriptions that are intelligible to agents qua agents, which is to say, agents within the circumstances of justice. Justice must tell the individual actor, given the circumstances that they cannot perfectly predict or control the actions of others, and yet must share action space with them, when they must defer to the choices of others and when they may force their choices upon others.

Natural justice therefore becomes a question of compliance with natural rights. As Hugo Grotius famously observed, recognising what acting *rightly* requires of us leads us to recognise that persons have *rights*.[42] The enquiry into where the moral need for justice arises can therefore be translated into an enquiry into what moral quality persons have that gives rise to their need for rights.[43] Persons have rights in virtue of their being essentially purposive and social agents, embodied in a scarce and uncertain world.

Moreover, since one's duties of justice are all those duties that correlate with the rights of others, doing one's duty is directed towards those others. All forms of injustice are injustices against a person or set of persons; that is in violating one's duties to those persons. Whatever the other kinds of wrongdoing that acting unjustly might also entail, it always entails wronging another person.

Other than that all rights of justice must ultimately authorise the use of force in order to override the choices of others, what more can be said about the structural content of our rights?

Compossibility[44]

Now we are in a position to say more about the structural content of justice, or as should now be clear, about the structural content of individual rights. Given that justice assigns rights and correlative duties to all individuals, the structure of an individual right must be dialectically established in light of the fact that it is part of a *set* of rights.

Steiner argues that the set of rights demanded by justice is necessarily a compossible set.[45] A set of rights is necessarily compossible when the actions it variously permits, prohibits, and requires are mutually performable. That is to say that is possible for every person to act within their rights and comply with their duties without thereby preventing another from exercising their rights or complying with their duties. If *A* has a right to φ, and φ is mutually unperformable with ψ, then no other person can be assigned a right to ψ and moreover must be assigned a duty not to ψ. This duty not to ψ must, in turn, be compatible with all their other duties. If *B* has a duty not to ψ which correlates with *A*'s right to φ, then no other person, for example, *C*, can be assigned a right that correlates with a duty *to* ψ in *B*. If such were the case, it would not be physically possible for *B* to comply with both her duty to *A* (to not ψ) and her duty to C (to ψ).[46]

If our rights were structured in a way that made this a possibility, we would, once again, arrive at the scenario that we started with: the need for guidance in how to overcome interpersonal practical conflict. If *B* was to ψ, then *A*'s right has been violated and is authorised to use force to stop *B*'s ψ-ing. However, this use of force by *A* would violate C's right that *B* can ψ, and therefore C would be authorised to use force against *A*. They cannot both prevail and we cannot expect one to voluntarily yield to the other. Justice cannot tell them both to fight it out because that was the position they were in before the question of justice arose. Justice has to tell one of them to yield and, in so doing, tells us that one of these rights was a demand of justice, and the other was not.

If we are content with the idea that rights of justice can conflict, and in such cases of conflict we invoke a second-order moral principle to say which one should prevail, then the ultimate site of justice is now simply located at the second-order level. Justice tells us how to deal with the moral question over how to deal with the circumstances of justice. If first-order principles of justice simply re-ask that question, then they do nothing, and ultimately second-order justice does all the work. If we want to know how to avoid *having* to kick the "can" any further down the road, we need to know what the end of the road would look like. Ultimately, rights must be structured so as to avoid the very possibility of conflict; this is the structure of rights as determined by justice. To simply say that rights of justice can conflict, at which point we appeal to a meta-principle, is simply to equivocate over the meaning of the term. Justice arises precisely because in a socio-economic context the moral actions of persons can conflict, so they need an interpersonal principle to tell them when to yield to one another.

Imagine if a designer of a traffic light system thought there was no need for green lights facing one plain of a four-way intersection to correlate with red light facing the adjacent directions. We would say that she had misunderstood the task in front of her. "Ah ha!" she says, "But whenever two conflicting directions of traffic both face a green, a second set of lights will pop up to give one direction priority over the other." We would tell her not to bother about the first set of traffic lights and just design a single set that performs the function of the latter – a function that is indispensable regardless of the function of first.[47]

If we start with a set of rights that stands in need of partial correction if not outright replacement in circumstances of conflict, then it is *that* further moral principle that constitutes justice because it is that moral principle that ultimately tells us whose choice may prevail and hence who is authorised to use force against another in those circumstances.[48]

Hart believed that a legal system that assigned rights that could conflict gave rise to a "Nightmare" in which the following takes place.

> Litigants in law cases consider themselves entitled to have from judges an application of the existing law to their disputes, not have the law made for them. . . . The Nightmare is that this image of the judge, distinguishing him from the legislator, is an illusion. . . . [T]hat judges make the law which they apply to litigants and are not impartial, objective declarers of existing law [but rather exercise] what Holmes called the "sovereign prerogative of choice."[49]

If we think that natural justice is a matter to be settled by those adjudicating disputes between conflicting, putative rights, then justice assigns ultimate authority to those adjudicators, rather than to the putative rightholders themselves.[50] The point to be taken away from Hart is that, to say justice can coherently lead to conflict because we have means of dealing with conflict is simply to push the question back a step. In order to have moral authority to adjudicate conflict and determine whose prima facie right gets to stand and whose does not implies that an adjudicator has some right to make such determinations. In order to avoid an infinite regression of further orders of adjudicators, that right must be compossible with all other rights held within the set.[51]

To say that rights must be compossible does not mean that it would be incoherent for a system of law to contain potentially conflicting legal rights. It means that the *just* way of adjudicating any such conflicts is morally final. Indeed, a positive institutionalisation of natural rights may be achieved through a process of such adjudication, learning, and improvement. But at least one symptom of that system of law becoming more just would be that the rights it recognises come closer to being compossible.

So, what structural conditions can we specify about individual rights in order to guarantee that no conflict of rights or duties occurs? What is the logical structure of the kind of things rights can be rights to?[52] Steiner argues that every right must be extensionally differentiable; that is the time-indexed objects that feature in the description of any person's right cannot also feature in the description of any other person's right. This, Steiner argues, is a *necessary* condition of rights-compossibility.[53] Every person's action takes place in space–time, and as such involves the disposition of a certain range of time-indexed objects. These are the action's physical components. Steiner argues that where two persons' actions share one or more of their physical components, those actions are mutually unperformable:

> [Two or more] actions are incapable of jointly occurring if there is a partial coincidence between their *extensional* descriptions – if those actions simultaneously have at least one . . . of their physical components (objects or spatial locations) in common.[54]

Where two persons engage in actions that are mutually unperformable, interpersonal practical conflict arises. The mutual unperformability of their respective actions means that they simultaneously interfere with one another. Their rights, therefore, cannot protect their respectively engaging in actions that share one or more of their physical components. Since both actions cannot mutually take place, they cannot have a right to engage in them at the same time. Likewise, if two persons have rights that are not extensionally differentiable, then the duties that third parties have towards them cannot be simultaneously complied with. To engage in the action required by one duty will constitute an action that violates the other.

Specifying rights as pertaining to time-indexed objects that do not feature in the description of the rights of any other persons ensures that any action taken by the rightholder within her rights will only have physical components that feature on that list, and not that of any other. The physical components of the rightful actions of all other persons are placed outside of her rightful domain, guaranteeing that any exercise of her rights does not conflict with any other's exercise of theirs. The extensional differentiability of rights guarantees their compossibility:[55]

> A rule or set of rules assigning the possession or exclusive use of each particular physical object to particular individuals, will, if universally adhered to, exclude the possibility of any individual's actions interfering with those of another in any respect.[56]

In order to guarantee compossibility any right to some kind of action must, at bottom, be a right to exclusive possession of the physical components of that action. If rights were not extensionally differentiable, but merely specified in terms of types of action the right protects tout court, they would be incompossible.

For example, if *A* (and many others) have a right to protest, *B* has a right to her flower delivery on time, and *C* has a duty to deliver flowers to *B* on time, as specified, these rights do not guarantee that if they are followed, interpersonal practical conflict is avoided. If *A* (and many others) choose to exercise their right at a particular time and place, namely, on the street where *B* is located and *C* is duty-bound to deliver her flowers, then *C* will not be able to fulfil her duty to *B*. Hence, *A*'s (and many others') and *B*'s rights are incompossible. A situation of conflict arose while everyone acted within their rights. The only way justice could have told us how to guarantee that everyone acting within their rights will not come into conflict of this sort is if the "right to protest" were specified in terms of a particular time and place the right to protest pertained to, and if those time-indexed locations were wholly differentiable from those time-indexed locations that feature in anyone else's rights.[57] Or, alternatively, if *C*'s rights were constituted such that she could not acquire a duty to deliver flowers to *B* on time if *A* and others were protesting at that particular time and space. It needs to be the case that those time-indexed objects in one person's domain of juridical incidents are not in the domain of another, in order to guarantee the aversion of conflicting uses of those objects being ones that are simultaneously protected by justice.

If all rights are rights to particular spatial objects at particular times to the exclusion of all others, then all rights are *property* rights. The substantive question then turns on who has property rights to what and why. On this view, it is not that justice entails we have a right to property, but that all our rights whatever just are property rights.

The precise nature of these property rights is not as Steiner has it, however. They need not be rights of exclusive possession to time-indexed objects, wholly differentiable from those time-indexed objects featured in the rights of any other. Extensional differentiability is indeed a sufficient condition of a set of compossible rights, but it is not a necessary one. What this means, as we shall see, is that rights can be categorically compossible, while being specified in terms of particular actions with regard to specific time-indexed objects, rather than exclusive possession of those time-indexed objects. All rights then are rights to non-interference in particular uses of particular time-indexed objects,[58] rather than rights to those time-indexed objects tout court. In what follows I will explain why this is the case, and why it matters.

Steiner's starting point – that partial coincidence of the physical components of two or more actions is a sufficient condition of their being mutually unperformable – is too strong. Actions can spatio-temporally overlap without thereby frustrating each other. Actions that use the same objects or spaces at the same time do not necessarily interfere with one another. While all actions subsume a certain range of time-indexed objects, their modes of subsumption are not *necessarily* rivalrous – that is mutually exclusive with another use of them by another person's action. Whether or not two person's uses of a particular object at the same time are rivalrous depends upon the type of actions in question.

Consider the following example.[59] *A* has a right to practice yoga at a specific location, S_1, at any time. *B* has a right to set up a Wi-Fi network at an adjacent location, S_2, at any time. The radio waves from *B*'s router permeate the space in which *A* has a right to do her yoga practice. Given that the actions that *A*'s and *B*'s rights permit each of them to engage in without interference both simultaneously share physical components, they are, according to Steiner's strong formulation, mutually unperformable. Therefore, on Steiner's account, *A*'s and *B*'s rights cannot both feature in a compossible set because the actions specified therein "conjunctively suffer from . . . extensional overlap."[60] An extensional description of *A* acting within the bounds of her yoga right will not be wholly differentiable from that of *B*'s acting within the bounds of her Wi-Fi right. Nonetheless, these two activities do not interfere with each other. One knows this so long as one knows what kinds of activities they respectively are, not merely as configurations of objects and spaces at particular times, but as purposive activities. *A* moving her body into the posture of downward-facing dog, for example, does alter the physical disposition of *B*'s Wi-Fi signals, but it does not interfere with the network; it does not frustrate its purposes. Likewise, *B*'s transmission of radio waves through and around *A*'s body does not frustrate her activity, despite the fact that it does alter the disposition of atoms in her body and the space she occupies while moving her body. These two actions, specified in terms of the space and time at which they may occur, are non-rivalrous because of the kinds of actions they are. Of course, if *A*'s right to practice yoga pertained to the particular area of ground upon which *B* had a right to place her router, then the two actions would be mutually unperformable and their rights thereto incompossible. But this relation of mutual frustration between the actions is not borne merely of the spatio-temporal coincidence of them, but also due to the kind of action they are. A hand placed on a particular area of ground to support the body is rivalrous with that area of ground being used to place a router, but the use of the same air-space by a yogi and an internet user is not.

In order to test for compossibility, we need to know whether the protected actions are non-interfering or not. Specification of their physical components is part of that enquiry, but it does not exhaust the enquiry; we also need to know what kinds of actions they are qua purposive activities to know whether their spatio-temporal overlap generates mutual unperformability or not.

Steiner argues that so long as the actions that a set of rights permits, prescribes, or proscribes are given in extensional terms, we can know whether they are categorically compossible simply by checking if the extensional terms in each right are differentiable. Meaning that our rights to any action are really just rights to act in any way as long as the action only subsumes those time-indexed objects to which we and no one else have exclusive right to. Steiner refers to this notion of rights as being title-based domains – tethered to specified physical components – as opposed to action-based domains – rights to engage in certain actions, untethered to any particular physical components. He says that while we may find it useful to refer to our title-based domains using action-based language, such terms can only ever be surrogates for the extensional specification of what our rights are really rights to: the physical components of that action. For example any right to free speech must ultimately be a right to one's vocal cords and to the particular space one occupies at a given time, and a right over the airwaves through which the sound travels, etc.[61]

However, action-based domains need not be untethered from their physical components. If rights are specified in terms of particular actions with regard to particular time-indexed objects, we can check whether or not those actions are mutually performable with others, and hence know if a right thereto could be part of the compossible set.

It is not, however, merely from the differentiability of the physical components that we know whether mutual performability obtains, it is through an understanding of the action itself qua purposive action. Many actions can spatio-temporally overlap without thereby rendering one another unperformable. What Steiner identifies as a necessary condition is in fact only a sufficient condition.[62]

So, all rights give the individuals they are assigned to a right to engage a certain set of time-indexed objects, S_t, in a certain activity, φ. All such rights are such that, given both the nature of φ qua intentional activity vis-à-vis S_t, it does not interfere with those activities others have rights to engage in. Knowledge of whether or not this is the case is borne out of, not merely what is included in S_t, since differentiability of the time-indexed objects that feature in each person's set of rights is not necessary for compossibility, but also an understating of φ as the kind of intentional activity that it is, and hence what it would take to interfere with it.

I believe that there is good reason to think that, when enquiring into the content of justice and of individual rights, we should push up against the necessary conditions of their compossibility rather than being satisfied merely with sufficient conditions. Deploying Steiner's account of compossibility would leave open space in the realm of rights and hence demand more exclusion that is necessary to avoid ex-ante and adjudicate ex-post interpersonal practical conflicts. Steiner's account would assign individual's exclusive possession of time-indexed objects where a more limited right to non-interference in specified use thereof would serve to avoid conflict. This enlarges the scope for individuals to exclude third parties from action space where that exclusion is not required for human activity to proceed in a socio-economic context. Hence, it results in a greater partition of action space than the circumstances of justice call for. For *A* to have the right to do yoga uninterfered at S_1, she does not need a right to exclusive possession of S_1 and only needs a right to non-interference in this particular use of it, which is compatible with *B* having a right to use parts of S_1 when she uses S_2 to set up her Wi-Fi network. To introduce more exclusion into justice than that which serves its moral purpose would be for rights to overstep their brief as the elementary particles of justice. To return to Hume:

> For what purpose make a partition of goods, where everyone has already more than enough? Why give rise to property, where there cannot possibly be any injury? Why call this object *mine*, when upon the seizing of it by another, I need but stretch out my hand to possess myself to what is equally valuable? Justice, in that case being totally useless, would be an idle ceremonial, and could never possibly have place in the catalogue of virtues.[63]

All rights, then, are rights to some specified activity in relation to a specified range of time-indexed objects. The particular actions that are protected in one person's rights cannot stand in a relation of interference with that of any other person's rights. That relation of non-interference, however, can be known in light of the kind of activity it is, as well as the time-indexed objects it subsumes, rather than merely the latter.

Given that claims protect us in making a choice as to whether that claim-protected activity takes place or not, it follows that our capacity to make such a choice cannot be something that falls within the domain of another person's original claims. In order to engage in a claim-protected activity (or not), we must, as a matter of priority, have a claim to make use of ourselves. One could not have a claim to walk down a public road or to have healthcare provided to them if one did not have a claim to make decisions as to what happens to one's person. All our activities involve the use of our person. Even inaction involves the use of one's body, namely, in doing whatever constitutes the negation of the relevant action. Using things involves using ourselves. Therefore, A's right to engage S in an action φ must include the right to use her own body in the way required, however she chooses to exercise her right to engage S in φ. A right necessarily endows its holder with some sphere of choice over our bodies.

At this juncture, it may be objected that having a claim does not presuppose the juridical liberty to act on it.[64] It is often said that to have a claim is merely to be identified as the passive beneficiary of non-violation of that claim. The distinction between passive and active claims – the latter being that claims just presuppose certain liberties and powers to act on them and the latter being the negation of that assertion – leads theorists into occupying one of two positions in a broader debate over rights: the will theory and the interest theory. The will theory says that a condition of having a right is that it protects one's will, and the interest theory says that it protects certain interests that are normatively strong enough to be protected by right.[65]

However, what I say in the foregoing is not to beg the question against the passive view of claims or the concomitant interest theory of rights.

Where claims are all claims to non-interference in a particular activity, it is the case that, unless we arrive at some reason to accommodate rights that somehow obstruct this, it has to be the case that persons are permitted to engage in actions that others have duties to not interfere with. Otherwise, it would be the case that claim-holders are under an enforceable duty to not act on their claims, which is impossible.

Moreover, it is not clear what it would mean to be the passive beneficiary of a claim against interference in an activity that did not entail the permission to act within that sphere of rightful non-interference. That is to say that, where rights protect spheres of non-interference, as I am advancing here, the will-theory of rights becomes the only plausible way of understanding such rights.

In order to have any right whatsoever we need a right over ourselves, to make our own choices, and to act in accordance with those choices.[66] Our very capacity to make a choice cannot be the subject to the original rights of any other. We need a right over ourselves in order for us to even in principle be able to exercise any other right that justice may bestow.

As discussed in the previous section, rights of justice are enforceable, meaning that if *A* interferes with an activity to which *B* has a right to engage in, *B* may use force, if necessary and proportional, to bring an end to *A*'s interference. Rights provide an answer to the circumstances of justice by giving a determination of whose activities get to override others and who therefore has the right to impose their choice over whether their activity should prevail over others or not upon others who might not comply. *A* having a right that some particular activity of hers gets to trump others *just is* a right to force others to *not* interfere with that action. Enforcements are interferences,[67] so it follows that justice should authorise interference with unjustly interfering actions.

A question that the reader may feel lingering is whether or not such rights can really be considered property rights after all. On Steiner's account, rights to exclusive possession of time-indexed objects can clearly be meaningfully understood as property rights. But can the action-based account that I defend in preference to Steiner's physicalistic account also be understood in the same way? Over the course of the rest of the book I will answer this query and show how an action-based account of rights does ground property rights, most importantly, myriad forms of property rights beyond the narrow full liberal ownership model that Steiner's account is constrained to.

Conclusion

In the following chapter, we turn to the question of the substance of justice; now as we know what kind of thing a right is, we enquire what particular rights people actually have.

Justice makes demands on all persons in their relations to all other persons. The rights it assigns are therefore "global" in nature. Of course, between parties who never know each other, never meet, and never interact, justice will not apply to them *insofar* as it will not ultimately positively guide their action with regard to one another. But this is of little to no import since in this case there is no interaction to guide. As soon as persons interact in a socio-economic context, which is to say whenever the potential for interpersonal practical conflict arises, justice applies to them. Whether or not this potential for conflict is on a merely "interactional" or "systematic" basis is immaterial to the question of whether justice morally constrains their interaction.[68] Robinson Crusoe is not constrained by justice *until* man Friday's arrival.[69]

Notes

1. Steiner (1994).
2. He uses the term "co-possible"(Nozick 1974, 166).
3. Hume (1739, sec. III.II).
4. Menger (2007, chaps 1–2); Walras (1954, sec. 21).
5. Hume (1902, sec. III.I); Cf. Walras (1954, sec. 23).
6. Hence, F. A. Hayek's insistence that large and complex societies in which people are strangers require general rules that apply to persons and circumstances in general, irrespective of all those things that make persons, groups, and their circumstances distinctive (Hayek 1982, chap. 7; Epstein 1997; Mack 2006).
7. Our limited benevolence also plays a positive role, since without it we could not be expected to moderate our conduct so as to bring it in line with rules of justice. If we were totally benevolent, justice would be unnecessary, but if we were totally malevolent, justice would be *impossible*.
8. Tebble (2016).
9. As Jacob Levy says, a fundamental fact of political societies is that they are made up of *strangers* (2017a, 2017b).
10. Waldron (1988b); Tomasi (1991); also see note 3.
11. For accounts of how rules become conventionalised that are consistent with the Humean account, see Lewis (1969), Bicchieri (2006).
12. Hume (1739, sec. III.II); Sayre-McCord (2016).
13. Karl Marx also believed that the normative significance of justice was relative to the mode of production at the given point of history. Marx believed that justice was purely remedial, namely, of the fact that the mode of production reproduced material scarcity, and that individuals are alienated from each other (Marx 1970, 1994; Geras 1989). Of course, overcoming scarcity and limited benevolence would still leave the epistemic issue, so even a post-scarce, post-self-regarding world would need rules of justice to deal with the knowledge problem.
14. Korsgaard (1996, 8); Ripstein (2012, 45).
15. Hume's is a secular notion of the *fallen* state of humanity.
16. Ronald Dworkin, for example, took justice to be a virtue of the sovereign, rather than of persons as such (Dworkin 2000). There is indeed a prevalent tendency among political philosophers to regard justice just as *that which the state should do* (Byas and Christmas 2021).

17. Hence Bernard Mandeville's ironic assertion that interpersonal virtues are merely the invention of politicians (Mandeville 1988, 41–57).
18. Ripstein (2012, 44).
19. Mises (2007, 100–4); Rothbard (1976, 61); Block (1977, 383); Hoppe (2010, 19–20).
20. Aristotle (2009, sec. I.I).
21. Rothbard (2006, 36–37, 1998, 47); Steiner (1994, 231–48); Ripstein (2009, chap. 3); Stilz (2009, 38–41).
22. Aristotle (1981, sec. 1253a).
23. Kant (1991).
24. Kant (1991, sec. 6:306); cf. Waldron (1993, 2011).
25. Den Uyl and Rasmussen (2006); Christmas (2019b, 279–80).
26. Long (2000, 49–50).
27. Whether the rules of justice therefore need to be *constructed* (Rawls 1980; Korsgaard 1996) in view of what constitutes our humanity, or they need to simply be *discovered* (Den Uyl and Rasmussen 2016, 2020) in light of what constitutes our humanity is not something I can see a material difference between for my purposes here.
28. Den Uyl and Rasmussen (2005, 2016, 2020, chap. 2).
29. Christmas (2018a); Den Uyl and Rasmussen (2018).
30. Mack (1989, 1998).
31. Rawls (1999, sec. 26); Kamm (2013, 261); Quong (2018, 308–9).
32. Dworkin (1984).
33. I use Wesley Newcombe Hohfeld's conceptual taxonomy of juridical relations (Hohfeld 1913, 1917). My understanding of Hohfeld is owed largely to Duarte d'Almeida (2016) and Frydrych (2019).
34. I use "right" to refer specifically to claim-rights, as per the Hohfeldian analysis, unless otherwise stated.
35. Hence Thomas Hobbes's assertion that under a system of mere liberties, where everyone has permission to interfere with everyone, a state of affairs akin to war would ensue (Hobbes 1983, pt. 1, 2012, chaps 13, 14).
36. It seems perfectly consistent with the structure of justice, however, that it could assign the respective rights and liberties to φ to separate persons, and that the claim to φ, therefore, is not partially constituted by the liberty to φ. All that can be deduced from the mere structure of justice is that if it assigns a permission to φ to *anyone*, it must also assign the right to φ to *someone*. I therefore do not take up either side of the conceptual debate over whether claims are "passive" (Salmond 1902, 223; Williams 1956, 1145; Finnis 1972, 377, 380; Wellman 1985, 65; Halpin 1991, 271, 293; Kramer 1998, 13–14, 22 n.8; Finnis 2011, 200) or "active" (Radin 1929, 903–4, 1938, 1148, 1152; Horwitz 1979, 155; Singer 1982, 986; Simmonds 1998, 223, n.137; Eleftheriadis 2008, 123). Thanks are due to David Frydrych for helping me understand the terms of this debate (Frydrych 2018a). In the next chapter, however, we will see that the substance of justice turns out to be such that all permissions to φ and rights to φ are originally assigned to one and the same person.
37. Hart (1982, 171–73); Steiner (1994, 75–76, 87–91).
38. Once again, the "may" in the former two sentences should be understood as that of moral permissibility not modal possibility.
39. Steiner (1974, 198).
40. More will be said about the nature of force in the next chapter.
41. Waldron (1996, 1555, 1999, 52).
42. Grotius (2005, vol. 3, sec. I.I.IV); Haakonssen (1985).

43. We need not, however, think of natural rights as displacing or "usurping" the sphere of natural justice, as Richard Tuck appears to Tuck (1979, 67). It is simply that there is more than one set of discursive tools that describe the same domain of morality.
44. The following argument is also presented in Christmas (2019a).
45. Steiner (1977, 1994, 74–101); a different rationale for the compossibility requirement of rights comes from Robert Nozick: that our rights must involve the right to do wrong, and therefore cannot be said to violate any duty to another, so long as we act within our rights (Nozick 1974, 106; Waldron 1981).
46. A different description of the compossibility requirement is that we each have a duty to let others do their duty (Goodin 2020).
47. Schmidtz (2006, 211, 2009, 4, 2010); Brennan and Schmidtz (2010, 33); Schmidtz (2011); we must make a distinction between theory and practice. First, in any given situation where there is uncertainty as to what rights two parties have, we may not *need* to know what structural conditions ensure compossibility in order for them to avoid interpersonal practical conflict. They may voluntarily acquiesce to one another in ways that avert such conflict, or they may demand respect for their rights as they understand them, but fortunately the manner in which they act on their duties to each other as they understand them does not give rise to any further interpersonal practical conflict. Second, acting on their rights as they understand them, coming into conflict, and then bringing the matter before an impartial third party to adjudicate may be one among many practical discovery procedures for arriving at what their real rights of justice in fact are. While compossibility is a necessary condition for any set of rights of justice, it may not need to be the starting point of any actually existing institutions of social and legal constraint (Schmidtz 1996). A virtue of such a system is that it arrives at compossible sets of rights *after* adjudication. What is crucial is to recognise that such an institution would only serve as a mechanism for discovering rights, not for creating them.
48. Mack (2018, 52).
49. Hart (1985, 126–27).
50. Steiner (1994, 101).
51. Steiner (1998a, 131–32).
52. Note that only rights and their correlative duties need to be compossible, not liberties. Since liberties merely grant a permission to engage in a particular action, they do not assign correlative duties to others to abstain from interfering in one's acting on that permission (unless one also has some other right that protects one from this form of interference, which gives rights to duties in others).
53. Steiner (1977, 1994, 74–101).
54. Steiner (1994, 91).
55. Strictly speaking, it is extensional *disjunction* rather than *differentiability* that does this work. But I will continue to use Steiner's term for the sake of terminological parity.
56. Steiner (1977, 769).
57. Steiner (1994, 78–85); Christmas (2019a, 221–22).
58. Where the use of a time-indexed object is understood broadly to just mean the subsumption of that object within an action at a given time or, that object's inclusion in a fully description of the action at a given time.
59. This example is taken from Christmas (2019a, 227–28).
60. Steiner (1994, 91).

61. Steiner (1994, 100).
62. James Stern argues, in a similar vein, that "rights to exclude" fails to capture the necessary conditions of rights that are guaranteed to avoid "incompatibilities" (Stern 2017). So long as the content of rights is structured such that their content be mutually exclusive, they are compossible, but this does not need to mean exclusive rights to physical objects; it could mean a right to an object that no one else has, even it is not a right to exclude others from the object tout court.
63. Hume (1902, sec. II.I.II).
64. See footnote 33.
65. Expositions and defence of the will/choice theory can be found in Kant (1991, pt. 1); Hart (1982, chaps 7–8, 1994), Feinberg (1980); Wellman (1985, 1995, 2000); Simmonds (1998); Steiner (1998b); Frydrych (2018b; Forthcoming); those of the interest/benefit theory can be found in Raz (1986, chap. 7, 1994, 258–65); Kramer (1998, 2010, 2017); MacCormick (2008, 129); those of putative hybrid theories can be found in Sreenivasan (2005, 2010); Wenar (2005, 2013); Rainbolt (2006); for criticism of the possibility of a hybrid account, see Kramer and Steiner (2005); Frydrych (2018b, 580–84).
66. Steiner (1994, 231); Pallikkathayil (2010, 136).
67. Flanigan (2018, 6, 10, 11).
68. Valentini (2011); Huber (2020).
69. Rothbard (1998, chaps 6–7).

2 The Substance of Justice

Introduction

So far, I have only argued that rights of justice have a certain structure – enforceable claims to non-interference in particular activities with regard to particular objects at particular times. This account of the form of justice could potentially be consistent with a vast variety of accounts of the substance of justice. All that has to be done is to give some argument for why particular persons have rights to the particular actions they do, in relation to the particular time-indexed objects specified therein. However, a substantive account of justice can be drawn from its form on its own. The original rights – or rather, original *right* – that I argue justice assigns each individual is derived from a minimalism about the moral function of justice. In order to coordinate human action in a socio-economic context, it need not introduce any more constraints than a constraint on the initiation of interference against others. While this is a substantive liberal account of our rights, it is one that complies with the overarching moral brief of justice itself. As I will suggest, it is for this reason that I think justice itself is a liberal idea, since it does not prescribe particular purposes for agents but, rather, simply gives rules for averting and adjudicating the conflicts that occur when purposes of different people are incompatible. The coordination of diverse ends in a context of scarcity and potentially disinterested sociality is a liberal goal. While I do not argue that a liberal approach to rights is the only coherent one grounded in the circumstances of justice, I do argue that it is the only one that is motivated *purely* by the circumstances of justice. That is without invoking ad hoc intuitions that justice is deemed to need to reflect.

The Right to Non-Interference in Our Non-Interfering Actions

The previous chapter argued that justice assigns claim-rights against interference in certain activities with regard to particular time-indexed objects. The remaining question, then, is which activities are protected for whom? This chapter will argue that individuals each have a claim-right to non-interference in their ongoing, non-interfering activities.

The first thing to note in establishing what the content of rights is, is that justice authorises interference in certain cases precisely because not all activities that individuals might choose to engage in a socio-economic context are mutually performable, and hence moral pronouncement regarding which are to prevail is morally necessary for moral actors. That is to say that the exclusion of certain activities is introduced into the scheme of justice because and therefore *to the extent that* such exclusion is necessary for human action to proceed in a socio-economic context. The structure of rights is such that they pertain to particular activities with regard to external objects, rather than to those objects tout court, because such expansive exclusion is not necessary for human action to proceed in a socio-economic context, even if it is sufficient.

The second thing to note is that the correlativity of enforceable rights and duties means that the admission of a particular right into the system admits the authorisation of interference. Any right to engage *S* in φ authorises interference in the action of any third party that itself interferes with such φ-ing with regard to *S*. In other words, necessary and proportionate interference with any action that is a violation of a duty is authorised.[1]

Given that enforcements are a kind of interference, it is essential that rights only protect activities that themselves do not constitute the initiation of interferences in other ongoing activities. For them to do otherwise would be for rights to introduce an authorisation of interference into a situation in which the coordination of action does not require it. Since which actions constitute initiations of interference in other ongoing actions depends upon the prior activities that have been initiated and are ongoing, justice authorises only interference in those activities that introduce interference into a pattern of otherwise mutually non-interfering social actions. Hence, the only right is a right to not be interfered with in those actions one initiates which themselves do not constitute interference with any action anyone else has already initiated. In order to abstain from authorising excessing interference and hence exclusion, justice must be blind in its assignment of rights to engage in particular activities – it must delegate that work to the actors themselves. That is to say, whatever activities a person chooses to initiate, so long as they do not interfere with anyone else, they are protected by right. Justice gives us each a claim-right to non-interference in our non-interfering activities.

If justice were to be purpose-directive and, prior to any person taking any particular action, justice laid down a list of particular activities and objects each person had a claim against interference in, it would introduce more exclusion than is necessary. Assigning original rights to engage in specific activities without interference, rather than a general right to non-interference in those activities that persons in fact choose to pursue – which we only know when such choices are made real through action – would authorise the use of interference in activities which may in fact turn out not to interfere in any activity that a person has chosen to engage in. Such a conception of justice would involve more interference (and therefore exclude more activities) than is called for by the circumstances of justice. It authorises interferences in a larger volume of cases than it needs to.

It may be thought that making non-interference the exclusive purview of justice privileges first-movers. Imagine *A* φs in conjunction with *S* at *t*, and this does not interfere with anyone else's ongoing activities. In this instance, *A* has a claim against interference in her φ-ing in conjunction with *S* such that were *B* to ψ in conjunction with *S* at t_1, and φ and ψ are mutually unperformable in conjunction with *S*, then *B* would be the rights-violator. However, had the temporal order of *A* and *B*'s respective actions been reversed, *A* would be the rights-violator. It might be deemed arbitrary for time to play such an important role in determining whose actions count as just and whose as unjust. Perhaps *B* had been considering or desiring to ψ from t_{-1} and is now no longer at liberty to ψ simply because *A* φ-ed at *t*. However, there is good reason for justice to operate in this way.

Justice protects actual choices made real by being acted upon. It cannot protect mere psychological intentions. Justice is an *interpersonal* virtue and hence the empirical facts that tell us how to apply it in any given context cannot be something that is logically private, such as psychological intentions or desires. Only the individual herself can be the authority as to whether or not she had an internal state of mind or not and, as such, can alter the empirical veracity of that fact at will.[2] The determinants of what is to count as just or unjust in a particular instance must be things that can be intelligible to all who are subject to justice; there must be objective criteria for determining that a particular action was just or unjust.[3] This is how I understand Kant's insistence that rights regulates our *external* relations.[4] Relations that are internal to the self are the province of other virtues, duties, or moral reasons. All actions must occur at some time; justice must therefore, in a sense, privilege earlier actions because and to the extent that, being earlier, they do not interfere with later actions, whereas later actions can interfere with earlier ones.

This temporal aspect of the right to non-interference also helps to clarify an important distinction between the way interference is prohibited on my view and the way interference is often treated in the philosophical literature on freedom.[5] Freedom as non-interference is often taken to be the fact of not being interfered with, whatever one's actions in fact are. For example, imagine that at t_1, *A* is fishing in a pond, and *B* is pondering on what she should do with her day. At t_2 – a point at which *A* is still fishing in the pond, *B* decides that she would like to go for a swim in this pond. Let us stipulate that the simultaneous performance of these actions is impossible, and that they are therefore rival with regard to the pond in question. Let us further imagine that *B* is stopped from swimming, either by *A* or by a third party (let us say, to protect *A* from interference in her fishing). While it is true that stopping *B* from swimming interferes with her, it is not the case that violates her right to non-interference, since that right can only protect one from interference in one's non-interfering actions.

A right to non-interference tout court is not one that can be made sense of. It is not clear what the correlative duty imposes on the rest of the world. It cannot correlate with an enforceable duty in all others abstain from interfering with each other, since the enforcement of that duty would interfere with them and thereby violate their right.[6] Any attempt to set in place a universal right to any notion of freedom that did not discriminate between licit and illicit actions will result in a set of rights that is incompossible. Kant referred to this a "wild, lawless freedom," which he took to be no freedom at all because it is not susceptible to protection by rights.[7] On Kant's view, one is not morally free to hinder the freedom of others.[8]

The approach favoured by Isaiah Berlin to rescue freedom as non-interference from this absurdity was simply to say that some interferences are worse than others, so we can engage in some of the milder interferences in order to stop the more serious interferences:

> [A]ll coercion is, in so far as it frustrates human desires, bad as such, although it may have to be applied to prevent other, greater evils; while non-interference, which is the opposite of coercion, is good as such, although it is not the only good.[9]

For example interfering with would-be murderers is worth the gain in freedom as non-interference experienced by the would-be victims; murder is a greater evil than depriving murders of their freedom. Implicit in Berlin's remarks here is that interference with interference violates freedom as non-interference. But this is not so. It does not violate the murderer's liberty to stop her from murdering because the murder's right to liberty does not and cannot extend to interfering with others, in this instance by murdering them.

If we believe that justice protects freedom, and justice consists in a set of compossible rights, then there must be a disjunction between the class of actions we have permission to engage in and those we are prohibited from engaging in. There must be a dichotomy between liberty and licence. To put this another way, according to Gerald MacCallum's triadic schema of freedom, an agent *x* is free from constraints *y* to do/

be/become *z*.[10] To be compossible, a set of rights must assign rights to actions in the *z*-parameter, but, moreover, actions in the *z*-parameter must be disjoined from the *y*-parameter.

At this point, an objection lies in waiting. Persons have a right to freedom, and freedom is defined in contradistinction to licence. However, if we already have a dichotomy between liberty and licence, and, by extension, an account of the class of actions persons have permission to engage in and a wholly disjoined set of actions they are prohibited from engaging in, then we already have a set of rights and the insistence that people have a right to freedom is thereby circular and the argument is question-begging.[11]

However, when one recognises the temporal nature of liberty, this problem is dissolved. If *A* φ's in conjunction with *S* at t_1 and *B* ψ's in conjunction with *S* at t_2 and φ and ψ are mutually unperformable in conjunction with *S*, then *B* violates *A*'s liberty since it is *B* that *interfered. A* does not interfere with *B* for the simple fact that she was there first and initiated a non-interfering action; *B* arrived later and initiated an action that, whatever else it was, interfered with *A*. Interfering is licence, acting in a non-interfering way is liberty – and it is liberty we have a right to. A right to non-interference in one's non-interfering actions is a right to liberty and a correlative duty of non-interference.

Liberty as non-interference has been subjected to other challenges. Philip Pettit[12] has argued that one's liberty as non-interference is not violated when it is that case that one *would* be interfered with if one was to φ (an action one has a right to engage in), but if one chooses not to φ, therefore the interference does not take place. While it is trivially so that an interference does not occur in this scenario (assuming no threat was issued), it is not the case that this individual enjoys a right to her freedom. For a right to be respected by institutions, it must be the case that one is free to exercise one's rights however one chooses to do so. That one *would* be interfered with if one exercised one's right differently means that one is subjected to institutions that do not respect one's rights. Any set of institutions that does not protect one's right to non-interference are necessarily unjust. The protection of a claim-right presupposes the counterfactual respect for its exercise however it may be exercised.[13] Institutional respect for a right to non-interference presupposes that whatever non-interfering actions one *might* take *would not* be interfered with. Any set of institutions that sets in place patterns of action such that, counterfactually if one were to φ (and φ is a non-interfering action), one would be interfered with would be an unjust set of institutions since it includes rules that demand initiatory interference and thus rights' violations. The questions of what actions commit injustices and what institutions[14] are unjust qua institutions are distinct but inseparable. They are distinct because the fact that no unjust actions occur at t_1 does not entail that institutions in place at t_1 were just. But they are inseparable because we need to know which actions are unjust in order to know which institutions are unjust in virtue of the actions they permit, prohibit, and require.

Pettit's introduction of counterfactual interferences here merely indicates the distinction between individual actions and social institutions. An individual who never interferes with anyone never violates anyone's rights. However, a set of institutions that demands they do so under certain circumstances is an unjust set of institutions, regardless of whether those circumstances arise or not. However, persons only act unjustly if those circumstances *do* arise and act as the institutions demands – unjustly.

Pettit's second challenge is that if one happens to not be interfered with due to the choices others happen to make (rather than one's own), one is technically free from interference, but undeniably unfree. And therefore, freedom cannot consist in non-interference. For example the institution of chattel slavery presupposes the legal right of the master to interfere with the slave in any way and at any time the master chooses. If the master chooses not to ever interfere, then it is true that the master does not engage in any action that violates the slave's right to non-interference. Yet, the institution that legally permits that master to interfere with the slave is unjust because it permits the master to interfere with the slave and hence permits injustice. Pettit wants to say that the slave is unfree because their non-interference is subject to the master's discretion. Freedom has to mean not merely the fact of non-interference, but also that the fact of non-interference is not owed to some person or persons' exertion of their discretionary will. However, it is not clear how any institution could remove the possibility of discretionary action in the way Pettit requires. Even if institutions were perfectly aligned to justice, all institutions depend upon a substantial degree of acquiescence from those who are subject to them.[15] Whether it is an individual or a group, there is always the possibility that they could unjustly interfere with one another simply because they choose to.[16]

Living under unjust institutions wrongs subjects in virtue of leaving them exposed to risk of being a victim of injustice. However, Pettit's insistence that there being a risk of one's liberty being violated or that one would find one's liberty violated if one acted differently is itself a violation of one's liberty is double-counting. There are actions that constitute interference, and there are institutions to attempt to secure a pattern of behaviours that exclude interference. Since justice demands that we abstain from actions that constitute interferences, it demands of our institutions that they secure that pattern of behaviour. When there are no such institutions, one is likely at greater risk of having one's liberty violated. While exposure to such risk is a kind of wrongdoing perpetuated by whomever is responsible, the risk of losing freedom is not itself a loss of freedom, any more than the risk of losing the pound coin in one's pocket reduces the purchasing power of that pound coin. Of course, when one's rights are at risk, one has greater authorisation to use defensive interference than if one's rights were not at risk. However, this is precisely because one's freedom is in jeopardy not because one is unfree.

The One and Only Right

Not only are all persons endowed with an original right to non-interference in their ongoing, non-interfering activities, but they are endowed with *no other* enforceable rights in addition to this. The nature of enforceable rights is such that no further right can be admitted into the scheme. An enforceable right to non-interference does not leave any space for any further, enforceable rights. To add any other enforceable right alongside the right to non-interference would introduce grounds for interfering with persons who are not engaged in interference. Take, for example, a putatively enforceable right that others promote one's happiness. This would necessarily introduce correlative duties in all others to promote one another's happiness. Were someone to fail to promote the happiness of others and yet not take any action that interferes with others, they would be liable to have their activities interfered with in order to make them comply with their duties of beneficence. This would constitute initiatory interference and hence would not be compossible with an enforceable claim to non-interference.

Of course, one could adjust the contours of the right to non-interference and change it so as to protect one's activities from non-interference so long as those activities promote the happiness of others. Perhaps steps could be taken to formulate this basic right so as to render its universalisation a compossible set of rights. What I press is that this would shrink the scope of non-interfering activities persons could rightfully initiate. And therefore the admission of any extra right into a system of rights to non-interference is not possible.[17] That is not to say that persons would no longer be free *whatsoever*, but simply that they are not as free as justice has the capacity to make them. That is free to set their own purposes, within a socio-economic context.

The foregoing is not to entail that there are no duties of beneficence or, for that matter, no duties of any other kind besides non-interference. It is only that there are no *enforceable* such duties. Since enforcement is a type of interference, there can be no enforceable duties (or correlative rights) to do anything other than abstain from interfering with others.[18] One right to non-interference, by extension, entails one has an enforceable right to violate one's non-enforceable duties.[19]

I think there are broader considerations regarding the nature of justice that lend plausibility to this liberal conception thereof.

The fact of potentially diverse and conflicting human purposes is part of the circumstances of justice. It is because of the fact of human purposiveness (in a socio-economic context) that justice arises. However, unlike other kinds of virtues, duties, or moral reasons, it does not tell us which purposes to pursue over other ones. Justice does not prescribe particular purposes to be pursued but rather adjudicates between the purposes of different agents when they conflict as they do in a socio-economic context. It does so by assigning authority to particular persons in particular circumstances to interfere with interferences in their purposes. In assigning claim-rights to individuals, it abstains from giving purpose-directed moral guidance and instead gives the rightholder the authority to choose how to proceed; namely, whether or not to let another person's conflicting action prevail or to use force to stop it in order that her own rights-protected action proceed. Justice's telos is the socio-economic nexus of teloi itself.[20] It is in this sense that it stands above other moral purposes as an overriding, functionally metanormative,[21] or deontological demand, whatever other demands are placed upon us by the rest of morality. It delegates purpose–direction to purposive agents themselves. For this reason, the actions it permits are those actions which individuals in fact embark upon, so long as they are mutually non-interfering.

Liberal approaches to justice that claim that liberty as the only or the primary value to be considered a matter of justice are often seen as arbitrarily narrow.[22] However, justice arises because of the interpersonal practical conflicts that arise in a socio-economic context, given the variety of other values individuals should pursue. To elevate those values that generate conflict for and between moral agents in a socio-economic context is to engage in double-counting. If we do not think insurmountable conflict ought to arise, and really it is just that certain values and purposes ought to prevail over others because they are more important, then we do not really think there are any such thing as the circumstances of justice. The common response that "liberty is important, of course, but so are many other things" is to misunderstand the position the liberal account of justice attempts to stake out: liberty is important *because* so many other, potentially conflicting things are indeed important.

I think, therefore, that herein lies the essential liberalism in taking justice seriously whatsoever: if we do not think that persons are such that what is prima facie good for them needs moral adjustment in a context of scarcity, uncertainty, and diverse sociality, then we have no call for justice nor freedom.[23] Indeed, the circumstances of justice, in part, give voice to the liberal concern of the separateness of, or distinctions between, persons.[24] Understanding the potential for a plurality of ends coming into practical conflict as a moral problem to be overcome *not* through seeking to change those ends, is to understand the liberal problem.[25] How to find singular moral guidance for society, given the plurality of morals guiding individuals and groups is the challenge liberalism simultaneously assigns itself and resolves with the idea of individual rights.

Justice provides moral finality to questions that arise due to practical conflict in our respective pursuit of our purposes; as such, it must assign compossible domains of action.[26] That justice assigns spheres of freedom does not mean that any exercise of our freedom is morally appropriate or permissible in a broader sense, but it does mean that it is morally inappropriate or impermissible to interfere with another person's exercise of their freedom.[27]

Justice demands that each person be given the same sphere of freedom qua non-interference. They may therefore choose which (non-interfering) actions they wish to pursue and when to yield to others or enter into joint activities with others. This likeness of juridical powers that each person has over themselves reflects the moral equality of persons, by giving them each such moral authority over a particular sphere of matters that is consistent with the moral authority of others over a particular sphere of matters. Hart describes holders of such rights as small-scale sovereigns, in other words, subjected to themselves only rather than morally superior human powers.[28] There is not sufficient space here to do justice to the claim that the value of equality is rightfully understood just as a right to non-interference.[29] But it is worth noting that giving non-interference such pride of place within a theory of justice does not necessarily come at the expense of equality. It only comes at the expense of applications of equality that presuppose our equality must be realised, in part, in demoting freedom. It is also worth noting that this was not an exotic notion to many proto-liberals.[30]

Kinds of Interference

Each person has a right that their activities not be interfered with, so long as those activities do not themselves constitute interference in other persons' activities. Given that these rights are enforceable and therefore authorise interference in actions that violate them, justice does not prohibit *all* interference, but all *initiatory* interference. While initiatory interference can come in many forms of varying moral severity, varying moral severity does not alter the fact they are all forms of injustice. That variation ought to be regarded as occupying different scales of wrongdoing *within* injustice. There are no forms of initiatory interference that are so minuscule so as to no longer be injustices. However, proportionality does demand that minor interferences may only be met with proportionally minor counter-interferences, whereas major interference may be met with more serious counter-interferences qua means of enforcement.[31] An injustice does not licence its victim to use whatever means they wish to repel it. Even as victims of injustice, we are still bound within moral limits.

What all kinds of interferences have in common is that they involve the use of force by an interferer against a person's actions such that they fail to align with interferer's choices at the expense of the victim's. Interferences get in between a person's capacity for choice and her actions and forcibly insert the interferer's will there between.

The most serious forms of interferences are those referred to as *aggressions*.[32] Aggressions are serious and immediate interferences with one's ability to pursue one's chosen course of action whatever it might be, often involving pain or injury or risk thereof. Battery under common law does a good job of covering those interferences we generally regard as aggressive: assaults and forceful seizure of personal property such as a hat off of the head or a wallet out of the pocket. They are deeper interferences in a person's control over her own actions because they generally interfere with a more important class of actions; they block a greater variety of further actions the persons may wish to engage in; and the means used is particularly painful, harmful, or unpleasant. It is not for these reasons that they are unjust, but for these reasons that they are relatively more morally serious forms of injustice.

Imagine you are walking across a meadow and find an easel with a canvas on it, a stool, paint brushes, and paint. Someone is in the middle of painting a landscape and has just left to go fetch a drink of water. Destroying or removing or tampering with these objects interferes with that person's ongoing activities, but they are not aggressions. It would be aggressive if when one stumbled across the scene, the painter was still there, and one snatched the easel and broke it in half, yanked the paint brush from her hand, and pushed her to the floor. The victim would be authorised to take more morally serious counter-interfering action in the latter case than the first. Proportionate use of force in the former case might involve entering your home to forcibly take the items back into her possession or the wherewithal to procure replacements, as well as a little bit more for her trouble. Proportionate use of force in the latter case could involve immediate violence against your person, even with a non-deadly weapon, and then the forcible seizure of means of restitution after the fact.

Restitution ought not to be regarded as *undoing* the rights-violation. Rather, the rationale for restitution is that the interference is still ongoing until the victim has what they need to proceed in the activity that was interrupted. If I take your easel, I am engaged in an interference for as long as I fail to return it. But if I break your easel, giving it back does not bring an end to my interference. The interference I present by breaking it is continuous until I enable you to continue the activity of painting. As Waldron puts it, "it is a continuing state of affairs" until the item is returned in tact or restitution is made.[33]

Physical force is clearly a violation of one's right to non-interference. However, another important form of coercion is volitional coercion.

The latter is a form of coercion that does not involve the application of force but nonetheless constitutes an interference in someone's actions. Certain kinds of threats constitute volition coercion.[34] While threats are ways of getting others to do things they otherwise would not do, they are only coercive in the sense of violating one's right to non-interference when what they threaten is itself an interference. The reason for this is simple: threatening a person with an interference unless they engage in actions they are not duty-bound to engage in constitutes an initiation of interference in non-interfering actions.

Threats are varieties of credible contingency announcements. *A* threatens *B* when she issues announcement of the form "unless you φ, I will ψ" where *B* prefers not-ψ to φ, but would prefer not-ψ and not-φ, were the option there. *A*'s threat removes the latter option, so *B* opts to φ in order to avoid ψ. The contingency announcement can be inverted and still constitute a threat: *A* says "if you φ, I will not ψ" where *B* prefers not-ψ to φ, but would prefer not-φ and not-ψ. *A*'s threat removes that latter option, so *B* opts to φ in order to avoid ψ. Both threats constitute actions that alter the options that *B* has and predictably impacts her actions.[35] Given that *A* can effect *B*'s actions through making threats, it is often argued that threats are therefore forms of coercion and are by implication at odds with freedom.

Debate has ensued over whether or not what is threatened is something that presumptively damages the victim's welfare or enhances it. There may be welfare-enhancing actions that are so irresistible to the victim they will predictably comply with the threatener's will in order to get them. Such threats are often referred to as "throffers"[36] since they technically add an option to the set before an actor rather than remove one. They are taken to nonetheless be coercive in that they predictably affect the victim's actions.[37]

Offers and threats are no doubt interventions into deliberations of persons. But that does not necessarily mean that they are always interferences in person's actions. Asking someone not to eat a salad introduces a new reason into their deliberations and therefore intervenes in that sense. Yet, it does not interfere with her act of eating it, even if it ultimately causes her not to. Grabbing hold of the plate and holding out of reach, however, does interfere because it affect a physical change in at least some of the physical components of one's actions against one's will in such a way the rediverts them to alternative ends.[38]

It is not that threats can be efficacious in getting others to comply with one's wishes that makes them coercive, since this is symptomatic of all reason-giving. What is important is *what* is being threatened. If *A* threatens *B* with some interference in her non-interfering actions, say stabbing her in the thigh if she does not hand over her wallet, she has *initiated* an act of interference. Threats constitute initiations of the actions they threaten, so when one credibly threatens an interference one initiates an act of interference by announcing one's willingness. Of course, the interference may not come to full fruition when the victim complies, but that does not mean that no interference was initiated. Just as pointing a gun at someone and threatening to pull the trigger constitutes an initiation of the act of murder even if the murder does not come to pass. For threats to be effective and credible, they must be ostensibly intelligible as initiations of the act they threaten; just like pointing a gun. Contingency announcements of the form "unless you φ, I will ψ," where the victim has no duty to φ and the threatener has a duty not to ψ, are qua speech acts, unjust as they constitute initiations of interferences in non-interfering actions. Whether the threat is ultimately effective or not does not alter the injustice of it.[39]

Self-Ownership

Can or should the claim to non-interference in one's ongoing, non-interfering activities be construed as a right of self-ownership or property right in one's own person? Many theories of property and justice, especially ones that take themselves to draw on Locke, believe that our original rights are ones of self-ownership and that our acquired rights to extra-personal objects are, in some way or other, acquired by an application or exercise of these original rights. I take the original claim to non-interference to be – as far as motivating intuitions might go – in the same spirit as self-ownership. The reason, however, that I do not attempt at the outset to frame this right as one that constitutes self-ownership, is that the latter idea is fraught with controversy over what has to be true of a right to qualify it as a *property* right or a right of *ownership*. There are accounts of self-ownership that are, more or less, equivalent to a claim-right to non-interference in one's non-interfering activities; these I have little quarrel with. However, I think it is important to understand property rights in external goods as a function of the rights we have over our person, rather than attempt to establish some coherent conception of property and then understand our personal rights through that lens. So, I will show why the most prominent views of self-ownership are problematic within my view and give some indication of how any conception of self-ownership could be coherent.

The account of self-ownership that is most common is that imputed to Nozick by Cohen,[40] carried forward for more rigorous development by Steiner, and adopted by Michael Otsuka and Peter Vallentyne. Nozick does not give anything like a developed account of self-ownership; he only suggests that it is a classical liberal notion and that the coercive redistribution of wealth that is required by patterned or end-state principles of distributive justice violate the spirit of it, because they demand that people sometimes be deprived of the fruits of their labour and to that extent are rendered mere tools to others.[41] Cohen, being a Marxist, was intrigued by this claim and subjected the idea of self-ownership to more rigorous scrutiny because he thought, intuitively, it might explain why capitalist exploitation of labour is a rights-violation.[42] The Cohenite account is as follows:

> Each person is the morally rightful owner of himself. He possesses over himself, as a matter of moral right, all those rights that a slaveholder has over a complete chattel slave as a matter of legal right, and he is entitled, morally speaking, to dispose over himself in the way such a slaveholder is entitled, morally speaking, to dispose over his slave.[43]

The analogy to *chattel* slavery was an unfortunate one for many reasons.[44] Chiefly, it meant that focus was drawn to the idea that just as chattel slavery implied owning other persons qua physical objects, it gave rise to a discourse that focussed on what it meant to have ownership rights over one's physical body. As we will discuss in the following chapter, the quest for what it means to own *physical objects* as such leads to an account of ownership as being as exclusive as is logically possible. Given Steiner's higher-order commitment to all rights being to time-indexed objects tout court (discussed in the previous chapter), it is expected that his account of self-ownership involves an exclusive claim to one's physical body for the duration of one's life[45] – not just any ownership, *full liberal ownership*.[46] However, the idea that owning oneself as an object must mean some totalising, logically complete, saturation of physical space with rights held by one individual was embraced also by Cohen, who later said that he understood self-ownership to be "the fullest right a person (logically) can have over herself provided that each other person also has just such a right."[47] And by Otsuka:

> [A] person's right of self-ownership is full if and only if that person possesses, to the greatest extent and stringency compatible with the same possession by others, the . . . rights to decide what would become of himself and what he would do . . .[48]

And by Vallentyne:

> The core idea of full self-ownership is that agents own themselves in just the same way that they can fully own inanimate objects. This maximal private ownership includes (1) full *control rights* . . ., (2) full *rights to transfer* . . ., and (3) full *payment immunities*.[49]

This account of self-ownership has come under attack for being too strong. However, such attacks do not say that self-ownership should be regarded as some different set of rights – a set less "full" or "stringent."

Rather, they say the idea of owning oneself is altogether implausible, merely because under this articulation it renders the claim-right too strongly. Peter Railton and David Sobel's objection to it is that it is mutually disabling to have such strong protections over our respective bodies (and extended rights with the same protection).[50] *A*'s emission of minute amounts of particulate pollution that *B* inhales or her gently grazing *B*'s arm as she passes her on a crowded street are violations of her self-ownership, and she is therefore duty bound not to engage in actions that have (or are at serious risk of having) this result. In fact, the problem can be stated even more strongly. If *A* really has a claim that no physical changes be made to anything within or on the physical perimeter of her body, even *B* moving on the same plane in the presence of light will alter the refraction of photons that hit *A*'s body and thus violate her self-ownership. So, *A* and *B* cannot even move their bodies without violating each other's self-ownership unless they are separated by a wall or otherwise on either sides of a sufficient lip of the gradient of the planet.

The extent of their duties is such that both *A* and *B* have vanishingly small space in which they are permitted to exercise the liberty rights that their claim-rights are supposed to protect the free exercise of. As Eric Mack puts it, they are "morally hog-tied."[51] This critique has received many replies that countenance a meaningful version of self-ownership that does not include such needless stringency.[52] However, I think the answer lies in revising the account of ownership more generally that is being applied to the person. Indeed, among many of those replies is the observation that the account of ownership in self-ownership that is invoked by Cohen, Steiner, and Otsuka is not one that is familiar with regard to other kinds of property. Indeed, we do not think private ownership of houses is impossible because it strikes us as permissible that people might graze the wall or fly planes overhead without our permission. If self-ownership is going to accurately represent our natural rights, we must understand the ownership involved not as a right to a physical object tout court, in this case our bodies. Rather, as a claim against interference in a particular circumscribed set of activities in conjunction with our bodies, as I have argued all rights must be. That we have a claim against interference in whatever non-interfering use we make of our bodies seems sufficiently expansive as to be captured by the term "ownership."

A claim against interference in whatever actions we in fact initiate is both broader and narrower than the physicalistic account of self-ownership adopted by Cohen, Steiner, and Otsuka. It is broader because it implies *some* claim to the disposition of objects outside of one's physical body. For example it implies certain claims to the spaces around one's body that one needs some degree of open access to in order to for one's activities to occur. Moreover, it implies non-interference with the use of whatever extra-personal objects are subsumed into one's activities.

This notion of self-ownership necessarily includes a right to make use of external objects, so long as it does not interfere with any existing use being made by others. The wedge between self-ownership and world-ownership that Cohen, Steiner, and Otsuka are so keen on is therefore removed under this account of self-ownership. Of course, we can still distinguish between objects which are part of one's body and therefore part of the object that *acts* rather than part of the subject that is *acted upon* or *used*. But there is no fine line between our biomass and our tools.[53] As physically embodied actors, there is an overlap between that which is part-and-parcel of the actor and that which is used in the action. The following chapter will discuss putative wedge between self-ownership and world-ownership, and between use-rights and ownership rights, in far more detail.

On the other hand, this account is narrower than the physicalistic one because it involves lesser claims over one's physical body. Because it is not a claim-right *to* one's physical body tout court, but rather a claim against interference in one's use of it. Therefore, there are some "uses" of one's body that others are free to make. I put "uses" in inverted commas because it is only under a rather stretched notion of use that this is the case, but it is important that this action space within one's body is left open to others. For example it does not interfere with one's activities to have harmless radio waves pass through one's body (created by the next-door neighbour's Wi-Fi network), nor does it interfere with one's activities to be exposed to negligible levels of particulate pollution, which means insensible particles land on one's skin or clothing. Where the claims only extend so as to protect the actual activities one engages in from interference, rather than to the total physical disposition of a particular object, they do not correlate with duties that are morally hog-tying.

There is a sense in which it is not that the rights of self-ownership on the physicalist account are too strong or stringent, but rather that their content includes too much. I take the claim to non-interference to be as stringent as possible; yet that does not make its correlative duties hog-tying because it leaves open action space that it does not need to enclose. It is rendering individual rights as exclusive rights to objects tout court, as opposed to right to use those objects for particular activities, which brings the trouble.

Necessity

A claim-right to non-interference in one's ongoing activities also implies a claim to non-interference in one's internal bodily processes, as they naturally proceed or as they proceed as a result of one's own intervention (medical, or otherwise). One does not purposively bring about the oxygenation of one's blood, for example. Such processes, therefore, are not typically the *subject* of one's action as such. Nonetheless, the subsistence of one's body and hence the non-frustration of these processes is a necessary precondition for one's initiation of action whatsoever. So, while it would be clumsy if not downright false to say that one's natural bodily processes are actions that one takes, they are nonetheless incorporated and subsumed into one's activity *generally*. They are the necessary conscripts of the possibility of one's activity whatsoever.[54]

Of course, one can hold one's breath, install internal medical appliances, or control other bodily functions through deep meditation, perhaps. Indeed, the entire notion of taking care of one's health, fitness, and well-being presumes the bringing of bodily processes under at least partial conscious control. Nonetheless, their ongoing occurrence even when they are *not* rendered the subject of our action is a necessary condition for our taking action *per se*. Without being bodies, we could not act, so that which is necessary to our bodies' being is necessary to our action.

An implication of the fact that we are physically embodied actors means that a claim to non-interference presupposes a claim to the necessary preconditions of our actions – the subsistence of our bodies. This has straightforward implications for the protection of our bodily integrity. For example, it protects us while we sleep: one might think that a right of non-interference means that when one is asleep, others are duty-bound to do nothing other than not wake you up. Meaning that if medical technology allowed them to do so without waking or killing you, others could make use of your internal organs while you sleep and so forth.[55] It also explains further protection that does not involve others making direct use of one's internal physiology. Imagine that you take shelter in a wood overnight and sleep on the ground. You wake up to find someone has erected a cage around you which they refuse to move. Indeed, it would putatively interfere with their activities for you to break it open or remove it! It is true that the construction of this cage around you did not interfere with your sleep, but I think it is wrong to say that it does not interfere with your activities. It prevents one from initiating any activity whatsoever beyond remaining inside the cage. It interferes with whatever long-term projects that one punctuated with sleep. One does not abandon all one's project every night and start them again in the morning. Certainly, not in a way which would mean they were unobstructed by one's imprisonment.

I believe that a claim against non-interference, inclusive of the preconditions of action, offers superior protection than a physicalist account of self-ownership when held up to common intuitions about what self-ownership *should* protect. It is true that a physicalist account makes it very easy to see how others have a duty not to harvest your blood while you sleep. However, it cannot explain why it would be unjust for someone to erect a cage around you while you sleep, so long as they did it without touching you. Nor indeed, as recognised by Edward Feser, why it would violate self-ownership to vacuum all of the air out of the surrounding atmosphere, causing you to suffocate.[56] As long as no air was taken directly out of your lungs, and only out of the surrounding external atmosphere, no violation takes place.

We do not need to know what actions a person pursues in order to know that they need their body to subsist, we only need to know that they are an actor. The subsistence of one's body requires that others not interfere with the reach of one's bodily processes both inwardly and outwardly. A claim against interference gives superior protection to our internal bodily integrity as well as the use we make of the external world. Human actions and processes must be understood as such through the lens of rights, rather than as mere arrangements of physical objects in space–time. It is not that we are objects that have rights, it is because we are particular kinds of being that act and because of the context in which that action take place.

The claim against interference in the natural or directed configuration of the preconditions of our acting whatsoever I believe captures what has been referred to in the natural law tradition as the "right of necessity."

The right of necessity refers to the right that each person has to take what would ordinarily be regarded as the property of another to save themselves from peril. For example taking food to avoid starvation or taking shelter in someone else's home to avoid exposure to the elements. St Thomas Aquinas said that it does not count as *theft* to take food out of another's possession under such circumstances because, strictly speaking, the food *belongs* to you – you may take it because the relevant property right has reverted to you. You already have a right to that which is implicated in the sustenance of your body:

> It is not theft, properly speaking, to take secretly and use another's property in case of extreme need: because that which he takes for the support of his life becomes his own property by reason of that need.[57]

Grotius also supported the right of necessity and argued that it justified raiding food stores on the high seas and pulling down houses to prevent the spread of fire.[58] He claimed to simply be following Roman Law and Aquinas in this vein. However, it is consistent with his theory of external property more generally. He argued that, in part, property rights in external objects arise to secure our subsistence.[59] If the security of subsistence is one justification for property rights, it would not make sense for those rights to exclude people from the means to their subsistence. The right of subsistence entitles everyone to non-interference in their attainment of standing space, breathable air, a minimal amount of food and water, as well as any action that they need to take in order to avoid expiration.

Much of what is interesting about this right is just how it sits next to property rights in extra-personal resources, so we will return to at the end of the following chapter once original acquisition has been fleshed out.

While what I have said here has been critical of the physicalistic account of self-ownership that has become so prominent and which received extended treatment by Cohen, Steiner, and Otsuka. There is another account of self-ownership that is also significantly developed and is more in keeping with the idea that it is a right to non-interference: that is Eric Mack's account.[60] He argues that self-ownership is not merely a right to exclusively determine the physical changes that occur within one's body but rather a liberty to bring one's world-interactive powers to bear on the world and a claim-right *just* strong enough to protect one's exercise of that liberty; namely, that others not interfere with said exercise. He has shown how this version of self-ownership both avoids the kind of absurdities that Sobel and others are critical of[61] and how it furnishes something like a right of necessity in protecting one from having one's world-interactive powers disabled by others, including by their exercise or enforcement of their property rights.[62] Indeed, the development of my own account of natural rights is significantly indebted to Mack's writing. However, my account of the claim to non-interference and Mackian self-ownership come apart at the level of original acquisition. In the present theory, original acquisition is, and must be, merely the application of the claim to non-interference. Whereas for Mack, one has the power to acquire property rights in extra-personal resources in virtue not only of having a natural right of self-ownership, but also a natural right to private property which one particularises through acts of original acquisition in accordance with some social convention.[63] On my view, there is no need nor any space for such an independent right. Moreover, the resultant property rights are strictly structured so as to protect one's from interference, rather than to protect some separately justified form of property.

Conclusion

In order to introduce no more exclusion into the system of rights demanded by justice than is called for by the circumstances of justice, we each have a right to non-interference in our ongoing actions and a correlative duty not to interfere in the actions of any other. Threats of interference are prohibited as acts constitutive of the initiation of the interference they threaten. While the account of freedom that justice affords each person is moralised inasmuch as we are free only within our rights, our rights themselves are rights to freely act without interference, so long as such actions are consistent with other persons' like rights. Therefore, the moralisation is not circular. The right to non-interference presupposes a right to non-interference in those processes which may not be under our direct control, which are nonetheless preconditions of our taking actions whatsoever. Hence, a right of necessity is internal to the right to non-interference. While a right to non-interference is akin to the protection afforded by certain accounts of self-ownership, property rights in external objects – insofar as they are just – inherit their structure from the rights we have over ourselves, rather than vice versa. Therefore, while this account of original rights is broadly in keeping with the spirit of self-ownership, I do not go to any lengths to defend it as an account of self-ownership.

In the following chapter, the right to non-interference will be shown to entail the possibility of original acquisition. Through acting within our rights in the world, external objects become subsumed into our actions we have rights against interference in, and hence, we come to acquire property rights over them.

Notes

1. In Kant's terms, having a right presupposes an authorisation to coerce someone who violates it (1991, sec. 6:231).
2. Wittgenstein (1986, secs 198–99, 201–2, 243–44, 258, 261–62, 268–69, 293).
3. Elements of this kind of idea can be found in Kant (1991, sec. I.I.VI.VI); Fressola (1981, 321); Barnett (1986, 302); Long (1999); Hoppe (2004, 87, 2006, 320–27, 2010, 23–55, 160–63); Ripstein (2009, 105); Stilz (2009, 52, 2019, 70).
4. Kant (1991).
5. Drawn from Hobbes (2012, sec. XXI.II).
6. Even if the right were unenforceable, a similar problem arises. They have a duty to not-φ as well as a right to φ; even if not both wrongful and rightful in a sense of rendering the actor liable and immune from interference, it would still be both right and wrong. Of course, it is perfectly coherent to say that a person has a right to do wrong (Waldron 1981); but this particular wrong is one that others have an equally strong right against, so a paradox – if not an outright contradiction – remains.
7. Kant (1991, sec. I.II.XXXXVII).
8. Ripstein (2008).
9. Berlin (2002, 175).
10. MacCallum (1967, 314).
11. Nagel (1975); Scanlon (1976, 13–14); Smith (1976, 89); Ryan (1977); Cohen (1989, 252, 256, 295, 1995, 60–62); Waldron (1991, 308); Steiner (1994, 12); Valentini (2012); Zwolinski (2016, 66–68); Bader (2018, 162–63).
12. Pettit (1999, chaps 1–2, 2012, chap. 1).
13. Layman (Forthcoming).
14. By "institutions" I understand rules that are conventionally followed (North 1991).
15. A diverse range of historical authors makes versions of this observation. Étienne de la Boetie argued that political power can only be successfully exercised with the help of a critical volume of *voluntary* acquiescence, since the subjected outnumber the powerful and hence cannot each be coerced into compliance (Boétie 1942). Similarly Hume argued that collective

actions such as political processes never proceed automatically no matter how formally circumscribed but always depend upon individual's choosing to comply (Hume 1987). Carl Schmitt argued that all conceivable legal constitutions depend upon *some* exercise of personal discretionary power. For the constitution to operate as intended, it is required that this discretionary power be exercised in the right way, but there can be no legal or constitutional guarantee of this Schmitt (1996).

16. Dowding (2011); Simpson (2017).
17. Long (2014).
18. Flanigan (2018).
19. Thomson (1971, 60, 1986, 171); Waldron (1981); Enoch (2002); Øverland (2007); Herstein (2012); Flanigan (2018).
20. Mack (2006, 277–84).
21. Den Uyl and Rasmussen (2005, 2016); Christmas (2018b).
22. For a typical, if pedestrian, example, see Nagel (1975, 192).
23. "If the differences are not very important, then freedom is not very important" (Williams 1953, 70; Hayek 2011, 149).
24. Rawls (1999, sec. 5); Nozick (1974, 32–33); Lomasky (1987, 99); Spector (1992, chap. 5); Vallentyne (2006); Zwolinski (2008); Mack (2018, 41–55).
25. Den Uyl and Rasmussen (2005, 271, 2016, 91–92).
26. Den Uyl and Rasmussen (2005, 83, 90, 100–6, 143, 162).
27. Long (2014); Flanigan (2018, 13).
28. Hart (1982, 183).
29. For defence of the idea that a right against interference is at least a necessary condition of realising the value of equality, see Long (2001, 2005); Hodgson (2010b); Flanigan (2018); Christmas (2019b).
30. For example Richard Overton said that "For by natural birth all men are equally and alike born to like propriety, liberty and freedom" (Overton 2014). Locke understood our natural equality to consist in the parity of our rights; that "all the Power and Jurisdiction is reciprocal" (Locke 1764, sec. II.4). Thomas Jefferson (in the first draft of the Declaration of Independence, but not the final one) said that "We hold these truth to be sacred and undeniable: that all men are created equal and independent; that from that equal creation they derive rights inherent and inalienable, among which are the preservation of life, and liberty, and the pursuit of happiness" (Jefferson 1950, 423).
31. Long (1993, 1999); Quong (2015, 2017); Ripstein (2017).
32. Christmas (2018a, 309–11).
33. Waldron (1992, 14).
34. Pallikkathayil (2011).
35. The standard template of analysis is Nozick's (1969, 441–45).
36. The term is owed to Steiner (1974, 39).
37. It is on this basis that Serena Olsaretti has argued that market transactions are often not robustly voluntarily and are therefore coercive (1998, 2004, chap. 5, 2013, 2007).
38. Thomson (1990, 53).
39. An alternative lens through which to view this analysis of threats is the following: threats are only coercive if they threaten a rights-violation and therefore remove an option that the victim has a right to. This is the analysis given by Ralf Bader (2018; n.d.). Such moralised accounts of coercion are often dismissed because they presuppose a set of rights in determining what counts as free actions and coerced action. However, where the prior set of rights is one in which each person has a claim to freedom as non-interference in their

non-interfering actions, there is no question-begging. It is not problematically circular to define coercion as rights-violating, when the rights in question are rights to freedom.

40. Cohen (1985b, 1986, 1995).
41. Nozick (1974, 179).
42. He argued that it cannot Cohen (1979, 1995) and thus sought different grounding for his socialism (Cohen 1982, 1983, 1985a, 2009).
43. Cohen (1985b, 109); Steiner (1994, 232).
44. It is difficult to make sense of slavery without some notion of something like self-ownership. I do not mean that in order to grasp the *injustice* of slavery one necessarily has to grasp the justice of self-ownership. Rather, it is difficult to understand how one person could own another person and therefore control every aspect of their person and life without some notion of how that person rightfully makes their own choices over courses of action for themselves. One cannot legally order about a slave unless one can also legally order one's own affairs. If we already understand the idea of one person owning two people, then surely we already understand what it would mean for them to own just one – themselves. The second problem is that it gives one the idea that the practice of chattel slavery is juridically coherent notion that one can clearly understand and use to make sense of self-ownership. However, chattel slavery is juridically incoherent. For a slave to be owned as a chattel would mean the slave herself lacks any rights and duties whatsoever, meaning that she has no duty not to kill her master, run away, refuse to work, etc. A chattel slave cannot commit theft, murder, fraud, or assault, any more than a table, house, or stone can (Steiner 1994, 232 n. 4). However, real experiences of chattel slavery involved slaves having legal duties and liabilities, meaning that they could not be simultaneously classed as chattel, even though they were. In order to be juridically coherent, chattel slaves would have to lack any legal personality whatsoever, meaning that they could not even have the liability of being given their rights back and being freed, just as tables, houses, and stones cannot be transferred rights and become free.
45. The reason the term is limited to one's lifetime is not because a dead body cannot be owned, but rather that a dead person cannot be an owner (Steiner 1994, 249–58).
46. Steiner (1994, 232).
47. Cohen (1995, 213).
48. Otsuka (2003, 12; also see 1998, 2006).
49. Vallentyne (2000, 2).
50. Railton (1985); Sobel (2012, 2013, 2016); also see Friedman (1989, 168); Zwolinski (2014, 10–12).
51. Mack (2015).
52. Mack (2015); Brennan and van der Vossen (2018); Flanigan (2019); Mulkeen (2019).
53. Wheeler (1980); Gillis (2009); Russell (2010); Long (2012); Carnegy-Arbuthnott (2019).
54. Ludwig von Mises said that involuntary bodily processes are not subjects of human action but rather the "general conditions of human welfare"(2007, 93).
55. I am grateful to Bas van der Vossen for pressing this objection.
56. Feser (2010, 263–64).
57. Aquinas (1947, IIa IIæ, Q66, A7).
58. Grotius (2004, 65) Locke also seems to have given the right of necessity a similar status: "charity gives every man a title to so much out of another's

plenty as will keep him from extreme want where he has no means to subsist otherwise" (Locke 1764, sec. I.VI.42). Although Locke says "charity" rather than "justice," the use of "title" indicates that it is a *right* rather than some less stringent moral claim.

59. Russell (2010) This is further supported by the fact that he argues that more extensive forms of exclusion only be introduced when societies became sedentary and more socioculturally complex – because only then did this extent of exclusion serve their use of the external world for their (now, more sophisticated) subsistence (Christmas 2019a, 32–36).
60. Also see Russell (2010).
61. Mack (2015).
62. Mack (1995, 2002).
63. Mack (1990, 2010, 2013).

3 Original Acquisition

Introduction

Many or even most theories of property and justice understand there to be some parity between our person rights over ourselves and our rights over external objects. However, private property rights are typically taken not to be justifiable purely on the bases of these personal rights alone. This chapter argues that this is mistaken. The dichotomy that is invoked in support of the justificatory distance between personal rights and property rights (or internal rights and external rights) is between *use* and *ownership*.[1] Our personal rights over our body – rights that protect us from interference in our action – can protect our uses of external objects but not our ownership of them. This chapter contests this claim. The acquisition of private ownership of external objects and spaces can occur simply as an application of our right to non-interference.

This removes the need to invoke some independent right to, or power to acquire, private property. The place of such independent rights or powers within theories of property and justice is at once symptomatic of the fact that no robust relationship between personal liberty and private property has been established, since liberty itself is not the ground for particular private property rights. It also renders the theory unable to make distinctions between how private property operates in different socio-economic, ecological, and technological contexts. It creates what have been come to be known as *boundary problems* and does not contain the tools to overcome such problems.

On the view developed in this chapter, not only is private ownership's relationship to liberty demonstrable, but the mode of acquisition determines the content of the rights acquired. Private property is not an all or nothing matter. The precise scope of the rights acquired is moulded to the activity within which one subsumes the acquired resources. The fine-tuning of private property rights in terms of the resources' various *uses* is something that has to be done in the final analysis, even on the view that strongly differentiates ownership from use. This view, however, builds in such fine-tuning from the ground floor. This is indicative that it is a more accurate account of the relationship between liberty and private property generally. While the account I offer is similar in spirit to principles of first possession[2] or first occupation, the activity through which one acquires property itself determines the rights acquired. Hence, it does not delegate the work of delineating boundaries elsewhere, but builds them into the basic justification.

Use, Exclusion, and Ownership

A natural claim-right against interference in one's ongoing activities gives one a right to use the external world. On a broad enough conception of what it means to use some object or space in the external world, acting in the world *just is* making use of it in some way. One is therefore at liberty to take up use of any resource, so long as that act of use does not interfere with some other person's prior initiated use of that or any other resource.

Kant believed that, at least provisionally,[3] the innate right to freedom entailed that each individual has permission to make use of the external world since this is inseparable from their permission to act freely of the will of others whatsoever:

> For an object of my choice is something that I have the *physical* power to use. If it were nevertheless absolutely not within my *rightful* power to make use of it, that is, if the use of it could not coexist with the freedom of everyone in accordance with a universal law (would be wrong), then freedom would be depriving itself of the use of its choice with regard to an object of choice, by putting *usable* objects beyond any possibility of being *used*; in other words, it would annihilate them in a practical respect and make them into *res nullius*, even though in the use of things choice was formally consistent with everyone's outer freedom in attendance with universal laws. But since pure practical reason lays down only formal laws as the basis for using choice and thus abstract from its matter, that is, from other properties of the object *provided only that it is an object of choice*, it can contain no absolute prohibition against using such an object, since this would be a contradiction of outer freedom with itself . . .
>
> This postulate can be called a permissive principle (*lex permissiva*) of practical reason, which gives us an authorization that could not be got from mere concepts of Right as such, namely to put all others under an obligation, which they would not otherwise have, to refrain from using certain objects of our choice because we have been the first to take them into our possession.[4]

Grotius and Locke, both believing we have a natural right to use the external world, however, grounded that right in the idea that the external world is originally commonly owned by all of humanity. In a radical departure from the doctrine of the divine right of King's defended by Robert Filmer, Grotius and Locke believed that the natural social equality of all persons means that no individual could naturally have any superior claim over the world than any other. Filmer defended patriarchy and monarchy as naturally just on the basis that God originally gave the Earth to Adam, to be inherited by his first-born son, and so on through the generations such that the territories of monarchs were their rightful private property.[5] The common ownership that Grotius and Locke supported against Filmer entailed that each individual, as member of this common, has the right to make use of it. Grotius wrote the following on the matter:

> Almighty GOD at the Creation, and again after the Deluge, gave to Mankind in general a Dominion over Things of this inferior World. *All Things*, as *Justin* has it, *were first in common, and all the World has, as it were, but one Patrimony*. From hence it was, that every Man converted what he would to his own Use, and consumed whatever was to be consumed; and such a Use of the Right common to all Men did at that time supply the Place of Property, for no Man could justly take from another, what he had thus first taken to himself; which is well illustrated by that Simile of *Cicero, Tho' the Theatre is common for any Body that comes, yet the Place that every one sits in is properly his own*.[6]

Similarly, from Locke:

> Whether we consider natural *reason*, which tells us, that men, being once born, have a right to their preservation, and consequently to meat and drink, and such other things as nature affords for their subsistence: or *revelation*, which gives us an account of those grants God made of the world to *Adam*, and to *Noah*, and his sons, it is very clear, that God, as King *David* said, *Psalm* CXV. 16. *has given the earth to the children of men;* given it to mankind in common. . . . God, who hath given the world to men in common, hath also given them reasons to make use of it to the best advantage of life, and convenience. The earth, and all that is therein, is given to men for the support and comfort of their being. And tho' all the fruits it naturally produces, and beasts it feeds, belong to mankind in common, as they are produced by the spontaneous hand of nature; and no body has originally a private dominion, exclusive of the rest of mankind, in any of them, as they are thus in their natural state.[7]

Both take the common ownership of the Earth to imply that each person may freely make use of it. Richard Schlatter refers to such an account of original common ownership as a "negative" commons in contrast to a "positive" commons.[8] A positive commons, rather than endowing its members with a right to freely use without the leave of the community, endows them with a duty to consult the community prior to use. Samuel von Pufendorf, for example, seemed to believe that a social contract was necessary before any use of the external world whatsoever was legitimate: "[W]e cannot apprehend how a bare corporal Act, such as Seizure is, should be able to prejudice the Right and Power of others, unless their Consent be added to confirm it; that is unless a Covenant intervene."[9]

Grotius and Locke's negative account of common ownership is coextensive with original non-ownership; that is the idea that no one originally owns the world, thus individuals are free to make use of it, so long as they do not interfere with other's use of it. Neither Grotius nor Locke, however, believed that this use-right was the sole ground for the acquisition of private property. Grotius notes that the right of use supplied the "Place of Property" but did not constitute a fully fledged right of private property. For reasons that will be elaborated later, Grotius believed that a social contract was necessary to justify private property, and, prior to that point, the right of use grounded merely "primitive" property.[10] Likewise, Kant believed that his *lex permissiva* could, on its own, only ground the protection of empirical possession and not intelligible possession.[11] The former simply just meant a physical connection with an object, whereas the latter meant a right to the object, which extended beyond mere physical connection – the kind of right that is typically understood to be at the heart of private ownership.

Indeed, the notion that a right of private ownership departs from a right of use in kind and not merely degree is typically taken to be a truism of the philosophy of property rights. What is taken to be an essential characteristic of a full right of private property is that it includes an extensive right to exclude others from the object. This right of exclusion is extensive in the sense of going further than being the mere corollary of any particular right on the part of the owner to use their property. The natural claim against interference in one's use of property allows one to exclude others from the object of one's use only to the extent that this is necessary for one's use to be uninterfered with. The right of exclusion that is deemed to be essential to private ownership is not tethered to any particular use or set of uses but rather gives one the right to exclude others even when one is not using it, and in a way which may be completely irrelevant to one's interest in using it.

David Schmidtz makes a useful analogy to characterise this idea.[12] Ownership is often likened to a "bundle of sticks,"[13] where each stick represents some particular right or juridical incident pertaining to the owned thing and the bundle as a whole representing what we call full ownership or private property in the fullest sense. Schmidtz says that ownership is better viewed as a tree, with the trunk representing the right of exclusion. Without the right of exclusion, it is just sticks; the trunk not only adds significant substance to the set of rights but also transforms them into branches, united into something of a distinctive character. If some of the branches are removed, the tree is still a tree – a different tree perhaps, but a tree nonetheless. Likewise, if some of the other rights within the set of ownership rights are removed, we still have ownership because we still have the residual right of exclusion that is greater than the sum of other rights, just as the tree is greater than the sum of its branches. This extensive right of exclusion – untethered to particular use-rights in the owned thing – is well-established as a key component, if not the defining component, of private property within the jurisprudence literature.

William Blackstone famously pronounced that private property constitutes "that sole and despotic dominion which one man claims and exercises over the external things of the world, *in total exclusion* of the right of any other individual in the universe."[14] In Anthony Honoré's famous analysis of private ownership, he defines it as being composed of 11 distinct incidents. The first of these is the right to possess, the nature and priority of which he clarifies in the following way.

> The right to possess, *viz.* to have exclusive control of a thing, or to have such control as the nature of the thing admits, is the foundation on which the whole superstructure of ownership rests. It may be divided into two aspects, the right (claim) to be put in exclusive control of a thing and the right to remain in control, *viz.* the claim that others should not without permission, interfere. Unless a legal system provides some rules and procedures for attaining these ends it cannot be said to protect ownership.[15]

James Penner argues that the right of exclusion constitutive of private ownership does not protect some specific or restricted set of uses of that which is owned but rather gives the owner "a protected sphere of indefinite and undefined activity, in which an owner may do anything with the thing he owns."[16] J. W. Harris describes the right to exclude as being "open-ended," by which he means that it does not protect specifically enumerated uses.[17] Thomas Merrill and Henry Smith claim that "the right to exclude others" constitutes the core of property ownership better than any "ad hoc 'bundle of rights' without any distinguishing features."[18]

Sometimes, it is the expansive right of exclusion per se that is taken to be the sole distinguishing feature of ownership,[19] or that exclusion is ontologically prior to any right of use.[20] Often though, it is emphasised that exclusion is not the end of private property but rather should be understood as strictly *serving* use. For example Larissa Katz argues that the "central concern" of private property "is not the exclusion of all non-owners from the owned thing but, rather, the preservation of the owner's position as the exclusive agenda setter for the owned thing."[21] As much as these nominal dissenters from the exclusion-based account try to distance themselves from it,[22] one has to note that the account of use that exclusion is invoked to serve is strictly *exclusive* use. Eric Claeys argues that what is essential is that the owners have a right not merely to some particular use, but "a right to determine exclusively how a thing may be used."[23] Therefore, the account of the extent of exclusion that is essential to ownership is the same in the accounts that emphasise the protection that such exclusion gives to use and those that emphasise exclusion as an essential characteristic per se. Whether or not we take the fundamental role of exclusion to serve use or not, the central notion of use is exclusive use; so the expansive account of exclusion is central in any case. When exclusion is there only to protect exclusive use, we end up with the same kind – that is extent – of exclusion. Given that the focal point of the right becomes such extensive exclusion and not any particular uses, the focal point of a property right becomes the physical thing itself, rather than any particular use of it. The limit of a property right, therefore, is not borne out of any account of the activities it is subsumed within but rather identified with the physical limits of the owned thing itself. The exclusion-centric account of property, therefore, is coextensive with an "ownership of things" account.

A use-right to an object is often regarded as a *kind* of property right vis-à-vis an interest in a particular use of an object protected under property law but is typically taken to be categorically distinct from a right of private property, private ownership, or a *fully fledged* property right. Often referred to as "usufruct," rather than property, it is seen as an exception to the usual form that property takes as in the case of private ownership. Related to the fact that private ownership is taken to necessarily include an expansive right of exclusion, whereas a use-right only permits one to exclude others from uses that would conflict with the rights-protected use, is that ownership pertains to a particular physical object tout court, whereas a use-right pertains to a particular activity vis-à-vis a particular physical object. While both accounts of rights and correlative duties are taken to exist between moral agents, their objects are different. Ownership pertains to things, whereas usufruct pertains to activities in relation to them.[24]

Early natural rights theorists of property – as well as their contemporary proponents – took such a distinction to be paramount as well. As noted earlier, Kant took it that his *lex permissiva* allowed one to make use of external objects but no right to exclude others from objects at any time at which one was not in physical possession (and hence direct use) of those objects.[25] Kant believed one's right to freedom could only (outside of the proper political institutions) protect one's possession of external objects so long as they were physically ("empirically") connected to one's body.[26] Therefore, physically severing the connection between oneself and the object in question was sufficient for one to lose any right to exclude others and hence any claim to recover possession.[27]

Grotius similarly believed our use-right in the commons permitted us to freely take possession but not to *recover* possession once we had relinquished it. However, he seems to have believed that use had a further extension than mere physical connection, but could nonetheless not extend so far as to ground a right of exclusion that resembled that which constituted private ownership.[28] For example Grotius uses Cicero's analogy with the theatre: "*Tho' the Theatre is common for any Body that comes, yet the Place that every one sits in is properly his own.*"[29] One's use-right to the theatre entailed that one could use a seat for the duration of the play. Presumably, this means that if one stands up to remove one's coat or makes an intermission trip to the bar or lavatory, one's use-right is violated if someone takes over one's seat at that moment – because one was still using it even though one was not at that point in contact with it.[30] Nonetheless, there was no right to recover possession in a broader sense. One could not occupy a seat during the matinée and then lay claim to it during the evening performance on the basis of one's earlier occupation of it alone. Nor could one remove the seat and sell it nor destroy it. So although Grotius deployed a less physicalistic conception of use than Kant, he did not think it extended so far as to give the user an expansive exclusion right. Blackstone explains the Grotian view:

> For, by the law of nature and reason, he, who first began to use [a resource], acquired therein a kind of transient property, that lasted so long as he was using it, and no longer. . . . Thus the ground was in common, and no part of it was the permanent property of any man in particular; yet whoever was in the occupation of any determined spot of it, for rest, for shade, or the like, acquired for the time a sort of ownership, from which it would have been unjust, and contrary to the law of nature, to have driven him by force: but the instant that he quitted the use or occupation of it, another might seize it, without injustice.[31]

This is very much the orthodoxy in the contemporary natural rights literature. Peter Vallentyne notes that since one's right to use a park bench does not give one a right to exclude others from it – except that part of it which one uses and when one uses it – a right to use external objects can never ground private ownership of them more generally.[32]

The expansive right to exclude – untethered to the protection of the exercise of any set of use-rights – would impose new duties upon those who are subject to them. The duties of non-interference that are correlative with natural use-rights are not imposed when a person makes use of an external object. Rather, the natural duty to not interfere with others is given a more specific application in the face of rightholders taking particular actions.[33] While the enumerated list of actions that others are now at liberty to take has changed,[34] their juridical incidents remain unaltered: they are still at liberty to take any action that does not interfere with that of any other, have a duty to not take any action that does, and a claim that others not interfere with any action they take. Therefore, no new duties of exclusion are created through a mere act of use. The unilateral creation of a right of exclusion that goes further than this, however, would require explanation via the introduction of a power–liability relation within the set of natural rights. In order for a person to create new duties that others exclude themselves from external objects beyond the original duties they already have, she must have a power to do so and, correlatively, a liability to having such duties imposed upon her by others.

Grotius invokes a hypothetical contract in which all rightholders (hypothetically) willingly submit their residual right to use that which others initially occupy but do not maintain physical possession of and therefore cement the right to recover possession of all those objects we intend to make future use of and invest in.[35] Grotius takes it for granted that it would be rational for all persons to consent because he takes it for granted that private property is essential to the full development of natural resources and hence human capacities.[36] Kant invokes an appropriately constituted state that can act on the omnilateral will and authorise private appropriations. Such appropriations are essential to our innate right to freedom for Kant, yet their unilateral acquisition violates the freedom of others since it imposes upon them duties to abstain from external objects that they might have had for themselves. The creation of new duties is compatible with the innate right to freedom when it is omnilateral rather than unilateral.[37] Hence, private property outside of an appropriately constituted state is merely "provisional."[38]

On the other hand, those in the more Lockean tradition invoke a distinct juridical power to acquire private property that can be justly exercised outside of a state and without the presumption of hypothetical consent.

Such theorists deploy various strategies for justifying such a power that hinges upon stating the conditions under which its exercise is just and those under which it is not. But they disagree with Grotius and Kant in taking it to be prima facie problematic in a state of nature; that is in lieu of a social contract or legitimate political authority. Invariably, though, they recognise (if implicitly) some prima facie problem with taking that power to be *unlimited*.[39] As Jeremy Waldron notes, the idea that individuals can, by their own unilateral actions, impose moral duties upon others to refrain from using certain resources . . . is a very difficult idea to defend *in an unqualified form*.[40]

There is a two-prong argument that surrounds the putative power to acquire private property. The first is the positive argument for why we should have such a power in the first place, and the second is the negative argument: an account of the conditions under which such a power may justly be exercised.[41] An act must positively do something to acquire the rights and must not do something else in order for those rights to survive. The positive arguments are fairly uniform: either it is assumed that a certain amount of private property is necessary for freedom per se, to have a sphere of totally unrestricted action, or it is taken that private property is a necessary institution for the development of natural resources needed for the socio-economic flourishing of humanity generally,[42] or some combination of the two.

For example Eric Mack argues that in addition to a natural right of self-ownership (grounding our right to liberty as non-interference), we also have a natural right to private property which we may unilaterally exercise to create private property rights in the hitherto unowned objects of our choice, so long as we do not disable anyone else's exercise of their self-ownership or natural right to private property.[43] Bas van der Vossen likewise argues that we have a natural right to private property, which we have a power to exercise at will, so long as such a practice produces economic opportunities for others to make valuable use of their productive capacities.[44] Murray Rothbard argued that in addition to the non-aggression principles (grounding our right to liberty as non-interference), we have a right to "homestead" unowned resources.[45] Rothbard, however, rejected any substantive limitation on homesteading beyond that which is formally compatible with non-aggression.[46]

Left-libertarians also believe in such a natural right to acquire private ownership; however, they have similar concerns to Grotius and Kant that the exercise of this right involves an inegalitarian, unilateral imposition of duties upon others. They do not argue that a state is needed to omnilaterally authorise acquisitions,[47] nor that our hypothetical consent to such subjection justifies it but, rather, insist that we may unilaterally take only an equal share of resources into our private ownership, thus leaving an equal portion of valuable property for others to have.[48] There are a variety of different approaches, but each reaches this conclusion. Fabian Wendt stakes out a middle ground in which so long as each person has a "sufficient" amount of private property for the exercise of their capacity to pursue long-term meaningful projects, new acquisitions are just.[49]

What unites Lockeans against Grotius and Kant is that they take unilateral acquisition – prior to the convention of any political institutions – to be potentially just. Private property, then, can come before we set up political institutions, rather than being dependent upon them.

The debate among Lockeans over the negative side of the principle of just acquisition – the conditions under which private acquisition is just – harks back to Locke's statement that one could appropriate from the commons "at least where there is enough, and as good left in common for others."[50] Many Lockeans frame that argument as an interpretation of what Locke meant or should have meant by this sentence. It is clear that Locke was concerned that one person's private property right does not unjustly entrench upon others' like interests.[51] But the precise normative mechanism at work is the battleground of many Lockeans.

I believe that all of these strategies are mistaken. One can acquire a right to exclude others from external objects that is as expansive as that which is taken to characterise private ownership, *yet* which remains strictly parasitical upon those use-rights one has in them. Hence, the distinction between property in activities and ownership of things is an unnecessary one, at least for the purposes of describing different kinds of justified property rights. In the following section, I will argue that a right to use external objects just is a right to privately acquire ownership of them, at least with a certain class of uses.

I have, thus far, left out substantial discussion of Locke's own account. Some possible interpretations of Locke's theory of acquisition are mentioned above, but there is another interpretation that does not depend upon an independent power to acquire private property but rather begins with a different set of natural claim-rights, the application of which enables the acquisition of private property. Such an account is not compatible with the set of natural rights I have argued we have, therefore that approach to private acquisition is not available to this theory. However, it is worth giving more attention to because it fails on independent grounds in a way that lends motivating support to my general framework. I will therefore address such accounts on their own in the penultimate section.

Extended Activity

One can immediately see that Kant's account of empirical possession falls short of what should properly be regarded as use, especially for the purposes of what kind of use is protected by a claim-right against interference in one's activities. In a wide range of cases, it is manifest that our activities can be interfered with by actions on the part of others which do not constitute the severing of a physical connection between our bodies and the objects we use. Grotius's notion of what is protected by a use-right is more on the mark: our use of a theatre seat is not constituted merely by its physical contact with our body (hence, we have a right to recover possession of it if someone tries to sit in after the interval). Grotius was also right to note that our use-right to the theatre seat does not extend to anything that looks like private ownership of it, since one cannot come back another day and claim it on the basis that one sat in it once, nor can one remove it, sell it, and so forth. The extent of one's right to exclude others from the theatre seat extends only so far as is necessary for us to use it qua theatre seat, that is by subsuming it into a particular activity: watching a play in the public theatre. Our activities extend beyond that which we have physical contact with and beyond that which is under our direct or total physical control. In *De Jure Belli ac Pacis*, Grotius believes that a right to use external objects gave us a right to exclude others from them that went a little further than Kant did, but not so far as to give us private ownership of them.

There are many uses of external objects that, however, in order to remain uninterfered with, require extensive abstention from third parties. When one engages in such an activity, the right to non-interference one naturally has becomes functionally identical to the extensive right to exclude that characterises private ownership. A right of exclusion that resembles that of private ownership can therefore be borne of a right to exclude that is strictly protective of the particular use one makes of an object. Uses of things that are near-exclusive – leaving little or no action space for others to make use of them – require that others almost totally exclude themselves from the resource. A use-based account of property can therefore yield an account of property that turns out to be functionally equivalent to ownership of things.

Grotius took it that the right to use consumables was – for all intents and purposes – identical to having a right to acquire them privately. If *A* picks an apple from a tree and eats it, there is (almost) no use of this apple that can be made by *B* or *C* without interfering with *A* and hence violating her rights. In his earlier work, *Mare Liberum*, Grotius argued that this principle, by "the process of reasoning . . . next extended to" capital goods including land and chattels, and that this was not done "violently, but gradually, nature herself pointing out the way."[52] The right to exclude third parties, strictly parasitical on one's claim to non-interference, extends as does the spatial intensity and temporal reach of the particular activity within which one subsumes external objects. Naturally, then, one's use of a park bench does not give one a right to exclude others once one has gotten up and walked on. But, as Grotius noted, in societies based on settlement and agriculture, many of our uses of external objects are spatially intense and temporally extended. In the later work, Grotius believed that a social contract was needed to legitimise this. However, no change in rights take place, only a change in the kinds of activities individuals pursued in relation to natural resources.[53] With that change of uses, there is a change on the content of our use-rights.

Consider the use of land for growing crops. If *A* tills a plot of land on her own and plants seeds in the tilled soil, this activity (nearly) saturates that land as action space and continues to be ongoing long after *A* finishes planting seed for the day and goes home to rest. There are very few uses of this land that could be made by a third party without interfering with *A*'s use of it.[54] For example *B* and *C* are both duty-bound not to dig up the seeds, nor pull up the crops once they grow. They may not pour toxic chemicals into the soil, nor may they construct a well on the adjacent land and lower the water table in a way that interferes with the growth process, as determined by natural laws and *A*'s actions.

They may not construct a skyscraper nearby if it blocks out the sun and thereby interfere with *A*'s crop cultivation (her use of the land for agriculture also constitutes a use of the sun).[55] They may only walk across it if they do so in a way that does not disturb the growth of the crops. *A*'s natural right to exclude others from engaging in these kinds of activities vis-à-vis the plot of land is far reaching. Even leaving the land fallow for a year to allow the soil to rejuvenate constitutes a use that demands non-interference from others. And given that this use is partially constitutive of her broader and more long-term activity of growing crops, *B* and *C* are not permitted to take the kinds of actions that would threaten the future fertility of the soil or otherwise the natural fitness of the plot of land for future crop-growth.

The fact that we use external objects as direct consumables *and* as production goods grounds the potential for far more expansive rights of exclusion than might be initially thought. Take the use of clothes made from animal hides, silk, wool, or cotton. The subsumption of these objects into the activities of their users does not cease when they are hung up at night and one goes to sleep, nor when one changes out of one set and into another. Their use is typically longer term than that and, when it is, therefore demands that others not snatch them the moment we take them off. As Mack puts it, one cannot "deny the use that a hunter has for his bow even at the moment when it lies by his side, or the use that the philosopher has for his word processor even when he is busy cooking dinner."[56] Our lives are not punctuated lists of book-ended actions: one being necessarily over for another to begin. Rather, they are expanding nexuses of overlapping actions of various degrees of spatio-temporal extension. Some actions continue as long as we live, others are long-term but not indefinite, others are short-term, and some are near-instantaneously completed. Many of these actions subsume the others, so that interference in one more spatio-temporally discrete action also constitutes an interference in a more expansive one. Examples given by those who place a strong dichotomy between use-rights and private property are invariable kinds of objects and uses thereof which are comparatively less rivalrous or long-term than others. Consider Vallentyne's park bench example or the frequent invocation of Cicero's theatre seat.[57] Use-rights are clearly not coextensive with private ownership in all cases of use, but that does not mean that they never are.

For certain kinds of uses of external objects, the application of the claim to non-interference just is a private property right. One does not need to exercise any power in order to create such rights; they are merely what one's rights to non-interference become when one takes certain kinds of actions in the world. They are acquired insofar as one has them in virtue of acting in certain ways, rather than merely in virtue of existing. But they are acquired not through the exercise of a power, but just by acting within one's original claim-rights.

While the extent to which *A* may exclude others from her plot of cultivated land is greater than the extent to which she may, for example, exclude them from a path she walks down each day, it still does not give her an entirely open-ended list of activities that she may choose to pursue with the land, as many argue the ownership of an object must entail. She has a right of near-exclusive possession but not quite in the sense supported in the jurisprudence literature. However, even from outside of the perspective of the theory of justice being developed here, it is as close to exclusive as we could wish for. If exclusive possession is taken in physicalistic terms, as it is by Steiner for example,[58] then it would enjoin far too much. The right of exclusion pertaining to a physical object tout court, rather than being limited to the protection of particular uses, renders it excessive. If *A* had a right to exclusive possession such that she could exclude any physical change within the spatial boundaries of her land that was caused by a third party, then she could legitimately enjoin any action that, for example, altered the number of photons directed at her land. And since any movement of an object within visible range of the property would alter the trajectory of photons onto her land, every person between her land and the horizon would be duty-bound to not move without her consent. The emission of carbon dioxide particles onto the land by anyone breathing within proximity would be a rights-violation, as would the slightest vibration in the airwaves caused by movement. In typical property systems, these actions would not even constitute nuisances, let alone outright trespasses. But if we think that the right of exclusion must be physically totalising, then we have to think of these as violations of that right.[59] In the context of many proximate property owners, this would mean that all owners were reciprocally duty-bound not to make almost any use of their property whatsoever, since this would violate all their neighbours' rights. This notion of ownership is mutually "hog-tying."[60]

The notion of exclusive possession must be somewhat and somehow bound to certain uses and indeed in typical property systems they are. The purportedly open-ended and unenumerated list of actions that a property owner is free to take with regard to the owned object presupposes a "non-prohibited class of uses."[61] Property systems typically do not and cannot count all physical boundary crossings as nuisances. All uses of one person's property will have an effect on surrounding owners. According to Penner (1997, 72), "[n]othing in the world is naturally of exclusive interest only to the one most closely associated with it." But in order to know what counts as nuisance we need some conception of *use*, that is a restricted conception that does not account for all physical possibilities. What does the nuisance disturb? What activity with regard to the owned thing is that which the ownership is purported to protect? Given that any workable conception of ownership cannot be of the physicalistic type and must make exceptions along use-based lines, there is no reason ownership cannot just be an enumeration of use-rights.[62]

Returning to the farmer example, it cannot be emphasised enough that the activity in question not only implicates certain aspects of "the land" as a two-dimensional location, but also of the surrounding space in all three dimensions. In order to know the physical limits of the property right, one must ask whether or not some human intervention with the natural playing out of the laws of physics with regard to some particular object would interfere with the activity that *A* initiated. Whatever actions are taken by third parties at these locations there are that would interfere with *A*, *A* has a claim-right that these actions not take place and to that extent has a property right over those objects, whether they be in the topsoil of the land, in the stratosphere over the land, a mile away at the surface, or a mile away beneath the surface.[63]

Indeed, the question of how we actually define what counts as "the land" in regard to any putative property claim is altogether sidestepped. When property rights pertain to physical objects tout court, it is incredibly important what is included and excluded in the description of that object as such. However, when the property right consists in non-interference with a particular set of activities with regard to a range of objects, it is not the case a priori that whatever we include in "the land" will be owned and whatever we exclude with be not-owned. However, if we describe the physical plot, the farmer will have delimited rights within it, as well as some rights beyond it. Physical boundary problems do not apply.[64]

Rothbard argued that when delimiting the boundaries of an owned resource, one ought to seek a physical description of the resource – but a technological one. What is owned is not a discrete set of physical objects as such but a "technological unit." One acquires rights over whatever amount of the resource in question one needs in order to use it as the kind of resource it is.[65] This proposal, however, puts the cart before the horse: physical objects contain no information as such as to what resources they are. The question of what resources different physical objects constitute depends upon how they are in fact used. In order to know what kind of resource an object is, we need to know how it is in fact used.

Eric Mack, responding to problems with the notion of ownership as involving a total right of physical exclusion, argues that the claim-rights to exclude others must be defined so as to only go so far as protecting one's liberty-rights with regard to one's property. Structuring rights in this way ensures that they are reciprocally permitted "elbow room." *A*'s liberty-right to S_1 is protected by a claim-right against third parties engaging in any action that disables the exercise of those liberties, and, reciprocally, *B*'s liberty to S_2 is so protected, meaning they each have the moral space they need to exercise their liberties, without imposing any more disabling exclusion upon each other than is necessary.[66] This is in agreement with what I argue here. However, what is missing in Mack's account is some criteria for determining what liberties persons actually have with regard to specific objects. My answer is that everyone is at liberty to engage in any action with regard to any object that they choose, so long as this does not interfere with any action already initiated by anyone else. So, the liberties people have are whichever liberties can be historically vindicated by their non-interference with any other person's antecedent activity.

The physical world needs partition, but it cannot be partitioned merely physicalistically; the partition must serve human activity, and therefore the boundaries of delimitation must be in terms of particular persons' specific activities. The question of which objects are assigned to which persons is insufficient: we must ask which objects are assigned to which uses by which persons. The question of what is owned by whom therefore must be a question of who has rights to engage in relatively expansive sets of activities with regard to concentrated sets of time-indexed objects.

I do not argue that a use-centric approach is the best way of conceptualising property law for the purposes of positive legal analysis, but it is the conceptual framework any property system ought to follow in order to be just.

While one's right to exclude only extends as far as the actual uses one makes, this does not mean other uses are blocked off. It just means that one does not yet have a claim to any further activity. One is still at liberty to initiate any action that does not interfere with the actions of others, and others have a duty not to interfere once it is underway. So while one's specific property rights that one has acquired only protect specific activities, one's general right to non-interference protects the vast expanse of possibilities one is at liberty to take.

Property is therefore an open-ended system standing ready to protect any new activities and leaving space for those that do no conflict with existing ones.

Contra Labour-Mixing

In the Lockean tradition, it is believed that persons can fully own things in virtue of their full ownership of themselves. Persons are self-owners, and this total right of exclusion they have over themselves they are able to transmit into external objects.

> Though the Earth and all inferior creatures be common to all men, yet every man has a property in his own person. . . . The labour of his body, and the work of his hands, we may say are properly his. Whatsoever then he removes out of the state that nature hath provided, and left it in, he hath thereby mixed his labour with, and joined to it something that is his own, and thereby makes it his property. It being

> by him removed from the common state nature hath placed it in, it hath by his labour something annexed to it, that excludes the common right of other men. For this labour being the unquestionable property of the labourer, no man but he can have a right to what that is once joined to, at least where there is enough and as good left in common for others.[67]

Locke's notion of labour-mixing is not taken literally by most neo-Lockeans. Instead, they typically take it that the moral grounds for our self-ownership are moral grounds for ownership of external objects too. Since we need to make use of external objects in a similar way we need to make use of our bodies, any principle that says this interest grounds a right to exclusive control of our bodies must imply that we get exclusive possession of some external objects and spaces too. Moreover, since we own ourselves, we may do with ourselves whatever we wish with regard to unowned external resources. Once we start using those external resources, we can lay a claim to ownership of them, assuming certain conditions are met. Those conditions constitute the Lockean proviso and are often interpretations of what Locke meant or should have meant when he wrote "as least where there is enough and as good left in common for others."

However, a minority does endorse a theory that represents a literalist interpretation of labour-mixing or very nearly so.[68] Such accounts say that through some process, our rights over the physical materials that compose our bodies can be transmitted into physical materials external to our bodies. Such accounts therefore generate an account of property in which property pertains to physical objects. The starting point is our full ownership of our physical bodies, and after physical processes that stand in for labour-mixing, we come to have full ownership of external physical objects. I do not intend here to give a full rebuttal of such accounts. However, it is worth noting how this account, due to its embrace of something my own account explicitly rejects, runs into significant problems which can be resolved by pivoting to a more use-based notion of property. The account doubles down on physicalism and then ends up having to invoke use-based considerations.

The first problem is that labour is itself an activity and therefore cannot be physically mixed with physical resources. When someone, for example, mixes seeds with soil, the labour is automatically implicated in the action of mixing. It is not an additional subject of the admixture itself. The labour is what *does* the mixing; it is not a thing that *is mixed*.[69] Steiner has sought to dispense with this worry about the general approach by replacing the role of labour with physical energy. If one owns oneself, then one also owns the energy that is latent in one's body. When we engage in acts that might be thought of as labour-mixing, we transfer this energy into other objects. These objects, if initially unowned, come to be filled and connected with energy owned by the actor. Composed only of objects that are unowned and objects that are owned by the person who acts upon it, this object becomes owned by them. "Ownership seeps over into the rest," as Nozick parses it.[70] Jeremy Waldron notes that, in those cases we might typically think of as labour-mixing, or as uses of resources which might bring them under our ownership, energy is by no means necessarily *added* to them. Often, our putatively self-owned energy is used to counter the resource's own source of energy that defies our efforts at using it in the way we want.[71] Steiner accepts this and replies that while the expended energy may not reside within the resource after use, one cannot deny that the resource has been *transformed by* the energy transfer that took place. For example hunting a wild animal does not result in one's energy being transferred into the quarry but, rather, one's energy (as well as the animal's) being transferred into the surrounding environment. Nonetheless, it is that case that the quarry's capture is the result of one's exertion of energy.[72]

However, for the ownership of one's physical body to explain the ownership of external, physical objects, this account must be able to give a description the continuity between the person, her action, and the object acquired in physical terms. The fact that one's self-owned energy is part of the means employed to achieve the end of the animal being trapped tells us that both the energy and the animal are intentionally subsumed into the action, but it does show that there has been a physical admixture of self-owned and unowned materials in the way required for ownership of one's physical body to explain one's ownership of the animal's. Since in this case, it is the surrounding environment into which the energy is intermingled, why is it not simply this space that becomes owned by the hunter? Steiner acknowledges that there may be no one-to-one correlation between what our energy is transferred into and what we claim as rightly ours as the fruits of our labour. He notes that

> expended energy is simply abandoned by us in the course of this acting. It's absorbed into parts of the external environment that we make no consequent claim to. Other portions of our expended energy are infused into parts of the external environment, transforming their features in various ways. Sometimes we claim these things for ourselves as the fruits of our labour.[73]

It is quite clear, even from Steiner's own words, that no physicalistic story about the locations of change or the origins of energy can tell us what is acquired and what is not through a self-owner's actions. A vast range of objects can be said to have undergone physical change as a result of a person's actions;[74] and the physicalist account cannot identify which should be deemed acquired and which should not.

The full ownership of physical objects as such, then, cannot be explained by our antecedent ownership of our physical bodies.[75] Any identification of an object as being the focal point of an action will need to make reference to the action, not merely as a physical event, but as a purposeful, end-directed human activity.[76] Once we see that it is a person's activities, and not her atoms, that provide the normative bedrock of her claims to external property, we are then forced to asked to what extent a right to exclude others is necessary for this object to remain subsumed by her activities.

As alluded to earlier, a problem that arises with conceiving of property as pertaining to objects tout court is that of giving a determinate physical description of the object itself. According to this notion of property, determining the physical boundaries of the owned thing is normatively essential. Since the right pertains to the physical object, establishing what the object is both necessary and is sufficient for working out whether any particular action was permissible or not. As long as an action subsumes an owned object and no other-owned object, it is permissible. The physical boundaries of the object are the boundaries of one's right.

On a physicalistic account of acquisition, there can be no determination over which physical objects fall within the acquired rights. And yet it is essential that such a determination be made, since their falling within a person's right would make them totally off-limits to others.

Where the right pertains to the object as such, the normative content of the right is filled out simply by a physically exhaustive description of the object in question. This cannot be given, and therefore the normative content cannot be given.

Even if full ownership of objects as such, rather than rights to engage them in particular kinds of activities, could be explained by an antecedent, similar ownership of one's body, the question would simply be pushed back a step: why do we have this kind of right to our body? There are good reasons to think that property cannot be constituted by claim-rights to physical objects as such, whether internal or external.

Richard Arneson and Ronald Dworkin complained that self-ownership is an indeterminate concept because there are any number of sets of rights to the use and enjoyment of a thing that can all be meaningfully construed as ownership, and yet have very different implications for the kind of theory of justice that they would entail.[77] Eager to defend the determinacy of self-ownership, Cohen retorts that it should be taken as the logically fullest set of compossible rights each person can have over themselves.[78] As noted, this notion was adopted by Steiner, Otsuka, and Vallentyne.[79] The problem – for our purposes here – with this account of self-ownership and the concomitant rights in external objects that are commensurately strong is that rights to the physically exclusive possession of physical objects renders almost all action impermissible. As noted earlier, every human action results in some kind of physical change to the surrounding environment. Where persons' rights over their bodies and external property within that environment are so strong as to not permit any non-consensual physical change thereof by a third party, everyone is reciprocally barred from taking any action whatsoever. My simply moving my body at a location between the sun and another person would physically alter the set of objects they have a right to the exclusive physical control of and hence would be impermissible. Their claim-rights of exclusive physical possession are so strong, they are not at liberty to even make use of their own bodies or property.[80]

There are accounts of self-ownership, which are not accounts of the full ownership of our physical bodies but, rather, sets of claim-rights to non-interference in certain classes of actions.[81] I take such accounts to be heavily overlapping with the account of our natural rights that I am giving here. There is nothing inherently physicalistic about the idea of self-ownership; it is just that a physicalist account thereof is sometimes given to defend a similar account of external property.

Abandonment and Transfer

It is often taken to be essential to property rights that they be alienable – that is that they can be permanently transferred. In order to buttress my claim that the theory I defend is a theory of property, rather than of some alternative to property, this section will argue that the claim-rights we have to non-interference with particular uses of particular objects and spaces at particular times are transferable to others. Our natural rights, therefore, can underwrite a socio-economic framework of voluntary exchange.[82] In the language of the historical entitlement theory of justice, the rights acquired in accordance with the principle of justice in acquisition can also be transferred in accordance with the principle of justice in exchange. Of course, the extent of the market that is justified by our natural rights is wholly dependent on whether or not actually existing persons choose to transfer their rights. What I intend to show is that our acquired rights, as an ontological matter, can be voluntarily transferred. The normative implication is that it is permissible for persons to transfer their own acquired rights.[83] By this, I do not mean to be taking out any position on the spectrum of positions one can hold on the "moral limits of markets," which is the debate over the extent to which the contractual exchange, the monetary exchange, or the commodification[84] of certain goods or services degrades their moral value. When I say that it is permissible to transfer any acquired right whatsoever, I do not mean it is necessarily *good* to do so, only that it is *just*; it would therefore be unjust and to that extent wrongful to interfere with such a transfer. For any given transfer of rights to be permissible is merely to say it is an available move within a just set of rights.

The first thing to recognise is that acquired rights can be abandoned. When *A* initiates an activity φ which subsumes *S* at t_1 and then brings it to an end at t_2, actions on the part of *B* that would have interfered with φ at t_1 no longer constitute an interference at t_2, and *B* is therefore no longer duty-bound to abstain from such actions in conjunction with *S*. It may be inherent in the kind of activity that φ is that it comes to an end at a certain point; for example, a daily walk down to the river involves temporally punctuated use of the path, or a regularly scheduled radio broadcast at a particular time involves a particular frequency. Each time these activities end, the physical objects they subsume reopen to the activities of others – activities that would interfere had they occurred at the same time. These activities may come to a total (as opposed to a punctuated) cessation, which would open up their physical components in a way that they were not before. When *A* regularly uses a path, others are free to use the path at any time in ways that do not interfere. This means when she is about to walk down it they cannot block it up; but when she is not walking down it, they could set up camp, temporarily, so long as they clear out so she is not obstructed the next day. However, when *A* abandons her regular activity of walking down to the river each day, assuming the path has no other users, others are now free to do things with the path on a longer time horizon than they were before. Others are now free to, for example, build on that land since *A* has abandoned her use of it as a thoroughfare. Likewise, if a broadcaster abandons her daily broadcast, then the corresponding frequency on the spectrum is now opened up for others at that time. Whether or not an activity is presumptively permanently abandoned, rather than only punctuated is internal to the kind of activity in question. We know that if a farmer is using land for agriculture, he will let the land lay fallow for a period, at which time walking across it does not interfere with his farming activities. However, it is not internal to farming that cessation should be taken to indicate permanency. Activities like farming are presumptively ongoing. It is obviously the case that people *do* nonetheless often abandon their activities totally and in so doing give up their rights.

The ways in which presumptively ongoing activities are abandoned is either through some public sign given to inform others that they are abandoned to provide some public criteria for determining the alteration that has occurred in everyone's rights. Alternatively, if the presumptively ongoing activity is patently no longer ongoing because of an extended period of apparent cessation, then the presumption of continuity is defeated.

To the extent that their acquired right to non-interference in the particular activity is abandoned, others are now at liberty to initiate activities that would have interfered. In other words, those abandoned rights can now be acquired by others through their initiation of the relevant activity. Therefore, one way in which acquired rights can be transferred is simply by one individual abandoning them and another originally acquiring them.

Given than *A* can choose to abandon her activity, allowing *B* to pick it up after her, there is no reason why two parties could not deliberately plan this. Imagine *B* can inform *A* that he would be willing to abandon his stock of vegetables into *A*'s possession such that they are then immediately subsumed into *A*'s activities, on the condition that *A* do the same with her old farm equipment. If abandonment can take place at will, then individuals can abandon them in ways that ensure they are immediately acquired again by other designated individuals.[85]

Gerald Gaus and Anna Stilz have both explicitly dissented from this view and argued that property cannot be transferred in this manner and that the transference of property would require some other juridical mechanism in order to take place. Gaus argues that the juridical mechanism described earlier is a case of merely *waiving* rights as opposed to *transferring*. The difference between *A* waiving her rights over *S* and transferring those rights to *B* is given in the following way. While in both cases *B*'s use of *S* is made permissible, in the case of waiving third parties do not owe any duty of non-interference to *B* but only to *A*. *A* has simply waived her right over *S* such that she relives *B* of her duty not to interfere with it. But now others only owe a duty to *A* that they not interfere with *B*'s use, and moreover *B* is not able to permit others to use *S* without *A*'s permission. In the case of a transfer, all duties of non-interference would now be directed at *B*, and *B* would, therefore, in turn be empowered to waive them and determine which third parties can make use of *S*.[86] In the case of a waiver, *A* remains the owner while *B* is a guest or licensee strictly at *A*'s discretion. In the case of transfer, *A* loses all rights and *B* gains them all and can therefore create her own guests or licensees.

This cannot be true. If *A* ceases her activity and *B* initiates a new one in conjunction with *S*, *B* always maintains a right not to be interfered with by anyone else, and it is now up to her when she chooses to cease this activity. The fact that *A* made an agreement about when and how her abandonment of *S* would take place does not mean that she retains any power over the object or *B*'s right not to be interfered with.

Stilz argues that the only way one can transfer one's acquired rights in external objects is if exchange itself is taken to be a kind of use that others have to respect.

> The natural duty to respect uses of material goods that are essential other others' life projects applies centrally to *nonexchange* uses. If you appropriate land for the sole purpose of giving others an incentive to exchange with you (i.e. you are not otherwise using this area for your life projects), then you lack . . . rights over it.[87]
>
> Why shouldn't primitive right[88] extend to the claim to transfer, to earn income, to exploit a good for market exchange, and so on?

> I do not deny that there might be a limited natural right to alienate. Even in a state of nature, one might promise one's goods to someone, and morality might require one to follow through on that promise. And, surely, if I come across two people in the forest bartering their nuts and apples, it would be wrong for me to run up and snatch the goods as they are passing between them. If later, the recipient comes to incorporate those goods into her central life activities, I ought to respect her use and possession of them.
>
> But the institution of contractual exchange differs significantly from the prepolitical morality of promise keeping and non-interference. Contract grants the donor a power to create a new right in a recipient, altering the duties of third parties so that they are now required to respect the recipient's – and not the donor's – possession of the thing. Moreover, this new right is meant to bind independently of any roles that the thing might play in the donor's or recipient's projects, *other than the project of exchange*. To form a plan for market exchange, then, I must *assume* that both my recipient and I have the right to exclude others from things apart from personal use.[89]

Stilz is right to say that other persons' participation in some voluntary scheme cannot be presupposed when vindicating the activity within which one subsumes object.[90] However, it is not the case that exchange must be construed as a type of use in order for third parties to be duty-bound to respect the new agreed-upon arrangement of rights. If *B* has engaged an object in an activity, then all third parties are naturally duty-bound not to interfere with it. If *A* abandons the object into *B*'s possession, then no right is any longer owed to *A* but only to *B* in virtue of her use of it. If *A* can make it the case that *B* does not commit injustice in making use of *S*, then she can make it the case that no one does. Where *B* is the first to make use of this opened-up action space, the world now owes her a duty of non-interference in this particular activity.

Both these accounts of the limits of transfer take transfer to achieve something that is in their view unobtainable, but it is also necessary for the transferee to have property rights in the thing transferred.

Transfer of property is enabled simply by the fact that individuals can unilaterally abandon and initiate activities. This account of transfer piggybacks on the use-based account of acquisition. Such accounts are often thought to be unavailable where property is taken to *have to be* something more than it in fact is.

Do such transfers involve the exercise of a Hohfeldian *power*? A power is the juridical ability to alter the juridical incidents that others have. Judith Jarvis Thomson, for instance, says that, it is *powers* that "are at the heart of property rights,"[91] and not merely claims and liberties. Indeed, Gaus and Stilz also seem to think that unless one has powers over one's claim-right to an object, one does not truly have a property right and therefore cannot transfer it to others. A power is deemed necessary to remove one's own claims and liberties with regard to an object (and with them the correlative duties in all others) and to create claims and liberties in one's transferee (and with them, the correlative duties in all others). Powers are invoked to explain how claims can be transferred permanently to others. However, it is not clear how invoking some independent juridical incident does the work it is supposed to. If we must invoke a power to explain how *A* transfers a claim to *B*, how do we explain how *B* can then transfer that claim onto *C* or anyone else? Presumably, *B* would also have to have a power over her new claims transferred to her by *A*. But – within this logic – *A* would need a power over that power in order to transfer it to *B*. *B*, then, if she wanted to transfer that power to *C* would also need a power over her power. So, *A* would need three orders of power in order for it to be the case that *B* can transfer a transferable claim. The invocation of an independent power to make claims transferable would require an infinite regression, otherwise the relevant claim would not be transferable after it had been transferred the number of times that matches the number of original orders of power. Invoking a power to explain transferability or insisting in that a power must be justified before transfer can take place does not appear to be able to do the work demanded of it. Simply choosing to cease activities in a way that permits others to take them up is transfer enough.

While all acquired rights are transferable simply by abandoning the activity that grounds the right and surrendering objects into the activities of others, one's original right to non-interference itself is not transferable. One can transfer rights to non-interference in particular activities because one can abandon those activities, but one cannot – while remaining a living human being – abandon oneself as an actor. Given that no appeal to powers is required to explain alienability, there is no absence of powers with regard to one's natural right to non-interference that needs special accounting for.[92]

Conclusion

The right to non-interference sometimes entails that persons have private ownership of external resources – when they use those resources in a way that renders almost any use by a third party rivalrous with it. The right to non-interference then contains a theory of original acquisition inasmuch as when rightholders take action in the world their right to non-interference is particularised to those concrete actions and the specific objects and spaces they subsume at any given time.

In acting, rightholders constantly alter the content of their own rights and their correlative duties. This is not taken as problematic. Given that private property rights – are in fact justified – are nothing more than rights to non-interference in one's actions, those property rights do not represent *new* or *additional* duties that one subjects others to. Rather, one has simply altered the content of the rights one had all along. There is no power to create new rights and correlative duties, which needs to be invoked. Indeed, I maintain that such invocation is symptomatic of an impoverished account of the relationship between freedom and private property. While there is no power the exercise of which creates new rights and correlative duties, it is still true to say that such rights are acquired, since one has them in virtue of what one does and not in virtue of what one is. Hence, the right to non-interference contains a theory of original acquisition in that regard.

In the next chapter, we will discuss all those cases where ongoing activities are not sufficient to ground private property rights and generate various forms of commons.

Notes

1. In the legal literature, this is typically parsed as use versus *possession*, for example see Ripstein (2013).
2. Epstein (1979); Rose (1985); Lueck (1995).
3. Kant (1991, sec. I.I.IX); cf. Messina (2019) Kant believed that external property rights were only provisional until they were politically authorised. This meant that they did not yet correlate with duties in third parties. They are merely rights in waiting.
4. Kant (1991, sec. I.I.II).
5. An important part of Locke's contribution was to show that, even if monarchical territories were the rightful private property of their monarchs, this would still not give them moral authority over their subjects (Locke 1764, sec. I.XXXXI; van der Vossen 2015b).
6. Grotius (2005, vol. 3, sec. II.II.II).
7. Locke (1764, sec. II.XXVI–II.XXVII) Though both Grotius and Locke believed that the content of justice is revealed both through divine revelation and reason, Grotius believed that reason alone would be sufficient for its truth (Grotius 2005, Prolegomena).
8. Schlatter (1951, 154).
9. von Pufendorf (1934, sec. IV.V.IV).
10. Stilz (2018); Christmas (2019b).
11. Kant (1991, sec. I.I.I).
12. Schmidtz (2009, 7, 2010, 80, 2011, 599–600).
13. To my knowledge, the earliest uses of the bundle of sticks metaphor are in Lewis (1900, 56); Cardozo (1928, 129).
14. Blackstone (1893, vol. 1, sec. II.I emphasis added).
15. Honoré (1961, 108) A Steiner urges us, "control" here is to be understood in the following way: "one *controls* . . . a thing inasmuch as what happens to that thing – allowing for the operation of physical laws – is determined by no person other than oneself" (1994, 39 fn 44).
16. Penner (1997, 72).
17. Harris (1986, 144–45).
18. Merrill and Smith (2017, v); Merrill (1998); Smith (2012).
19. Douglas and McFarlane (2013).

20. Ripstein (2013).
21. Katz (2008, 275); Cf. Penner (1996); Mossoff (2003); Smith (2012, 1693).
22. Mossoff (2011).
23. Claeys (2009, 631); Cf. Mossoff (2009); Smith (2012, 1693).
24. Douglas and McFarlane (2013); Breakey (2011).
25. Kant (1991, sec. I.I.I).
26. Kant (1991, sec. I.I.IV).
27. Under both accounts, however, consumption of an object, such that use of it consisted in its being *used up*, necessarily permitted exclusion of others. Consumables are de facto inaccessible to third parties once they have been consumed, so one's use of them cannot be separated from permanent exclusion. Locke also made the same remarks regarding consumables (Locke 1764, sec. II.XXVIII).
28. John Salter, however, seems to take the Grotian view to be more similar to the Kantian one than I do (Salter 2001, 544).
29. Grotius (2005, vol. 3, sec. II.II.II).
30. Christmas (2019b, 25–29).
31. Blackstone (1893, vol. 1, sec. II.I).
32. Vallentyne (2000, 6); cf. Gibbard (1976).
33. van der Vossen (2015a), the objection raised against the possibility of unilateral original acquisition – that it involves the imposition of new duties on third parties and therefore the arrogation of moral authority – is altogether sidestepped. For a variety of version of this objection, see Gibbard (1976); Waldron (1988a, 265–67, 1996, 1999, chap. 3); Wenar (1998); Flikschuh (1999, 2000, chap. 4, 2008); Varden (2008, 2010); Ripstein (2004, 2006, 2009, chap. 6); Stilz (2009, chap. 2, 2011, 2012, 2014, 2018); Hodgson (2010a); Pallikkathayil (2010); Hasan (2018); Sinclair (2018); Spafford (2000).
34. Though there is no reason to think that it has *necessarily* been truncated.
35. Grotius (2005, vol. 3, sec. II.II.II).
36. The treatment of Grotius's account of property hitherto is distilled from his latter major work that deals with property, *De Jure Belli ac Pacis*. However, in his earlier worker, *Mare Liberum*, he offers a different account, one which is in far closer agreement with the one developed here and not making any invocation of a social contract (Grotius 2004; Christmas 2019b).
37. For combination of the Grotian and Kantian views, see Stilz (2018, 2019, chap. 3).
38. Kant (1991, sec. I.I.IX).
39. Christmas (2019a).
40. Waldron (1988a, 253, emphasis added).
41. Attas (2003).
42. For critique of this empirical assumption at work here, see McCall and Widerquist (2015, 2017).
43. Mack (1990, 1995, 2002, 2010).
44. van der Vossen (2009, 2015a, 2020, van der Vossen therefore joins libertarians who believe that the proviso can, to a significant extent, be fulfilled *by* private acquisition itself (Nozick 1974, 177; Schmidtz 1990, 1991, chap. 2, 1994; Epstein 1997, 63; Machan 2006; Kogelmann and Ogden 2018) For criticism, see McCall and Widerquist (2015, 2017, 2021).
45. Rothbard (2006, chap. 2, 1998, chaps 6–9, 1997, 127–53).

46. Rothbard (1998, chap. 29), Rothbard does, however, *hint* at a limitation along the lines of requiring actual labour or use on the part of the homesteader. One cannot acquire something merely through claiming it (2009, 170). He referred to the latter notion as a "Columbus complex" (Rothbard 1998, 47).
47. Steiner (2017) explicitly argues that concerns over unilateralism are averted so long as the distribution of acquired property is equal. Distributive justice pre-empts the need for a social contract or omnilateral political authorisation.
48. Steiner (1994); Vallentyne (2000); Otsuka (2003, chap. 1).
49. Wendt (2018).
50. Locke (1764, sec. II.XXVII).
51. Scanlon (1976, 23).
52. Grotius (2004, sec. V.VII); Tuck (1979, 61); de Araujo (2009, 358).
53. Christmas (2019b, 32–36).
54. Christmas (2018a, 314–15).
55. Block and Block (1996).
56. Mack (1990, 528–29); Simmons (2001, 239).
57. For example see Stilz (2019, 69).
58. Steiner (1994, 39 fn 44).
59. Many have discussed the issues raised for negligibly harmful physical impositions upon other persons' private property, such as mild pollution of or very low risks of very serious impositions (Railton 1985; Sobel 2012, 2016; Zwolinski 2014, 10–12; Mulkeen 2019); however, the problem extends further than that. The causal contiguity of the physical environment in which humans exist means that almost any action we take has a physical effect on the property of others: effects that we have a duty not to have upon others. David Friedman seems to indicate how much more serious the problem is (1989, 168).
60. Mack (2015).
61. Alchian (1965, 816).
62. Newman (2018, 75).
63. Lifshitz, (n.d.).
64. Nozick, commenting on Locke's notion of mixing labour with land, writes the following.

    > What are the boundaries of what labor is mixed with? If a private astronaut clears a place on Mars, has he mixed his labour with (so that he comes to own) the whole planet, the whole uninhabited university, or just a particular plot? Which plot does an act bring under ownership? . . . Building a fence around a territory presumably would make one the owner of only the fence (and the land immediately underneath it) (1974, 174).

    Also on the problems of establishing physical boundaries with acquired property rights, see Parry (1978, 52); Waldron (1983, 42); Simmons (1992, 268).
65. Rothbard (1997, 153–57).
66. Mack (2015).
67. Locke (1764, sec. II.V.XXVII).
68. Wheeler (1980); Steiner (1994, 233); Mossoff (2002); Long (2012); Claeys (2013, 2017).
69. Hume (1739, sec. III.II.II.VI n); Day (1966); Waldron (1983, 1988a, 184–91).

70. Leaving aside the distinct, if related, question of why the energy does not take on the unowned status of that which is it transmitted into, rather than vice-à-versa. As Nozick asked (rhetorically, we must assume),

    > why isn't mixing what I own with what I don't own a way of losing what I own rather than a way of gaining what I don't? If I own a can of tomato juice and spill it in the sea so that its molecules . . . mingle evenly throughout the sea, do I thereby own the sea, or have I foolishly dissipated my tomato juice?
    >
    > (Nozick 1974, 174–75; cf. O'Neill 1976, 471; Thomson 1990, 325–26; Steiner 1994, 233–35)

71. Waldron (1988b, 187); cf. Geras (1991, 70).
72. Steiner (1994, 233 fn).
73. Steiner (1994, 233).
74. Indeed, any given part of the universe can be truthfully said to have undergone a physical "Cambridge change" as a result of any action by any person (cf. Geach 1969, 71–72).
75. Something like a coherent labour-based account of acquisition might be available, but in order for acquired property to be construed as the "result" of a person's conscious will has to justify acquisition through showing how those kinds of actions justify the resultant rights as types of actions, rather than mere physical occurrences.
76. As Waldron notes, "entropy is not a process which is relative to human purposes" (1988a, 187).
77. Arneson (1991); Cohen (1995, 213); cf. Lippert-Rasmussen (2008).
78. Cohen (1995, 213) Whether or not determinacy is decisively borne out of the maximality and universality of the rights is not my concern here, I only mean to illustrate the genesis of this account. Barbara Fried, for example, argues that this move fails to yield determinacy. The notion of what makes a compossible bundle of rights "strong" is indeterminate. Given the correlative Hohfeldian incidents therein, the strengthening of one incident will result in a weakening of its juridical opposite. If everyone has relatively strong powers, correlatively they must all also have significant liabilities; strong immunities comes at the expense of disabilities, and so forth (Fried 2004).
79. Otsuka, Steiner, and Vallentyne (2005).
80. See note 59 above.
81. Flanigan (2018, 2019).
82. Benson (2019); Mildenberger (2020).
83. Normative "rabbits" can be pulled out of ontological "hats" when it is the ontology of legitimately enforceable *rights* that are under question, since the existence of a right presupposes the truth of a range of normative propositions regarding permissibility and force (cf. Cohen 1995, 121).
84. These three categories are often run together, but it is important to keep them distinct. Contractual exchange only means that one gives away on condition of receiving something in return. Monetary exchange simply means that one gets money in return of the good. And commodification implies the presence of commerce in that good: the existence of a widespread, perhaps, impersonal market on which it is exchanged, as opposed to the mere fact of two persons exchanging it at one time. The permissibility of exchange in no way guarantees commodification (Christmas 2017).
85. Penner (1997, 84–85).
86. Gaus (1994, 218).

87. In the following chapter, we will address the important issue over whether an intention to exclude constitutes a form of use sufficient for original acquisition. I do not believe that it can.
88. By "primitive right," here, Stilz means the natural right to use and thereby exclude others from objects in a state of nature.
89. Stilz (2019, 71 emphasis in original).
90. We will discuss this at length in Chapter 5.
91. Thomson (1990, 285).
92. For debate, see Steiner (2013); Biasetti (2015); Kurki (2017).

4 The Commons[1]

Introduction

The Lockean account of property acquisition places a dichotomy between property and the commons. Lockeans often take original acquisition to just *be* a process by which the commons are privatised. If the commons are what come before property, and original acquisition involves the unilateral creation of property rights, then the commons cannot themselves be a form of property. Rather, it must be a sort of property vacuum in the least, and a primitive chaos at worst. This is wrong. Commons are forms of property. They are unlike forms of private ownership, but they are forms of property in that they assign permissions of access to and control of particular resource to particular persons at particular times. Moreover, liberty is not a priori less compatible with common property any more than it is private property. All property rights must be assigned in such a way that they protect individuals from interference in their ongoing activities. Sometimes this means that private property is called for, sometimes it means some form of common property is called for, and everything in between. The point of a theory of acquisition is not merely to tell us when you can privatise resources and when you cannot, but also what kinds of property systems we should have in place for different kinds of resources that are used in different kinds of ways.

We should be very careful not to think that situations in which there are no *private* property rights and those where resources are open to private acquisition are the same kind of normative landscapes. Lockeans may not always make this conflation, but the terms of the Lockean framework are almost always put in a way that makes this conflation very easy to make. The discursive entanglement of this intellectual tradition with the enclosure movement in England and with American colonisation means that one should not merely be careful not to make the conflation, but should mark the distinction very explicitly and clearly. In developing a positive account of the commons, and analysing when and how they emerge as an application of our respective rights to liberty, this chapter attempts to do just that.

I argue that the right to freedom as non-interference means that resources which are used by an open-ended group in non-rival ways that leave considerable capacity for new users should be considered public property – no set of persons holds anything like a general right to exclude new users. At the point at which intensity or volume of use becomes so rivalrous that there is no action space for new users, it becomes collective property – where the set of current users holds a fairly broad right to exclude new users. There are infinitely many points between these two poles that a commons can occupy.

Liberty and Property After Ostrom

Many Lockeans, broadly construed, are implicitly committed to the view that there is one form of property – private ownership – and where there is no private ownership, there is no property. Freedom demands property, therefore freedom demands private property. This implicit presupposition explains, I think, the failure to satisfactorily analyse the relationship between individual liberty and private acquisition.

Consider Nozick's brief discussion of original acquisition. Nozick never offers a positive account of how or why it is that individuals can acquire private ownership over parts of the hitherto unowned world. Rather, he merely describes why private property is desirable for other reasons that have a tenuous connection at best to a right to freedom and then discusses potential limitations on the power of acquisition that might also be desirable.[2]

A premise of the discussion is that the antecedent principles just obviously entail that we need to be able to acquire private property; the purpose is to neutralise any putative moral remainders:

> Here enter the various familiar social considerations favoring private property: it increases the social product by putting means of production in the hands of those who can use them most efficiently (profitably); experimentation is encouraged, because with separate persons controlling resources, there is no one person or small group whom someone with a new idea must convince to try it out; private property enables people to decide on the pattern and types of risks to bear, leading to specialized types of risk bearing; private property protects future persons by leading some to hold back resources from current consumption for future markets; it provides alternate sources of employment for unpopular persons who don't have to convince any one person or small group to hire them, and so on. These considerations enter a Lockean theory to support the claim that appropriation of private property satisfies the intent behind the "enough and as good" proviso, *not* as a utilitarian justification for property.[3]

Nozick's assertion that this is not a utilitarian justification for private property implies that a rights-based justification has already been made. Indeed, he invokes the Lockean story but takes issue with the idea that "labour-mixing" can do the work required.[4] The result is that we are left with a presumptive power to acquire private ownership of extra-personal resources with no robust positive argument in its favour, only a negative delimitation. What this means is that an act of private acquisition is not justified due to its fulfilment of some general criteria that is necessary for it. Rather, an act of acquisition is justified in virtue of what it *does not* do. Namely, make other worse off. Private acquisition is justified because – and to the extent that – it does not violate the proviso. But we are left wondering what triggers the question of private acquisition in the first instance.

There is only a principle of what an appropriation *must not* to in order to be justified – it cannot make anyone else worse off. However, there is no principle for what an appropriation *must* do in order to be justified; something that can be positively attributed to it that merits its justification. As Daniel Attas puts it, this account includes only a "negative principle of just appropriation," but no positive one.[5]

The proviso, at least to a significant degree, evidences the weakness of the connection between liberty and private ownership within the theory. The connection is so weak that any given instance of private acquisition must undergo ex-post assessment to make sure it did not "entrench" upon the rights of overs, rather than only arising due to its being an entailment of rights generally.[6] This proviso is reflective of an implicit acknowledgement that the power of private acquisition does not have a very robust derivation from individual liberty.

The presumption is that we just need to get private property off the ground somehow, and as long as it does not flagrantly violate any of our prior rights-based commitments, then surely that must be acceptable. This is not in and of itself an unforgivable philosophical shortcut. It would be acceptable if there was a robust account of how a power of private appropriation at least in the typical case, in typical circumstances, was a direct entailment of individual liberty. But given that there are a subset of cases in which this does not hold sufficiently well, we should run an ex-post check as well.[7] However, this is not how the theory operates. There is no positive justification for private property based on individual liberty; all there is, is the ex-post check and that elevates whatever values are protected by that check to the primary level. The proviso – which protects people from being made worse off – encompasses the whole theory and liberty is forgotten.

More serious problems arise when it is combined with the equation of common property with no property. Often (or so I will argue), common property is strictly demanded by liberty, so when it is privatised based on a lazy assumption that private property must somehow be required by liberty, the result is that liberty is sacrificed for private property, rather than property strictly following liberty.

Why is common property implicitly, if not explicitly, equated with a lack of property? I think it is owed to a particular line of reasoning that goes back long before,[8] but was most clearly articulated by Garret Hardin.[9] His famous account of "the tragedy of the commons" took the paradigmatic commons to be an open-access pasture. Anyone may graze their cattle on the common pasture as much as they want, and no one may exclude others from doing so except by and through their grazing of their own cattle. The users are also incapable of communicating with each other, except by using or abstaining from the pasture. Given this set of open-access rules, users are reciprocally unable to restrain each other's use of the pasture. This means that they are collectively unable to obtain credible guarantee that if they individually abstain from use, the others will do so as well. Each, then, has no incentive to holding back on grazing their own cattle for the sake of the longevity of the pasture, since if they hold back themselves, all this does is leave more for others, who in turn have every incentive to take advantage of the extra grazing capacity one leaves for them.

This state of affairs is suboptimal inasmuch as each individual user's optimific strategy results in collective ruin. Each user has an incentive to over-graze the pasture since if they do not, it will get over-grazed by others anyway, and the only difference is that their cattle will not be fatted as a result. There is no pro-social or sustainable way for individuals to benefit themselves in this scenario.

What would be optimal is if each individual could graze their cattle in a sustainable way so that they can continue to do so season after season. Hardin offers a purportedly exhaustive list of two solutions to the problem as he frames it: parcel-and-privatise or command-and-control. Parcel-and-privatise involves dividing the pasture into spatially discrete units and assigning each parcel exclusively to each individual. This would mean that each individual is permitted to exclude third parties from their parcel, meaning that they get to reap the benefits of holding back for the sake of long-term sustainability of their portion of the pasture. Command-and-control involves empowering "Leviathan" to impose and enforce rules of use such that each user is no longer permitted to graze as much as they choose; each user would be forced to abstain to some degree in order to sustain the pasture season after season.

Both involve the imposition of enforceable rules where there were none before. Both call for Leviathan to impose rules exogenously, it is just that one in scenario it is private property rules assigning rights to individuals, and in the other it is duties owed to and enforced by the state; essentially making Leviathan the one private owner of the entire common. In both cases, what is sought is an agent who has final authority over a spatially discrete area in order for there to be socially reconcilable rules at all. Without one of the two of these scenarios being brought to bear on the situation, the commons will be brought to tragic ruin. If either Leviathan or private property is absent, each user is incapable of reconciling their own good with that of the community, and hence there is an inevitable tragedy of the commons.

Elinor Ostrom famously debunked Hardin's analysis, showing not only that his model applied to very few empirical examples but also that the success of his solutions was inconsistent with the assumptions of his model.[10] Hardin paints common-pool resources as prisoners' dilemma games,[11] and hence the outcome's suboptimality requires an exogenous intervention. However, common-pool resources typically are not prisoners' dilemma games: participants can communicate with each other and negotiate over rules of conduct; they can develop norms of conduct with regard to each other's use of the resource and enforce them; they can nominate third-party enforcers when endogenous enforcement through social sanctioning is insufficient. This should not be surprising. Why would we assume that persons who share essential resources and have repeated interactions should automatically lack social capital?

Moreover, the kind of information regarding the disposition of resources that a Leviathan would need to know in order to determine and enforce an efficient set of rules is already presupposed to be unavailable to the actors on the ground. How is it that Leviathan can pull this information out of the air, and yet the actors on the ground who are familiar with each other and the resource cannot even learn it? If the information is available, why can those resource users themselves not deploy it among themselves? Hardin's account lacks analytical symmetry.

The "familiar social considerations" Nozick refers to echo Hardin's account. Where there is no private property there is ruin, and the first priority is to get private property started – regardless of how these resources are currently being used. Nozick's formulation of the proviso makes it clear that he imagines resources that others have already engaged in ongoing use are open to unilateral privatisation by newcomers, so long as they are not made worse off by being deprived of access to this resource (as per the proviso).[12] Just because one did not make oneself the private owner of a resource when one started using it, one has no property right in it whatsoever. All one has is a claim to the level of welfare that one's previous use enabled one to achieve. Anthony De Jasay even more flagrantly disregards existing users' rights when they do not use the resource in an intensive or exclusive way. So long as an acquirer successfully excludes these antecedent users, she gets to privately own the resource in question.[13] Those who fail to establish private property in a resource and elect instead to use it in a way that does not involve the total exclusion of others fail to acquire any right to it whatsoever. The premise of the necessarily tragic commons is the most charitable interpretation for what motivates these ideas.

Locke's political theory of property has been attacked as a disingenuous justification for European colonisation of the Americas and the acquisition of Native American territories.[14] For example, the claim that one must "mix" one's labour with the land, tilling it and making a long-term investment in a fixed parcel, defined away the rights of many nations who depended less on sedentary agriculture and moved around with the seasons and natural cycles of ecosystem services. (They did engage in sedimentary agriculture and private property, but many commentators simply denied or overlooked this.)[15] There was a lot of disagreement between the interpreters and propagators of natural rights theory at the time over whether settlers or natives had established property claims,[16] so it would be wrong to say that Lockean principles are *obviously* designed to prejudice indigenous peoples' practices of resource use. Locke did say that the commons of his time *in England* could not be privatised because there is such widespread and established use,[17] but in the new world it was another story. In any case, I leave questions of author intent to biographers and intellectual historians. What I do say, though, is that Lockeanism, as it typically articulated, certainly contains the resources for strong prejudice against commons-based ways of organising natural resources.[18] There is a lack of a proper theory of why private property in particular is required by freedom and why other kinds of property have *no place at all* for reasons relating to freedom.

How would a Lockean approach to rights look if we actively embraced Ostromian agnosticism as to the a priori social costs and benefits of private property and rejected the neo-Lockean assumption that all property must be private property? This chapter attempts to show that in some detail. In Chapter 3, we saw that liberty does not always and everywhere necessitate that individuals acquire private ownership of the resources they use. That chapter argued for the precise conditions under which a person's claim-right to freedom as non-interference is coextensive with a right to private property in a particular set of time-indexed physical objects and spaces. Here we will see what kind of rights take up the rest of society's action space.

There are two forms of common property that can emerge through an application of the claim against interference. I refer to these as public property on the one hand, and collective property on the other. However, the distinction between them is a matter of degree and not of kind.

Collective property is when a resource is privately owned by a group of persons or almost so. Carol Rose refers to this form of property as "property on the outside, commons on the inside,"[19] and G. A. Cohen refers to it simply as "joint ownership."[20] Individual members may proceed in the established use of the resource, but may consult the collective if they desire to make any change that would affect the overall disposition of the resource, and hence present an interference to other members. With collective property, the group as a whole has the right to exclude (almost) any use of the resource by non-members.[21]

Public property, on the other hand, is when there is an open-ended, as opposed to closed, set of rightholders, each of whom has the right to use the resource in a particular way. The set of users at any given time does not use the resource in a way that gives the users a right to exclude newcomers *tout court*. As always, some new uses will be barred, but there is no presumption of exclusion, as is the case with collective property.

Public property is distinguished from what is often referred to as an *open-access* commons in which there are no persons nor any uses of the resource that are excludable.[22] On my analysis, open-access commons would best be understood as a state of *non-ownership* – a vacuum of property rights that lays waiting for persons to establish them through some use. The only resources that are in such a state are those that no one has yet subsumed into their ongoing activities in any way whatsoever. In Roman law, this is called *res nullius* and refers to resources, which are not yet subject to any property rights, are therefore sites of original acquisition by the first occupant. Both collective property and public property are varieties of *res communis*: resources that are not used in ways that make them suitable to private ownership by an individual but do remain in a settled state of use by many persons.

Property scholarship struggles to make a place for public property as I conceptualise it. Typically, property forms are differentiated by *who* is excluded from a resource, rather than what *uses* are excluded from them.[23] This leads to the conclusion that the property is either privately owned by one or few persons, collectively owned by society at large, either regulated by a state that purports to represent that society, or is left as unregulated open-access commons.[24] The cases studied by Ostrom represent property that is not subject to any single final authority (and hence, not state regulated, nor privately owned) and is yet regulated by endogenous norms and endogenously selected third-party enforcers. However, her cases always involved presumptive exclusion of outsiders at any given time. So, novel as they are, they still do not quite fit the bill of public property as I conceptualise it.

An important exception to the tendency I am critical of is Hanoch Dagan and Michael Heller's articulation of a "liberal commons" in which resources are owned by groups who have collective internal discretion over the resource's disposition, but each member has an individual right of exit.[25] They rightly observe that a concern with individual autonomy should not translate into "an exclusive preference for old-fashioned private property." Precisely how the individual's claim to non-interference in her liberty can result in various forms of commons is what the remainder of this chapter seeks to do.

Public Property

Public property can emerge through the unilateral and/or multilateral use of hitherto unowned resources via an application of the respective users' claims against interference.

When an individual uses a resource in a way that leaves action space open to others, her acquisition of the relevant use-right is consistent with the resource's use by third parties, so long as those new uses are non-interfering. In the case of cultivating a field of crops, the extent of that residual action space is extremely limited, so limited as to justify calling the farmer's property right *private ownership*. However, imagine that instead of cultivating a crop, the individual in question merely uses a beaten path to cross from one location to another on a regular basis. Her claim to non-interference implies that no third party may use the path or the land around it in a way that would obstruct the first user's use of the path as a thoroughfare; however, this leaves many uses open to all third parties. Others could use the path themselves as a thoroughfare, so long as they did not do so in an interfering way – say, by driving down it at a hundred miles an hour while the first user is also passing. Imagine now that more and more people start using the thoroughfare (given that it is hard to use it in any other permissible way). Each new person uses the thoroughfare in a way that does not interfere with any previous user. This may be quite simple with regard to the use of a thoroughfare. If each person simply uses it for walking down (one way or the other), the rules of use are fairly simple – not to obstruct the thoroughfare for others. Problems only arise where use gets to a scale at which the path is rendered less suitable for its current use either by congestion or damage to the path. We will discuss what happens in terms of rights at this stage shortly.

With resources that are used in other ways, a more complex set of rules will be required to protect each person's claim against interference. Consider a large fishing pond. When an individual starts fishing, she acquires a right to the pond. No one may take the fish she catches, nor kick her off of the embankment, nor engage in noise pollution that scares all the fish away or water pollution the kills the fish, etc. An additional fisher, however, would not necessarily interfere. At least, assuming the second fisher's rate of capture did not come at the expense of that of the first fisher's, then her fishing is non-interfering.[26] Or, an occasional swimmer who only comes when the fisher is not there or diligently swims around the area being fished.

For these kinds of uses of resources – walking across an expanse of land and fishing in a pond – there is action space left with regard to the resource such that there are relatively expansive uses of it that are still left open to others (at least, the same use being made by the present user). I call resources subject to this composition of acquired rights *public property* because of the extent to which they are more open to new users than with private ownership. Whereas with the privately owned farm, so many uses by others are not permitted that it is functionally equivalent for all third parties to be excluded altogether (or nearly so). With public property, there are so many potential uses that permissibly could be made by third parties that the required property rules do not exclude all other persons, but more closely permit access by anyone, and importantly regulate their use to those that do not conflict with pre-established ones. Such resources are presumptively open to new users.

Though I assign different labels to private and public property, the distinction is one of degree and not kind. The right to exclude is *always* contingent upon such exclusion being justified by the particular interest the user (or set thereof) has established in the resource.

One can imagine the resources that each member of a community uses in the more fleeting, less intensive ways must remain subject to public property rules. No one may privately appropriate the public square without the consent of all those who presently have established easement rights to it, which is the class of persons who frequently pass through it such that its privatisation would constitute interference with them. One can imagine public parks, streets, and squares emerging this way, as well as many rural, large-scale resources such as forests, fisheries, etc.

Collective Property

Whatever the use of the public resource, there will be *some* point at which an additional user (even making like use) will interfere with the existing users. There is an issue of establishing the cut-off point,[27] when there is a point at which another person along the path interferes with the existing users, or where another fisher in the pond, or another occasional swimmer in it, overcrowds the resource in such a way that the previously established users are now being interfered with.[28] At this point, the status of the resource *vis-à-vis outsiders* resembles that of private property: there is (almost) no use that can be made by an outsider that does not interfere with present users. The difference, though, is that the class of users with regard to what is taken as the unitary resource is greater than one. Between them, the group of users collectively own the resource since the admission of use by another would interfere, and hence they have a right to exclude all third parties. At this stage of development, the resource goes from public property to collective property. Margaret McKean and Ostrom note that stable commons often evolve in precisely this way:

> Historically common property regimes have evolved in places where the demand on a resource is too great to tolerate open access, so property rights have to be created, but some other factor makes it impossible or undesirable to parcel the resource itself.[29]

Where the use of a resource is not diminished by additional users, it remains open to new users. Existing users are free to negotiate with each other about how to mutually alter the resource's disposition, but they may not exclude other non-rival uses of the resource. At the point at which (almost) no additional use can be made, the group of existing users has far broader powers of exclusion and may govern the resource as their collective private property. This would give the users of an overcrowded thoroughfare the right to enforce a traffic management system and/or charge user fees, which they can use to maintain the path or build an alternative one to ease congestion. It would enable the users of an over-fished fishery to prohibit new fishers, sell a restricted number of licenses, or impose restrictions on the volume, age, species of fish that can be fished, or any combination thereof. If overcrowding was reached after both swimmers and fishers had acquired claims, then they would have to negotiate between themselves as to how to manage their respective activities.

The particular governance mechanism is entirely up to the users themselves. They may abstain from formally organising and simply negotiate with each as and when they need to. When an individual wants to augment her existing use of the resource (including admitting new users), in a way which would interfere with another existing user or the group as a whole, she needs to obtain their consent and may have to offer up something in exchange. Without any formal organisation of all the users together, it would be managed through a nexus of such spot-transactions. Depending on the nature of the resource and the use it is being put to, however, this may be extremely costly to the users as a whole.[30] Negotiations take time, but contractual agreements bring uncertainty. After all, no matter how well specified the contractual arrangement is, it is still possible for one party to renege on the contract ex post.[31] This will be a violation of the other's rights, of course, but that is no guarantee it will not happen. Moreover, there will be costs just in discovering whom one needs to get the consent of. Where the complexity of the resource is such that it is not obvious upon whom one's change of use imposes costs, and hence whom one needs to negotiate with, these costs will be prohibitive. Where such transaction costs are sufficiently high, it will be efficient for the users to collectively consent to a set of primary rules binding each individual. Rather than behaving like interdependent, individual users, they will then behave more like a firm: each following a set of agreed-upon rules and procedures, rather than bilaterally negotiating with one another each step of the way. Indeed, if the need to change these rules may be an ongoing possibility, it will be efficient for them to also consent to a set of secondary rules, so that certain among them are empowered to make changes to the primary rules when necessary, without the need for a new consensus. Indeed, it may be easier to obtain consensus on secondary rules rather than directly upon primary rules.[32]

We should briefly note that all this is also true of public property, except that the incorporated group of users cannot exclude newcomers whose uses would not in fact interfere. They may incorporate in order to coordinate and develop their own uses, but until the resource is rendered rivalrous by new users, they may not convene on the terms of those new users' exclusion.

Rothbard, Hoppe, Block, and Randall Holcombe recognise the place for public easement rights to the use of thoroughfares. Holcombe even explicitly notes that where the public use does not generate overcrowding, no user has the right to exclude any other user. However, they all maintain that such resources could nonetheless be privatised by an incorporated group of users, who could impose property rules and charge user fees. This is inconsistent with respecting the rights of newcomers.[33]

Almost any new disposition for the collectively owned resource is open to them from the perspective of their collective property rights in it. The only caveat is that it must be by each user's consent that she be incorporated. Prior to consensual incorporation and agreement to a set of primary and secondary rules, any decision to alter the disposition of the use of the resource that interferes with a non-consenter's ongoing use would be unjust. Even if she herself would "benefit" from being forced into a situation in which her use of the resource is governed by a set of overarching rules, it would still be a violation of her claim to non-interference to conscript her into the organisation. The fact that she might be compensated for this rights-violation *ex post* does not legitimise the violation *ex ante*.

The forgoing entails that individuals could strategically withhold their consent to incorporation in order to increase any compensation they might be offered in exchange for it. However, others may legitimately threaten the holder-out with sanctions falling short of rights-violations – for example through ostracism or abstaining from other future contracts that the holder-out is dependent upon. If this all proves ineffective, however, the holder-out remains free – normatively speaking – to hold out. This will present costs to other individuals, but that is the cost of dealing with individuals who have rights.

Each individual party to the common must therefore consent to any change in its disposition which would impact her ongoing use of it. Once a user has consented to incorporation, they will be contractually obliged to comply with the primary and secondary rules thereof. Once incorporated, the right of exit is limited in that users may not exit the organisation *with* their property rights, since they have been contractually pooled. Exiting outside of the parameters of the incorporation would result in their property rights being left behind. Each individual is always free to abandon their right to the common and exit, given that other uses cannot conscript them into maintaining positive contributions to it if they wish to simply leave.[34] Or they may simply transfer their right to another member of the common on terms of exchange both consent to and which is in agreement with the rules of the particular common.[35]

Collective owners may indeed agree to make parts of their resource partially open to the public for certain uses at certain times. The more ecologically connected resources are, even those resources subject to individual private ownership may be joined, to some degree, into a commons organisation in order to deal with common problems and determine rules to ensure they are able to coordinate the changing dispositions they may have of their respective resources. Combinations of collective, public, and private forms of ownership can overlap in space because all property rights are rights to certain kinds of actions with regard to time-indexed objects, rather than right to those object tout court. Over time, then, patterns of acquisition, exchange, and incorporation could mean that the property system becomes very complex indeed to the point that to an outsider, the property rules themselves are very hard to read in totality, since they are the function of so many different actions. James C. Scott's example of how pluralistic property forms that evolve endogenously is a useful illustration

> Let us imagine a community in which families have usufruct rights to parcels of cropland during the main growing season. Only certain crops, however, may be planted and every seven years the usufruct land is redistributed among resident families according to each family's size and number of able-bodied adults it comprises. After the harvest of the main season crop, all cropland reverts to common land where any family may glean, graze their fowl and livestock, and even plant quickly maturing, dry-season crops. Rights to graze fowl and livestock on pasture land held in common by the village is extended to all local families. The number of animals grazed, however, is restricted according to size of family, especially in dry years when forage is scarce. Families not using their grazing rights can give them to other villagers but not to outsiders. Everyone has the right to gather firewood for normal family needs of heat and fuel, except for the village blacksmith and baker who have larger allotments. No commercial sale from village woodlands is permitted.
>
> Trees which are known to have been planted are, together with their fruit, the property of the family which planted them, no matter where they are now growing. Fruit fallen from such trees, however, is the property of anyone who gathers it. When a family fells one of its trees or it is felled by wind, the trunk of the tree belongs to the family, branches to the immediate neighbors, and the "tops" (leaves,

twigs, fronds) to any poorer villager who carries them off. Land is set aside, exceptionally, for use or leasing out by widows with children or dependents of conscripted males. Usufruct rights to land and trees may be "let" to anyone within the village but not to anyone outside the village unless no one in the community wishes to use it.[36]

Conclusion

Given that the kinds of rights that are acquired are purely down to the kinds of activities individuals choose to pursue and that the kinds of commons arrangements will be a function of this, in addition to the kinds of agreements that they make with one another, the fact is that we just do not know how property would look if it spontaneously evolved in a just way. Visually speaking, all we know is that it would probably be highly pluralistic both between and within social groups of whatever scale.

The idea that property must take one particular spatial and visual form can be attributed to the need for bureaucrats to make the reality that they survey match the model they have constructed of it.[37] When drawing up a map of an area for the purposes of political administration – archetypally, counting heads for conscription, allocating responsibility for tax payment, calculating tax liabilities – simplifications of the reality on the ground are necessary. However, the limitations of the simplifications result in errors of administration, leading the bureaucracy to exert its coercive power to render the reality on the ground more like the simplification. The kinds of commons that Scott describes would be highly challenging for a bureaucrat to administer. There are a variety of different things produced that are not all necessarily monetised; there are variegated lines of responsibility and residual claimancy meaning that who is responsible for paying any taxes associated with the land and its produce would be very convoluted. It would surely be much simpler if the bureaucrat could just carve up the land into parcels and give each head of household exclusive rights and therefore tax liabilities to each respective parcel. Alas, just because it would be convenient for taxation does not mean property should take this shape by right. When thinking about what kind of property is demanded by justice we must ensure we are not "seeing like a state."[38]

The need for judgements regarding property to be only abstract and physicalistic is one that we should be critical of, especially when thinking about property normatively. The kind of knowledge that is involved in judgements regarding acquired property rights will be discussed in Chapter 8. As we will see, knowledge that is local, contextual, and not transmittable in propositional form is partially essential for fully delineating the constant and changing boundaries of our property rights.[39]

Peter Railton makes the following characterisation of the normative landscape from the perspective of the view that the elementary particles of justice are property rights.

> From this Lockean view emerges an image of moral space akin to a map at a registrar of deeds. Individual entitlements or rights determine a patchwork of boundaries within which people are free to live as they choose so long as they respect the boundaries of others. To learn one's moral obligations one need only consult the map. Would a given act involve crossing another's boundary? If so, it is prohibited; if not, permitted.
>
> If we take seriously the fact that we find ourselves situated in, and connected through, an environment, we are soon impressed with the inaptness of a conception of morality that pictures individuals as set apart by propertylike boundaries, . . . free to act as they please within their boundaries, although absolutely constrained by them.[40]

According to the view defended here, the content of justice could not be drawn on a map, at least, not particularly usefully. Our rightful actions physically overlap and are often mutually dependent on one another. Respect for property rights does not, a priori, drive physically apart individuals physically apart any more than it brings them together.

As I hope to have now made clear, rejecting the physicalistic account of property rights both demonstrates when property rights are strictly applications of one's right to be free and how that property rights can come in myriad forms.

Notes

1. The central argument here is also presented in (Christmas 2020a) and, to a lesser extent, in (Christmas 2018b, 315–16, 2017, 512–16).
2. He does however offer a negative account of why property system that permits the coercive extraction of wealth by one group from another involves partial ownership of the extractees by the extractors (1974, 172) and notes that this is surely contrary to liberty (1974, 160–64; cf. J. Brennan and van der Vossen 2018). This, then, does offer an argument for a natural right to external property, but not an account of how the right manifests (how it is acquired), nor of why it should always be in the form of private property in particular.
3. Nozick (1974, 177).
4. Nozick (1974, 174–75).
5. Attas (2003).
6. Scanlon (1976, 23).
7. For example van der Vossen's particular approach resembles this (2020).
8. Aristotle (1981, sec. II.III); Aquinas (1947, sec. IIa IIIæ, Q66, A2); Hobbes (1983, sec. I; 2012, sec. XIII – XIV); Lloyd (1833); Gordon (1954); Olsen (1965).
9. Hardin (1968).
10. Ostrom (1990); also see Levine (1986); Rose (1986).

11. In which participants cannot communicate with each other or have knowledge of one another's actions.
12. One of the ways Nozick says a person might be made worse off by another person's acquisition is not just that they are now unable to acquire it, but that this acquisition might render them "no longer able to use freely . . . what he previously could. . . . [U]sers might face more inconvenience, crowding, and so on" (Nozick 1974, 176).
13. De Jasay (1997, 171–80).
14. Tully (1994); Arneil (1996).
15. Anderson (1997, 2016).
16. Fitzmaurice (2014).
17. Locke (1764, sec. II.XXXV).
18. Tully (1994).
19. Rose (1998, 144).
20. Cohen (1995).
21. Much of what we think of as private property in the real world is in fact collective property in this sense. For example homes owned by married couples and corporations owned by shareholders (Ellickson 1993).
22. Ellickson (1993).
23. This naturally follows from any account of property that understands rights to be exclusive possession of physical objects as such.
24. Stevenson (1991); Ellickson (1993); Epstein (1994; Forthcoming).
25. Heller and Dagan (2001). It is worth recognising that they too draw strong inspiration from Ostrom.
26. This applies whether or not the first user's rate of capture was sustainable relative to the natural rate of regeneration of the fishery or not. Of course, if it *was* sustainable, and the second user rendered it unsustainable, this would constitute interference. However, if the initial rate was unsustainable and the newcomer hastened the depletion of the fishery, this would also be an interference. Determining the precise activities that are permissible by the newcomer may well require fairly sophisticated ecological knowledge as pertains to the particular resource.
27. Though it need not be as difficult as identifying the straw that broke the camel's back. Rather, the slightly less difficult task of identifying the straw that made the risk of the camel's break breaking intolerable.
28. The question of how bad foot-traffic has to be in order to constitute interference or how loud the swimmers in the pond have to be to count as interfering with the fishers, for example, is going to vary across social contexts, to the extent that the relevant activities (and what it takes to interfere with them) are differentially constituted across cultural settings.
29. McKean and Ostrom (1995, 6).
30. Coase (1937).
31. Klein, Crawford, and Alchian (1978).
32. Rawls (1955); G. Brennan and Buchanan (2000, vol. 10, chap. 2).
33. Rothbard (2006, chap. 11); Holcombe (2005, 22); Block (2009, 242); Hoppe (2011, 4).
34. Conscription will be discussed in more detail in the following chapter.
35. This therefore coheres with a "liberal" account of the commons, as per Michael Heller and Hanoch Dagan's account, inasmuch as free exit is always guaranteed (Heller and Dagan 2001).
36. Scott (1998, 33–34).
37. Scott (1995, 1996, 1998, chaps 1–2; cf. 2017, chap. 2); Carson (2011); Rozumalski (2017).

38. While the account of justice argued for in this book and applied in this chapter is highly abstract, even *simple*, that need not mean that its property application be visually rationalised. Rationalism at the level of moral principle can be consistent with pluralism as the level of institutions thereby justified (cf. J. Brennan 2015; Long 2015).
39. Scott (1998, chap. 9).
40. Railton (1985, 187, 219).

5 The Limits to Appropriation

Introduction

The principle of acquisition that I defend in this book has inherent limits. I have discussed at length what is included in this principle, so in one sense its limits have already been fully described. However, full understating of a limit involves understanding what is on both sides of it. So, here I will discuss what is not included; that is the kinds of acquisitions that are prohibited by the principle but not necessarily *obviously* prohibited.

First, the right to non-interference, being inclusive of the preconditions of acting whatsoever, constitutes a kind of right of necessity. Therefore, whatever turns out to be necessary to the subsistence of others can never, at that time, come under the acquired rights of another. Second, there are two related forms of land engrossment that may be thought to be paradigm cases of original acquisition but cannot in fact be vindicated in a non-question-begging way. That is when land is putatively originally acquired through acts of exclusion or by employing others to make it productive. Intellectual property rights cannot be acquired whatsoever. Both models of intellectual property – ownership of ideal objects and intellectual usufruct – are not the kinds of rights that can be consistent with everyone's right to freedom as non-interference.

Necessity, Revisited

As I noted at the end of Chapter 2, the claim against interference in whatever non-interfering action we might initiate includes a claim against interference with the necessary preconditions of our being an actor at all; namely, our obtainment of the subsistence of our bodies – air to breathe, food to eat, space to take shelter from the elements, etc. Such a right is typically referred to as the *right of necessity*. It has two important features. First, as part-and-parcel of our original right to non-interference, it is prior to any acquired right, which means it takes precedence over any acquired property rights. Second, it is a purely negative right to not be interfered with in the pursuit of one's subsistence rather than a positive right. It is therefore correlative with duties of omission rather than action in third parties.

What does it mean for the right of necessity to come before any acquired right? Obviously, the right of necessity means that no one may initiate activity and thereby acquire a property right that interferes with any other person's pursuit of their subsistence. However, it also means that any activity initiated by *A* at t_1 that did not interfere with anyone's means of subsistence at t_1, due to a change in circumstances, turns out to involve an interference with *B*'s subsistence at t_2, and *A* will incur a duty to stop this activity. Hence, any property right, the exercise or enforcement of which turns out to interfere with any person's subsistence, is extinguished. Strictly speaking, all activities are only allowed to proceed if they are non-interfering. It is just that, with regard to subsistence, this may take precedence even when it comes later in the temporal chain of events, unlike other activities. The reason for this is that though all property rights are strictly applications of the original right to non-interference, they are nonetheless *acquired* rather than *original*. Rights acquired through action exist on the coattails of the actions that acquired them, and where it is the case that those actions prove to no longer be non-interfering, they are no longer just.

Given that the right of subsistence that is original and the particular property right (or the right to continue any particular action) that is acquired, it is the latter that gives way to the former, rather than vice versa. Strictly speaking, it is the former that is automatically delineated so as to leave space for the latter. The right of necessity is often framed as a kind of *exception* to the rules of property;[1] on this account however it is partially constitutive of property, since the two are implications of the same basic right.[2] Therefore, as Aquinas said, it is not theft to take food that putatively belongs to someone else if you are starving since your starvation makes you the rightful owner of the nearest available food.[3]

The right to subsistence is a negative right, meaning that it is a right that others *abstain* from taking particular courses of action rather than and that others *proceed* to take particular courses of action.[4] Therefore, the duties that correlate with the right are negative duties of omission rather than positive duties to take certain actions. For example imagine *A* starts drinking from the only water hole in the desert and intends to drink every last drop (even though she is fully hydrated and can easily make the journey home without any more water). Under normal circumstances, any newcomer would have a duty not to interfere. Indeed, *A* has acquired a use-right to this waterhole. However, if *B* were the newcomer and was severely dehydrated, then a certain amount of water in the waterhole is automatically implicated in *B*'s subsistence and *A* has a duty not to exclude her from taking the water in a way that she would not had *B* not been in peril. However, *B* does not have a positive duty to *provide B* with hydration beyond abstaining from any action that would interfere with *B* obtaining hydration herself. If, for example, *B* is unconscious and *A* has the wherewithal to mainline a saline drip into *B*'s arm so that she is hydrated, she does not have an enforceable duty to do this. Her only enforceable obligation is not to interfere with or frustrate *B*'s efforts to get hydrated (or, for that matter, any third parties' efforts on *B*'s behalf).[5]

Now, it is possible for persons to have *derivative* positive duties to positively assist others in obtaining the means to their subsistence. For example, if *A* snatched away the water receptacle as *B* was about to drink from it and threw it into the distance, she has a positive duty to go and collect it and give it back. Since her throwing it into the distance was an act of interference, *A* has a duty to cease this interference and that means bringing the receptacle back to *B*. Once one initiates a rights-violation, it is now that case that one's obligation is cashed out in terms of specific positive acts that are required to bring it to an end. However, this is the case for all negative duties,[6] not just with the duty not to interfere with subsistence. For example, if *A* were to break into *B*'s home, while she is inside the home, she has a duty to do at least one very specific action: to leave as quickly as possible.

However, a non-derivative, enforceable positive duty would not be compossible with a claim to non-interference since it would permit non-interfering persons to be interfered with in order to make them provide for the subsistence of others.[7]

How would the right of necessity operate in practice? Imagine a world where all appropriations rendered *A* without any way of obtaining her means of subsistence via access to unused resources for acquisition or to her own private property or to public or collective property or via exchange. In this world, whoever was in possession of the most proximate resources required for *A* to subsist, call this person *B*, would be required to abstain from interfering with *A* freely using those resources for her subsistence. Though *B* has no original positive duty to assist *A*, there may be any number of positive actions that she is required to take in order to fulfil her negative duty to abstain from interfering with *A*'s subsistence, if she has already initiated positive actions which present interference – for example unlocking doors to let *A* into her house to get something to eat. Whatever one's ongoing activities include, for example, living in a secure home, one is required to abstain from those aspects of them which interfere with others' subsistence. This means that if *B* does lock the door, she has to unlock it. All these positive acts are parasitical on *B*'s prior negative duty not to engage in activities which interfere with another person seeking the available means of subsistence.

It is not relevant whether or not the most proximate means to *A*'s subsistence would not have existed but for *B*'s ongoing activities. We imagine that the food in *B*'s kitchen did not just grow there and then *B* erected a wall around it; rather, it is the result of a vast network of different persons' actions and exchanges. Under the view developed here, one does not acquire rights to objects because one produced them;[8] it is only their subsumption into one's actions which gives rise to a claim against interference in one's use of them. However, the food in *B*'s kitchen is subsumed into *A*'s sphere of action insofar as it is a precondition of her action, and therefore *B*'s use of the food now interferes with *A*'s right of subsistence.

The fact that *B* ended up being the one to give up – what would in other circumstance be considered to be – *her* property does not give her any right to, for example, demand that *A* compensate her, whenever she may be in a position to. *B* may not attach any conditions to *A*'s using of what were previously her resources. For *B* to be able to impose conditions that *A* must comply with before being given access to food or shelter from the elements would be for *B* to impose conditions on *A*'s exercise of her original rights.

Often it is thought that an obligation to make one's property available to others is always a positive duty. Allowing others to make use of one's property is on a par with allowing others to make use of oneself, which is equivalent to being required to take positive actions on the behalf of others. However, where all just property rights are strictly applications of one's right not to be interfered with, one's property ought not to be reified as falling under one's rightful jurisdiction beyond that. So that the right of necessity generates positive non-derivative duties presupposes precisely what that right partially informs: whose property is the relevant object?

A just property regime will likely involve instances of private ownership, punctuated with collective property, all connected up with public property, the details of which will depend upon the social practices which pervade the society. What one would hope is that this system provides ample opportunities for each person to flourish, rather than merely obtaining their means of subsistence. When people plan for the future, they can ensure that their subsistence and even comfort are provided for in times of uncertainty through mutual aid schemes at the level of family, neighbourhood, church, occupation, community, etc., or through for-profit insurance available through the impersonal nexus of the market.[9] However, the fact that one's original right includes the liberty to obtain the means of subsistence means that whatever the spontaneous order generated by a just property regime means, one is always permitted to take what one needs for one's subsistence. For example, if there is systematic discrimination against a particular class of persons in a society which deprives them from access to basic resources (and there is no possibility of exiting to another society) those persons are justified on grounds of their original rights in taking what they need with the use of proportional and necessary force. Or indeed, if persons face horrendously bad luck for which they did not make arrangements, they are likewise permitted to take what they need with the use of force.

It is often thought that, if one has the right to engage in actions which would ordinarily be classed as property rights-violations on the grounds that one would otherwise be in peril, then property rights must be "non-absolute."[10] However, under the view of original appropriation developed here, the right to interfere with someone else freely obtaining the means to her own subsistence is never a right one can acquire in the first place – it does not feature among any bundle of rights one could have over the external world because others come into the world with an original right to the means of subsistence.[11] The right of subsistence by no means "trumps" other property rights; it is rather the case that all property rights are acquired *around* each person's basic right to the means of their subsistence.[12]

This is all assuming the means of each person's subsistence is in fact available. If circumstances are such that, no matter what actions people take, there really is not enough food, space, or breathable air to go around, the circumstances of justice have fallen away. Justice no longer provides the moral function it arises in the service of. Coordination is no longer possible. One person acting so as to allow one person's access to their means of subsistence will result in their obstructing another person's means of subsistence. Rights become incompossible and hence cease to be rights. In such circumstances, justice has no application.[13]

The right of necessity presents an internal restriction to the extent of private appropriation that can be justified.

Against Engrossment

Two forms of original acquisition which might be thought to be justified are what I refer to as varieties of *engrossment*. Engrossment involves making a claim to land (or other natural resources) through forms of putative use that fail to justify the acquisition of property rights. To illustrate these two forms of engrossment and why they are not successful in acquiring rights, here are two cases: that of the land speculator and that of the aspiring agricultural capitalist.

Land Speculator

Someone who wishes to get rich off owning land stumbles upon a large swathe of land that she believes will one day be highly valuable. Perhaps it is on the periphery of a rapidly expanding city, perhaps it contains materials that will soon skyrocket in value, or perhaps it will be on the route of a major new highway or railway line that no one else knows is being built yet. The land speculator claims that this land is now hers. Anyone who does not respect her ownership of it is interfering in her ongoing activities, and therefore she believes she owns it by natural right. How is it that her claim could be vindicated? What is she doing with the land?

Well, the activity she claims she has engaged the land in is *withholding it from the market* in order to drive up its value. But this putative action cannot vindicate a property right because this action can only be said to be undertaken by her if she already has the relevant property right. That activity she is engaged in needs to itself be vindicatable without presupposing that she has the property right she is trying to vindicate. Perhaps, then, the activity she is engaged in is simply *excluding others from the land*.[14] This is certainly something that she can in fact do without having a right to the property. She could erect fences, hire guards, personally patrol it herself and physically remove people, or threaten them into staying away. However, this is not a use of the land that she has a right to initiate. The mere exclusion of others from unowned property is something that is only justified to the extent that it is required, as a necessary by-product, of an already ongoing use continuing uninhibited. Exclusion cannot be the activity that justifies itself. There must be some actual activity that makes exclusion necessary, and the extent of that exclusion will be strictly pegged to that required by the extent of use.

Perhaps if all third parties voluntarily abstain from the land, physical exclusion never turns out to be necessary because everyone just happens to stay off it. Since the speculator does not violate anyone's rights, could she not claim the land then? Well, this would only be possible if it were the case that she could be said to have a claim that all third parties *continue* to voluntarily exclude themselves from the land, and that would require the possibility that the speculator could justly conscript them into this activity for a moment longer than they chose to. There is no way a person can acquire land simply by willing that it be theirs.[15]

Aspiring Agricultural Capitalist

Someone who wishes to get rich off industrial agriculture stumbles across a large swathe of land that would make the perfect starting ground. It is covered in fertile soil, there are few trees and rocks that need removing, and it is in a location with ideal weather for growing popular foodstuffs. The land is incredibly large and far beyond that which the aspiring capitalist could actually make into a farm on her own, even with all the sophisticated machinery she owns. Nonetheless, she claims that it is hers. While she may not be actually using all of the land, her soon-to-be employees will make use of the rest. Clearly, she impresses upon those who question her, she has initiated use of the entire plot as an industrial farm. She has roped off the whole area and is now recruiting farmhands. However, the notion that *her employees* will till the soil, plant seed, irrigate, harvest gives her property rights to the land cannot work. If she has not begun use of the land at t and newcomers come and start farming it, the property right is theirs. The aspiring capitalist believes that since they are only permitted to enter the land with her consent, she determines the terms of the employment contract, and among them will be that all the land becomes (or, remains) her own. However, without a prior property right in the land, she would have no right to exclude her putative employees, and therefore they would not need to consent to any terms whatsoever before entering the land and unilaterally making use of it. Her claim to have initiated use of the entire plot as a commercial farm presupposes her right to exclude others from the land in the first instance and therefore presupposes her property right.

Both attempts to justify the land engrossment at will rather than through action turn out to be question-begging: the activities they claim to have subsumed that land in can only be true if they already have the property right in the first instance.

This restriction on acquisition ought not to be seen as some additional principle that imposes limits on the scope of a prior principle of acquisition – it is inherent in the principle from the start.

Against Intellectual Property

Intellectual artefacts such as works of art, discoveries, and inventions are often regarded to be so closely associated with a person's activities and projects that they ought to have rights over them in similar ways in which they have rights over the physical substrata of their activities and projects.

Broadly speaking, there are two accounts of the ontology of intellectual property.[16] The first takes it to be the ownership of an ideal – that is non-physical – object. The second takes it to be a kind of usufruct, or a right to use physical property in a particular way without external impediment, namely, in a *commercial* way. The unimpeded use of physical property in a commercial way often requires others to abstain from using numerically different but qualitatively identical objects in a commercial way in order to protect one's market position or the price one commands for commercial production of a good or provision of a service. Neither versions of intellectual property, I argue in this chapter, can be justified by a commitment to non-interference. Indeed, both are inconsistent with non-interference and are therefore prohibited as property forms by our natural rights. All intellectual property is therefore unjust.

Intellectual Property as Ownership of Ideas

Intellectual property rights are often contrasted to property rights in physical objects. A copyright in a poem or a patent in a pharmaceutical is not a right over any particular physical instantiations thereof. When the poem is written on a particular piece of paper or when particular chemicals are combined and pressed into a particular pill with a particular mark on it, persons can have property rights in those particular objects and use them as they wish. An intellectual property right may give its holder some rights over these physical instantiations, but it does not consist solely in those rights. Indeed, one does not need a prior property right in the physical substrata of a poem or a pharmaceutical patent in order to come to have rights over it once that poem or pharmaceutical patent is instantiated by them. Someone might write the poem out with their own hand, with their own pen, on their own piece of paper, and yet because the result counts as an instantiation of the copyrighted poem, the copyright holder has some rights over this object – for example that it not be sold. It is for this reason that intellectual property rights are often viewed as ownership claims to *ideal objects*; our rights to their physical tokens are explained by our ownership of their ideal type.[17]

Ideal objects are distinguishable – if not separable – from the physical objects in which they are instantiated. For example computer software can be distinguished from the particular disk it is installed on; a manufacturing process versus the machinery required and physical product that is manufactured in accordance with it; works of music versus the paper they are written on, the disk they are saved on, or the vocal cord they are sung with. Indeed, there is a sense in which any ideal object can be held in the human mind. One can recall a poem in one's inner voice, have the ability to hum a tune, execute a secret production process, assemble a patented microchip, or write a proprietary branch of code.[18]

Ownership rights in ideal objects do not, then, inhabit a separate normative space to rights in physical objects. Since ideal objects are instantiated by physical objects, allocating ownership to ideal objects restricts the uses of physical objects which are already the objects of rights. Allocating rights to ideal objects therefore comes at a cost to rights to physical objects no matter how those rights are allocated. We will, therefore, need reasons to allocate those rights which are grounded in our reasons for allocating property rights more generally, in order to justify making space for owning ideal objects when those rights are incompossible with rights to physical objects. Rights to time-indexed physical objects can only be attenuated – if then – if the grounds for attenuation are the same grounds for the rights in the first place.

Among the grounds for having property rights in physical objects as the elementary particles of justice is that fact of the rivalrousness of the physical world in which society finds itself. Since the physical world is rivalrous, there are times where there are actions physically coincide with one another, and therefore we need property rights to tell us who gets to determine who must give way to the other. If I pick an apple from a tree and eat it, no one else can pick and eat it; therefore if one person takes the apple and another tries to take it at the same time, they will frustrate each other's actions, and we need to know who gets to determine who gets to break the deadlock. Ideal objects on the other hand are non-rivalrous and therefore not subject to the same calamity. If I write a novel, no one else is *thereby* stopped from writing that same novel as such. Of course, if I write my novel on the only piece of paper in existence, or if I chose to write at the only point in the space where you are able to write it, then our respective novel-writing is mutually frustrating. However, this is not because we are writing the same novel, but merely because we are attempting to do so with the some of the same objects at a given time in a mutually frustrating way. It is not our simultaneous employment of the ideal object of the novel that renders these actions conflictual. If there were more paper and more space to write, we could both write the same novel without thereby coming into any conflict whatsoever. The question, the answer to which is individual property rights, does not arise with regard to ideal objects. No one need be excluded from the use of any ideal object so that another may proceed in her use of it. When it comes to the world of ideal objects, we live in a non-rival world. We do not need moral guidance on who gets to break deadlock because no deadlock can arise.

A's exclusion of *B* from making use of *S* at *t* can only be justified as a necessary side-effect of *A* proceeding in her occupation of *S* at *t* unimpeded. No more exclusion can be admitted into the scheme of justice than is necessary for the coordination of human activity in a socio-economic context.[19]

The introduction of ownership of ideal objects, lacking any common justification with the rest of our acquired rights, simply violates those rights, since it would make permissible exclusion from the use of objects which do not in fact conflict with any prior initiated action on anyone else's part.

Intellectual Property as Usufruct

Bryan Cwik has argued that intellectual property rights need not and should not be understood as ownership of ideal objects. Rather, they are rights to particular kinds of uses, with correlative duties in others to abstain from actions that hinder those uses.[20] Indeed, Cwik's analysis is reflective of that of the main philosophical defenders of intellectual property in the jurisprudence literature.[21] While some of those authors also defend intellectual property on the basis of something like a literalist labour theory of property, they do not conceptualise intellectual property as the ownership of ideal objects qua the product of physical or intellectual labour. Rather – and the subtlety matters here – it is a right to not be impeded in their *productive use* of physical property on the basis that *uses* of physical objects should be given rights-based protection where those uses involve physical and intellectual labour in the production of things of value.[22]

In order to see why property rights cannot take this particular shape, we must take a bit of a step back.

The action one initiates in conjunction with time-indexed objects and spaces in order to ground a property right must be vindicated without reference to the actions of others. If this were not the case, then it would be possible to *conscript* others into one's activities and to acquire a right that they continue. Such a right would correlate with a duty on their part and hence would grant one the right to interfere with their actions in order to bring their actions in line with those one has conscripted them into. It would come to constitute an interference for them to merely abstain from contributing to, or positively cooperating in, one's activity. For example, when *A* plant seeds in tilled soil, it may well be true that she is initiating the activity of *becoming a prosperous farmer*, because she does in fact end up growing produce that commands a high price at market, which she is successful in selling season after season. There is no doubt that her activity is, at least in a commercial sense, successful and lucrative. However, if we were to include those aspects of her activity into the description that we use to inform her acquired property rights, then she would have a claim-right to her success on the market. This claim-right to her success would correlate with duties in every other person to not interfere with this success; that is to abstain from actions that are not consistent with her ongoing success. However, constitutive of this success are the positive actions (as opposed to omissions) on the part of her cooperators, including her customers. This means that interference in her action could occur simply by her customers' *inaction*. Were they to withdraw their custom, they would be interfering with her *successful commercial food production*. This, in turn, would mean that our farmer would be justified in interfering with her would-be customers in order to bring them into line. She would have a right to a captive market, simply because she had a market share at some point in time. Rather than protecting each person from interference, this would render our natural rights as potential tools of conscription. Whenever we cooperate with others, we risk becoming duty-bound to cooperate with them for as long as *they* choose, and the same would be true in the other direction.

Failing to provide positive assistance in another's activities cannot count as interfering with them.[23] There is a quite formal reason for why the right to non-interference could not be formulated in this way. Recall from Chapter 1 that rights are *individual* rights so that justice always provides a *final* answer to questions of who should give way when actions collide in space–time, in lieu of any spontaneous coincidence of their respective wills. If rights were assigned to groups, the possibility of internal disagreement would give rise to indeterminacy over who has the final say as a matter of justice. If justice were to provide any further guidance as to who has the final say in cases of deadlock, it would thereby assign an individual with a right. In order to provide finality to interpersonal moral conflict, justice must, in one way or other, assign rights to individuals. Now, if our individual claims to non-interference correlated with duties in third parties to continue whatever cooperation is required for our activities to proceed, it would also go both ways. If the farmer decided she did not want to be a farmer anymore, but her customers complained that this was interfering with their ongoing activities which included the farmer's particular produce at the price they negotiated. Both therefore have an identical claim that the other not withdraw their cooperation. It seems *neither one* has the right to determine that this activity can come to an end, and yet cessation of this activity is something that occupies possible action space. They must both agree to *mutually* waive their respective claims to non-interference in this instance in order to free themselves from it. But in cases of disagreement, there is no *individual* who can make the decision. This kind of deadlock is precisely what justice provides moral guidance in; by telling us who may unilaterally break the deadlock; and by assigning complete decision-making authority to a single locus of agency in every given case.

The fact that our claim to non-interference only extends so far as our independent actions does not mean that our collective actions are not protected from interference. Our actions are frequently in tandem, even in purposeful cooperation with others. And our *respective* claims to non-interference in *our own* actions protect our liberty to continue these collective endeavours from third-party interference, since by interfering in any one of the cooperators' actions they interfere with the collective action in virtue of interfering with an individual contribution to it. No claim that cooperators continue cooperating is required in order for it to be the case that it is unjust for third parties to interfere with a scheme of cooperation.

Persons may very often initiate uses of objects such that an aspect of that use is commercial – implying that they intend and may well, in fact, be able to derive a living or even a fortune by selling objects on the marketplace. The commercial aspect of their activity can be undermined by people not being disposed to buying it or because someone else is selling something similar that people want with a greater intensity due to a lower price or a different quality. For this commercial aspect of their activity to be taken as in part forming the ground of their property rights, it must be the case that other persons' actions must be included in the description of her activities we take to be salient for her acquisition of property rights. And this would involve their conscription. For it to be the case that a competitor's actions interfere with her activity, it must also be the case that her customer's changing consumption habits also interfere. Markets, and beneficial use thereof, are never things that a person can have a right to. One's right permits the emergence of a market and the permissible beneficial use thereof only when others voluntarily interact with you in the relevant way.

Let us return more closely to the matter at hand. For an intellectual property to take the form of a commercial usufruct – a right to non-interference in commercial deployment of certain physical property, this could only extend to the same type of non-interference they already have in the physical property – namely, not to be stopped from transferring it to others, from transporting it to a place of exchange, and from advertising it (possibly in contract with others). But for it to correlate with duties in others not to sell similar kinds of physical property, or not to engage in similar kinds of uses of similar physical property, presupposes that one could conscript others into one's activities against their will, such that their omissions (rather than acts) constitute interference in one's projects.

Intellectual property rights as usufructs are on the face of it consistent with the general form of rights that is developed here, being in one sense a protection of activities with regard to physical objects, rather than protection of ownership of immaterial objects. But it turns out not to be consistent. The enforcement of a putative intellectual property right will involve interfering with another person's non-interfering activities in order to get them to assist the intellectual property holder in theirs. To the extent that they privilege their holder's market activities and positions at the expense of others, they are a variety of protectionist, monopolist, or mercantile right, rather than a negative right to freedom as non-interference properly speaking.

Conclusion

Having seen that acquisition of any property rights at all (not only private property, whose limits we discussed in Chapter 4) is internally limited insofar as one cannot acquire rights that conflict with any persons' subsistence, nor can one acquire rights through engrossment, nor can one acquire any kind of intellectual property right, we will consider whether any *further* limitations are called for. In the following chapter I will discuss, and reject, Lockean provisos that argue that further restrictions are either inherent to the principle of acquisition or must be imposed upon it ex post.

Notes

1. Epstein (1990).
2. For this reason, Dennis Klimchuk argues that the right of necessity is itself a property right, drawing on Grotian, and by implication, Thomist and Roman foundations (Klimchuk 2013, 2018).
3. See Chapter 2, section x.
4. Stephen Holmes and Cass Sunstein reject the distinction between negative and positive rights as spurious. They argue that what are referred to as negative rights depend upon positive actions of third parties for them to be

enforced, and therefore turn out to be positive rights after all (Holmes and Sunstein 2013). However, they conflate what actions are necessary to constitute a right (in other words, for it to be the case that the right is respected) and what it takes to regulate a right (in other words, what it takes to correct the behaviour of those who would violate it). It is true that enforcement of any right may empirically require positive action on the part of someone besides the rightholder, but this can clearly be distinguished from that fact that the moral duties correlative with the right itself are duties to abstain from specifically enumerated actions rather than to engage in specifically enumeration actions.

5. I think that *A* has a non-enforceable duty to rescue *B*; that is a duty of charity but not of justice. Thankfully, people do not only act out of enforceable obligations, and morality demands more than they only obey the rules of justice. It might be objected here that since the cost to *A* is so low and the benefit to *B* so very high, it has to be that the obligation is enforceable. But I question what is altered in the moral universe by making it enforceable? Making an obligation enforceable does not somehow guarantee that it is acted upon. All it changes in this scenario is that if a third party were present, *C*, and *C* lacked the ability to inject the saline *but* had the ability to threaten *A* with proportionate force to get her to comply with her putatively enforceable obligation, it would be permissible for her to do it. But this no more guarantees that *C* so threatens *A* nor that *A* acquiesces to the threat, than simply saying *A* has a non-enforceable obligation guarantees she acts on it. A reply might be that enforceable obligations tell us how to arrange coercive institutions, having coercive institutions ensure that people assist one another is a good guarantee that they do so, But, equally, our non-enforceable obligations tell us how to arrange our non-coercive institutions. If we are entitled to assume our coercive institutions operate well, then we are entitled to assume our non-coercive institutions operate well, and in both cases, the obligation is acted upon. Elevating a duty to the status of a duty of justice is not a way of guaranteeing it is acted upon.
6. Long (1993, 171–76).
7. Machan (2001); Narveson (2006); Long (2014).
8. See Chapter 3 section x.
9. Schmidtz (2008, ch. 10); Long (1993, 1994a).
10. Mack (2006).
11. I share Long's bemusement about what it means for a property right to be non-absolute, since any putative non-absoluteness can always be explained by a more complete description of the "absolute" right that was there in the first place (2012a, 2012d).
12. It ought also to be noted that the protection of the right to subsistence is not the only way in which self-ownership restricts appropriation. As Chapter 4 discussed in some detail, self-ownership prohibits the engrossment of natural resources – that is excluding others from a resource that one does not in fact use. It also prohibits the acquisition of property that is not owned by any particular individual but is nonetheless used by one or more others. One may acquire *some* property rights to these resources, but one may never deprive first comers of their free access to them. In the end, one may not unilaterally acquire intellectual property rights – that is one may not acquire the power to exclude third parties from certain uses of property one has no particular claim to, simply because this one undermines one's commercial interest in one's own property.

13. Rand (1964); Den Uyl and Rasmussen (1991, 145–46).
14. For authors asserting that one can legitimately acquire property merely through excluding others from it, see Nozick (1974, 174–81); Becker (1977, 27); De Jasay (1997, 171–80).
15. Rothbard referred to the idea that one can acquire at will as the "Columbus complex":

    Some theorists have maintained – on what we might call the "Columbus complex" – that the first discoverer off a new unowned island or continent can rightfully own the entire area by simply asserting his claim. (In that case, Columbus, if in face he had actually landed on the American continent – and if there had been no Indians living there – could have rightfully asserted his private "ownership" of the entire continent.) In natural fact, however, since Columbus would only have been able actually to use, to "mix his labor with," a small part of the continent, the rest then properly continues to be unowned until the next homesteaders arrive and carve out their rightful property in parts of the continent. (Rothbard 1998, 47).

    Rothbard was keen to emphasise that one cannot acquire property at will; however, he may have failed to see that this also meant one could not acquire property on the basis that one's employees will be the ones to actually "homestead" it.

    Columbus or Crusoe would have to *use* the land, to "cultivate" it in some way, before he could be asserted to own it. This "cultivation" does not have to involve tilling the soil, although that is one possible form of cultivation. . . . If there is more land than can be used by a limited labor supply, then the unused land must simply remain unowned until a first user arrives on the scene. Any attempt to claim a new resource that someone does not use would have to be considered invasive of the property right of whoever the first user will turn out to be. (Rothbard 2009, 170).

    The important phrase being "labor supply" which may imply labourers under the employment of the homesteader in question or may simply refer to the several homesteaders in their capacity as labourers.
16. For my purposes here, I am considering the four standard types of intellectual property rights: patents, trade secrets, copyrights, and trademarks. Patents and trade secrets are claims to exclusive (to some degree) commercial use of particular kinds of technologies, processes, and physical substances; copyrights and trademarks are claims to exclusive (to some degree) commercial use of particular communicative or artistic works and symbols.
17. The argument one finds for the view that persons can own ideal objects is that persons own the fruits of their labour, and ideal objects are often the *product* of the human mind (Spooner 1855; George 1929, 411; Rand 1967; DeLong 2002, 24–25) Given that the view defended here explicitly rejects a literalist labour theory of property, I will not spend any time interrogating its analogue with intellectual property.
18. In this sense, then, owning and ideal object could place far-reaching "blanket" restrictions on what other can do with their own minds and bodies (Palmer 1990, 831; cf. Long 1995).

19. Hettinger (1989, 34–35); Palmer (1990); Long (1995); Bell (2002, 1, 4); Attas (2008, 30–37); Kinsella (2008, 28–45) Lysander Spooner, an advocate of intellectual property, believed that the non-rivalrousness of ideal objects could not count against intellectual property, because he believed it would be absurd for property to only extend so far as use was rivalrous (Spooner 1855) He therefore saw the incompatibility of a theory of property such as the one defended here and intellectual property rights. Epstein similarly argues that the albeit very real conflict between liberty and copyright is no more problematic than the conflict between liberty and property generally is (Epstein 2005a).
20. Cwik (2016).
21. It is often conceived as a public right under statutory law, rather than a private right under common law. However, it is those who conceive of it as the latter that really take it to be a kind of property right, rather than some other kind of legal or regulatory artefact (Smith 2007; Mossoff 2019). It is these defenders of intellectual property qua property that I will discuss here.
22. Claeys (2009, 2013a, 2013b, 2017, 2018); Mossoff (2002, 2003, 2009, 2012); Mossoff and Claeys (2019).
23. Cohen (1995, 215).

6 Against the Proviso

Introduction

The acquisition of property rights is justified strictly to the extent to which it can be justified by an application of our original right to non-interference. The theory of acquisition, then, simultaneously justifies and limits the extent to which individuals can appropriate. The limits of the principle are internal to it. It is for this reason, I will argue, that Lockean provisos are either superfluous to a principle of non-interference or incompatible with it. They are superfluous when they reiterate restrictions already inherent in the principle of acquisition itself. And they are incompatible with a right to non-interference when they permit or demand interfering with a person's non-interfering actions.

Elsewhere I have referred to this rejection of the proviso coupled with strong internal limitations to appropriation as "ambidextrous Lockeanism"[1] to contrast it against the prevailing taxonomy of left- and right-Lockeanisms. Such distinctions are typically made at the site of the proviso. Right-Lockeans advocating limited or non-existent provisos and left-Lockeans advocating egalitarian provisos – placing very strong restrictions on the quantity of property any one individual can legitimately acquire. Such focus on the proviso is symptomatic of a problematic notion of original acquisition in the first instance; specifically, the principle of acquisition is implicitly (though, sometimes explicitly, as we will see) to be incredibly permissive and unbounded. Acquisition is often cast as a power that one can exercise at will, rather than simply the application of one's original rights. The principle of acquisition is therefore that one can exercise this power and thereby acquire property. Little reference is made to the actions (if any) that constitute such an execution, or to how such actions determine which time-indexed objects are acquired, and which rights in particular are acquired. This radically open-ended and permissive power, naturally, would need to qualify. Neo-Lockeans and quasi-Lockeans invoke the proviso as that which provides the ex-post check to ensure that acquired rights do not entrench upon the rights of others.

In Chapter 3, we discussed the reasons why authors often believe that original acquisition must be an independent power, rather than the mere application of one's original right to non-interference. Typically, it is motivated by a belief that private property involves a right of exclusion further than can be justified by any claim of use. I will not belabour these points any further here. It is however important to note that, at least in the cases of Nozick, Steiner, and Otsuka, the idea that original acquisition is, in itself, an open-ended power one can exercise at will, rather than a side effect of acting on one's original rights, quite clearly motivates the conceptual need for a proviso to exert some restrictive force upon it.

Where one bears in mind that property rights can only obtain where they represent the concretisation of one's rights to engage in one's chosen activities free from extra-personal frustration, the idea that one should have a bare power to acquire property becomes rather alien. The pre-occupation of Lockean theories of property seems to have been to just get to private property and deal with any moral remainders thereafter – by invocation of the proviso. As Chapters 3 and 4 showed, we need not and should not make any presumption that private property that categorically diverges from rights of use need be what we seek to justify.

In this chapter, I will reconstruct Nozick's theory of appropriation to show why a bare power of appropriation demands a proviso, and why grounding acquisition in non-interference altogether pre-empts any such demand, as it builds in those restrictions at the outset. I will then consider whether the far more restrictive egalitarian provisos of Steiner and Otsuka are warranted or even compatible with non-interference. At the end, I will discuss other approaches to the proviso that take it to be internal to the principle of acquisition itself. These are deontological accounts of the proviso (unlike Nozick's) but not egalitarian accounts (unlike Steiner and Otsuka's). They are broadly in-keeping with the substantive restrictions placed on acquisition argued for here. I give some reasons for resisting referring to these as provisos.

Nozick's Proviso

In this section, I will discuss one account of the proviso that casts it as an independent principle that limits the applicability of the principle of acquisition. We will find that it presents restrictions that are already inherent in an account of acquisition grounded in a right to non-interference. Nozick needs to resort to a proviso ex post because it fails to ground his theory of acquisition in any account of liberty in the first place. It is therefore superfluous to my account.

Nozick believed that any acquisition by *A* constitutes a loss of liberty for *B*. However, he did not see this as necessarily problematic – at least not to the point of it being a reason to invoke a proviso. What mattered,

Nozick thought, was whether or not *B* is made worse off by this loss of liberty, when costed against the potential benefits accrued to her from permitting *A*'s acquisition. If *A* acquires *S*, it may be the case that there are plenty of other *S*-type objects for *B* to acquire,[2] or that *A*'s appropriation makes *S* far more valuable than it would have been if it had been left unappropriated[3] or if it had been appropriated by *B*, "counter-balancing their loss of . . . liberty."[4] Nozick concludes that the only restriction on appropriation is that "the situation of others is not worsened" by the appropriation in question.[5]

Nozick's proviso could be dubbed a *Pareto* proviso, insofar as it requires an acquisition to be Pareto efficient in order to be just. However, even when *A*'s acquisition in itself makes *B* worse-off, if *A* accompanies the acquisition with ex-post transfer of compensation to *B*, an acquisition that initially looks proviso-violating will in fact be justified. Nozick's proviso could therefore be better described as a *Kaldor–Hicks* proviso.[6]

Before going into further depth on Nozick's version of the proviso, we need to first take some time to try to understand his overall account of original acquisition within which the proviso is situated. Mack and Steiner both start from a position that is familiar, given the discussion of self-ownership and labour-mixing in Chapter 3. However, Nozick seems to reject the idea that self-ownership *itself* implies one can appropriate through action.[7] Nozick only mentions self-ownership once in *Anarchy, State, and Utopia*, though he clearly did like the idea.[8] Nevertheless, Nozick *explicitly* leans away from using self-ownership as a foundation for original acquisition. As I noted in Chapter 3, Nozick claimed that the admixture of self-owned labour with unowned resources might just as well be a way of *disposing* of one's labour: "why isn't mixing what I own with what I don't own a way of losing what I own rather than a way of gaining what I don't?" he asks rhetorically.[9] Moreover, Nozick is concerned with what others would later refer to as "the boundary problem"[10] – for any given instance of labouring upon a resource, what are the physical limits of the labour's penetration into that resource? Again, Nozick rhetorically asks:

> If a private astronaut clears a place on Mars, has he mixed his labor with (so he comes to own) the whole planet, the whole uninhabited universe, or just a particular plot? Which plot does an act bring under ownership?[11]

After noting these two problems with using self-ownership (and labour-mixing) as a determinate basis for a principle of acquisition, he moves swiftly on to discuss the proviso. The problem with this move, however, is that a proviso is a constraint on the scope of a prior principle justifying acquisition. Nozick however does not appear to have an initial principle – only a proviso. He has a regulative principle but no activity to be regulated. We can only assume the principle he has in mind is a very broad one, something like "you may appropriate unowned property at will." Allan Gibbard calls this "bare appropriation," since it is simply a moral act of altering the rights of others with no accompanying physical activity.[12]

It may be objected that Nozick does not seem to altogether *reject* the central Lockean idea that self-ownership implies one can come to own initially unowned things; he just does not think this idea gets you very far. Perhaps one appropriates by labour-mixing, and in the face of the two problems that Nozick thinks this will often raise, we simply lean on the proviso to fill in the gaps and provide determinacy. The view might go something like the following. When is labouring on an unowned thing *not* a way of creating more unowned stuff? When claiming that which one labours on does not leave others worse off. Why does pouring tomato juice into the ocean not appropriate the entire ocean? Because appropriating the entire ocean will probably leave others worse off.

The foregoing does not, however, seem like a plausible reading when one recognises that Nozick believed that one could appropriate property that is *already* in use by other people. This, I think, places significant distance between self-ownership or liberty and Nozick's theory of property acquisition – distance which creates the urgent need for a proviso.

In his elucidation of the proviso, Nozick claims that one of the ways in which someone can be made worse off by another's appropriation is "by no longer being able to use freely (without appropriation) what he previously could."[13] This statement implies that one can privately appropriate property which others use, thereby making it the case that they can no longer use it, and that unowned property can be used by a person without that person acquiring rights to it.[14] Appropriation is therefore not a by-product of activity, for Nozick,[15] but rather a moral power that one can exercise at will, within the bounds of the proviso.[16] Acquisition becomes a mere move in juridical space, rather than a moral implication of action taken in real space.

There is therefore no other interpretation available other than that Nozick did indeed reject the idea that the justification for – and the mode of – acquisition can be gotten out of our basic right to be free itself.[17] The proviso therefore does all the justificatory work in his theory of appropriation. Let us now turn to the details of Nozick's proviso.

Nozick claims any acquisition that does not thereby worsen the situation of others is legitimate. He outlines two ways in which *B*'s situation may be worsened by *A*'s acquisition of *S*: by losing the opportunity to appropriate *S* or by no longer being able to freely use *S* (without acquisition). Nozick parses the prohibition of appropriations which make people worse off in the first way as a "*stringent*" proviso and ones which do so in the second way as a "*weaker*" proviso.[18] Nozick says that it "is arguable that no one legitimately can complain if the weaker proviso is satisfied."[19] Moreover, although he claims that one can be made worse off by losing an opportunity to appropriate *S*, he also claims that not all cases where one loses such an opportunity are cases where one has been made worse off.[20] He also seems to claim that the weaker condition will be satisfied because the development fostered by private property will expand opportunities for well-being in various important ways.[21] So a plausible reading of Nozick's intentions is that only the weaker proviso is the one that governs individual acts of appropriation.[22]

For Nozick, *A* can claim ownership of *S* as long as *B* (who was initially engaged in using *S*) is not thereby made worse off. Will Kymlicka offers an example of the proviso at play:[23] Both Amy and Ben use and live off a plot of land; Amy then decides to privately appropriate a portion of it, leaving Ben without enough to live off, thus making him worse off. However, as required by the proviso, Amy hires Ben to work on her land and pays him a wage such that he is no worse off than he was before.[24] The proviso has thus saved Ben from suffering a loss of welfare at the hands of Amy's appropriation. Nozick's proviso ensures that, where appropriations interfere with others' uses of resources, they do not *thereby* leave others worse off by excluding them from resources upon which they have established use.

The need for Nozick's proviso arises because his theory of acquisition lacks a "positive principle" that connects liberty and property acquisition. This means that Ben's ongoing use of land is not seen as grounding any kind of property rights that would protect him from expropriation. The principle of acquisition defended here – that acquisition can only take place when it is an application of one's claim against interference – does not need a proviso to protect people from the welfare-depriving effects of losing access to resources they use because they cannot be unilaterally deprived of access to those resources in the first place. That transfer of compensation to ensure the expropriation is Pareto optimal does not undo the injustice of having one's rights violated. From the perspective of justice, it is a far more serious thing to violate someone's rights than to merely lower their welfare. The proviso therefore falls short in insisting the lost welfare from expropriation must be compensated, rather than simply prohibiting appropriations that constitute interference with other people's ongoing use of resources.[25] Where one cannot be forcibly divested of one's access to a resource one has already initiated use of, the question of whether such divestments leaves one worse off does not arise.

Recognising the implications of a claim-right to non-interference means rejecting the idea of bare appropriation. One cannot legitimately claim property over spaces and objects by fiat: one only acquires rights over things by actually incorporating them into one's activities. This means that if someone incorporates some resource into her ongoing activities, insofar as they have a claim against interference, they will have some rights over this resource. These are rights to not be interfered with, not rights to merely have one's welfare considered in the expropriation procedure.

In Kymlicka's case, regardless of whether or not Amy compensates Ben by offering him a good job ex post, Ben has no duty to respect the rights that Amy is claiming for herself – he has the right to exclude Amy from interfering in his ongoing use of the land. No proviso is therefore needed to protect Ben from being made worse off by this appropriation, since his right to non-interference protects him from such an appropriation from taking place at all. All Nozick's proviso does is protect persons from having their well-being lowered[26] due to property they use being appropriated. The theory developed here already prohibits such appropriations, given that they are really *ex*propriations.

Anthony De Jasay makes similar claims as Nozick about the purported legitimacy of appropriating property that is already being used, but which, somehow, has not been appropriated by its users. De Jasay says that when appropriating property that is already engaged in ongoing use by some person or group (who have not appropriated it), they are due compensation for their loss of access.[27] We are told that this loss of access is not a tort,[28] that is not a rights-violation, since the harmed parties did not initially own the property in question. De Jasay claims that those who are deprived of access nonetheless "have some kind of reliance-based claim" the loss of which needs to be compensated. The existing users are not, however, free to turn down the appropriator's compensation and continue using the property as they always have done, since they do not ex hypothesi have any property rights to it. The paying of compensation seems, for De Jasay, to play the same role as Nozick's proviso.

De Jasay believes that one can only acquire ownership by taking on exclusion costs – through actually excluding others, including existing users. If existing users do not actively exclude other users, then they have not taken on any of the associated costs and have not acquired ownership of the property; hence it can be appropriated by anyone willing to exclude them from it.[29] A difficulty arises though when we ask what it takes to exclude someone; De Jasay readily acknowledges and allows that it includes threats and actual executions of physical violence against those who seek to use the property.[30] It is hard to see how this is not a tort and a rights-violation – even if we agree with De Jasay that the initial users do not have any particular rights over the property in question. Forcibly removing persons from land they are using is only legitimate if one already has rights to that land in particular, which those being forcibly removed are currently violating. It is not clear how one can acquire the right to forcibly remove others from land and simply by acting as if one does.

Even ignoring this issue, De Jasay has a more fundamental problem. Property rights arise to provide moral finality to questions regarding interpersonal conflict over the use of scarce resources. But De Jasay wants at least some of these rights to be acquired *through* conflict. If *A* decides to appropriate land which *B* is using or occupying, for De Jasay she can only do so by physically excluding *B* (and paying her compensation). But what if *B* wants to appropriate the land too? She can only do so by effectively fighting off *A*'s attempt at removing her. In the midst of this violent conflict, De Jasay cannot appeal to rights in order to adjudicate the conflict, since rights are only acquired once the conflict is over. De Jasay's theory of appropriation is inconsistent with the entire purpose of property rights. It is a theory of how to assign rights after conflict has ended, rather than how to morally adjudicate conflict in the first place.

Both Nozick and De Jasay have a notion of using unowned property without acquiring any rights over it, and this leads them to the need for a proviso and a compensation requirement respectively in order to protect the inevitable victims of appropriation. When one makes acquisition strictly an application of non-interference, it removes this problematic divorce of use from acquisition. The right to non-interference does not require first users to accept compensation; it gives them the right to simply say "no."[31]

Original appropriation is often conflated (evidently, even among its advocates) with the kind of land claims involved in, for example, the European colonisation of the Americas, the English enclosure movement of the late medieval to early modern period, and neo-colonial dispossession of land in the global South.[32] Resources that are already in sustained use are not regarded as owned and are therefore up for grabs. Yet, it is simultaneously acknowledged that the current users must have some kind of claim to consideration, so argument must be made for why the expropriation actually benefits them.

One can imagine that Nozick's view in 1974[33] might have been that, in both cases of colonial expropriation and English enclosure, there was legitimacy because those who were no longer able to use that land as they had before were not made worse off due to the net benefit they would likely experience from the development of "civilisation."[34] De Jasay would presumably have made the judgement that the peasantry's use of agricultural lands in pre-enclosure England was merely "promiscuous use."[35] Likewise, native Americans could be deprived of access to their hunting-and-gathering territories and religious sites since they were not excluding other persons from them in the way characteristic of private owners. Such theories of acquisition seem to be torn between protecting individuals' liberty through property rights and establishing justification for assigning the kinds of property rights that have been prevalent in the West since capitalism's inception,[36] with the function of making those communities more legible to increasingly rationalising states.[37]

Indeed, Locke believed that land that was not *cultivated* was unowned.[38] It has been argued that the entire *point* of the theory is to justify imperial expansion using proto-liberal rhetoric, rather than an attempt to formalise the moral rights to the world that people actually have.[39] Regardless of what Locke's intentions truly were, there is no doubt that placing too much distance between individual freedom and a principle of acquisition leads to the possibility that property becomes something that overrides individual freedom.

Theories of original acquisition have often been articulated and applied in ways that renders them blind to aboriginal modes of property,[40] but they need not. The extent to which they have done so is due to a misapplication of the idea of original acquisition and the role of individual freedom therein.

Given that such Lockean accounts of acquisition permit what looks so much like expropriation, it is natural to think that for it to even begin to be legitimate, there must be some proviso on it, such as ex-post compensation by the appropriator or some beneficial economic system that results from the practice of such appropriations overall. Expropriations of the colonial/enclosure type bypasses the principle of *quod omnes tangit ab omnibus tractari et approbari debet*[41] in that they non-consensually interfere with their existing uses of resources and, as such, call for some further justification, if they are to be legitimate at all. However, the theory of appropriation that is being defended here does not bypass this principle because it does not permit one to interfere with the ongoing activities of others – even if those activities do not conform to typical forms of agricultural use of land that give rise to private ownership.[42]

According to the view defended here, the medieval peasants had property rights to the village common, which were violated by the Acts of Enclosure.[43] Indeed, the overall use of the village common by all its users was usually such that any imposition by a third party would have constituted an interference, so the land was the collective property of the village.[44] Likewise, the hunting and gathering territories in America – while not fully owned by the natives who so used them since they are open to many other non-interfering uses by others[45] – were illegitimately appropriated by colonial settlers *regardless* of any purported benefit they may have received thereafter.

Jonathan Wolff suggests the possibility that Nozick posited the proviso not as a replacement for a prior theory of appropriation but as necessary condition for any appropriation to be just, while remaining agnostic on what the prior principle might be that justifies appropriation per se.[46] What should be clear from the discussion here, however, is that if that prior principle is a right to freedom as non-interferences, the proviso becomes superfluous. The theory of appropriation does not call for a

Nozickian proviso because the kinds of cases it applies to are already ruled out by the theory at a prior level.

The Egalitarian Proviso

So-called left-Lockeans invoke an egalitarian proviso, prohibiting acquisition of more property than is compatible with a scheme of equal distribution for all at a given time or at least not without acquiring a liability to taxation for the purposes of redistributing towards those who have appropriated less than their equal share.[47] Typically, left-Lockeans argue that this specific and stringent requirement on property distribution is simply a reflection of the fact that the extra-personal world starts off commonly owned by all of humanity, rather than any particular individual or group. Therefore, in order for our individual acquisitions of property rights not to prejudice humanity-at-large's claim to the world, no one can ever have rights over more than an equal share.[48] While they identify the original common ownership thesis with early modern natural rights theorists such as Locke, it is clear that almost no such theorist drew the stringently egalitarian distributive implications they do. Common ownership was taken, at least by them, to permit persons to acquire unequal amounts of property. Such theories owe more to Henry George's arguments than to Locke's.[49] Nonetheless, left-Lockeanism is a prominent position so it is crucial to show why their account of the Lockean proviso ought not to be embraced.

This section will begin with the weakest case: Otsuka's attempt to demonstrate the compatibility of an egalitarian proviso with self-ownership. I will argue that there is no such compatibility and supporting equal original ownership of natural resources to attenuate the content of self-ownership (or comparable set of rights) does not save the overall plausibility of the position. I will then turn to Steiner's stronger argument that self-ownership *demands* an egalitarian proviso and argue that the conclusion is underdetermined by its premises.

Otsuka's project is to show that self-ownership is compatible with material equality of outcome and, so, contra Cohen,[50] those concerned with distributive equality need not abandon self-ownership but are free to embrace it so long as they simultaneously embrace an egalitarian proviso on acquisition.[51] Otsuka does not attempt to show that this proviso is required on grounds of self-ownership itself: he is only interested to show the compatibility of the conjunction not its truth. His premise is the presumed plausibility of the idea that each person owns herself, and yet the external world is commonly or equally owned by all.[52]

Otsuka's proviso prohibits persons from acquiring rights in objects and spaces through subsuming them into their ongoing activities where such an acquisition would give them a more advantageous share of property than the equally advantageous share which the economy is capable of yielding at that time. The proviso licences the exclusion of persons from unowned resources,[53] which is to say that it licences the interference in self-owners' non-interfering uses of those resources. Otsuka argues however that no interference is necessary to ensure the proviso is honoured, so long as property is initially distributed in just the right way. If those who are worst at transforming resources into welfare are given ownership over all resources beyond what is needed by those who are best at transforming resources into welfare for subsistence,[54] the latter group would need to offer a steady stream of valuable resources to the former group in order to access luxuries (which, Otsuka presumes, they are disposed to doing). The invisible hand of the market would thereby ensure that everyone gets an equally advantageous share of resources, without the need for coercive intervention that would interfere in the ongoing activities of self-owners, nor threatening the abler with starvation if they do not come to the assistance of the less able. Otsuka claims then that a "robust" conception of self-ownership is therefore protected under his theory insofar as "one will not be forced by necessity to come to the assistance of others in a manner involving the sacrifice of one's life, limb, or labour."[55] They will always be able to access subsistence, and when they want anything more, they will have to seek it through exchanges with the lesser able class of owners.

However, this does not save the compatibility of self-ownership and the egalitarian proviso. The need for interference is only avoided in those possible worlds where there happens to be an initial distribution of resources such that the market process plays out in a proviso-respecting way. Where the initial distribution diverges, the market will have to be exogenously interfered with very systematically in order to ensure that the proviso is respected. This means forcing some to cease their ongoing use of resources in order to give them to others – a plain violation of the former's self-ownership.

Moreover, even in the set of possible worlds where no interference is required to achieve this, natural events that alter the relative value or productivity of the resources held by the respective groups will disturb the way the market process plays out, and in order for the proviso to be met, interference will be required.[56] The fact that it is in principle possible for persons to voluntarily engage in exchanges which end up bringing about an egalitarian distribution does not mean that self-ownership is consistent with that distribution being mandated by justice, which is precisely what a proviso does.

Where self-ownership is asserted as a natural right alongside a natural right to an equal share of resources, the only way for the two to be compatible is to rid self-ownership of any content that refers to rights beyond the physical body. It is trivially true that if one takes self-ownership to only include internal rights and no right to control one's body motions and activities in the external world, then one can support any distributive pattern as a matter of justice and it will be formally compatible. The lengths Otsuka goes to show that an egalitarian distribution of property can under very particular socio-economic empirical circumstances be compatible with a robust right of self-ownership show that even he sees the implausibly of an account of self-ownership that is so thin.

Given that a right to non-interference in one's ongoing activities goes further than a right to exclusive control over the physiological limits of one's body, it is clear that an egalitarian proviso is incompatible with a right to liberty as non-interference. Wherever *A* has a greater quantity of property than *B* because her activities subsume more time-indexed objects (or, however one quantifies property), she will involuntarily become liable to having her non-interfering activities interfered with in order to transfer control of some of those objects over to *B*. An egalitarian proviso on acquisition necessarily cuts into rights to freedom. To invoke a premise of equal original ownership of earth as part-and-parcel of our natural rights and therefore something which our right to liberty must be attenuated by is merely to assert that our right to freedom must be compromised whenever it is proven incompatible with freedom.

To assert original rights in the earth is just to assert original restrictions on liberty.

Steiner offers a very different argument for the egalitarian proviso. His argument hinges on the very recognition that self-ownership that does *not* include any rights to the external world results in absurdity and therefore insists that self-ownership must be combined with original equal ownership of the external world.

Steiner argues that if self-owners can appropriate parts of the external world, then there is the possibility that at t_1 all external property is privately owned by the extant generation of persons, and therefore at t_2, when at least one more self-owner comes into existence, there is nowhere for her to occupy other than other persons' private property. Her rights of self-ownership are therefore incompossible with the rights of those who have already acquired the world. They have a claim against her occupying their property without their consent, and she has a claim against having her body interfered with. Yet, the only space she can exist is on property owned by others, where she simultaneously has a right to occupy and a duty to exclude herself from. Herbert Spencer made a very similar argument against private property in land generally:

> [I]f *one* portion of the earth's surface may justly become the possession of an individual, and may be held by him for his sole use and benefit, as a thing to which he has an exclusive right, then *other* portions of the earth's surface may be so held; and eventually the *whole* of the earth's surface may be so held; and our planet may thus lapse altogether into private hands. Observe now the dilemma to which these leads. Supposing the entire habitable globe to be so enclosed,

> it follows that if the landowners have a valid right to its surface, all who are not landowners, have no right at all to its surface. Hence, such can exist on the earth by sufferance only. They are all trespassers. Save by the permission of the lords of the soil, they can have no room for the soles of their feet. Nay, should the others think fit to deny them a resting-place, these landless men might equitably be expelled from the earth altogether. . . . [M]en who cannot "live and move and have their being" without the leave of others, cannot be equally free with those others.[57]

What this argument seeks to show is that the self-ownership (combined with rights acquired in accordance with it) of the first comers is incompossible with the self-ownership of the latecomers.[58] In order for universal self-ownership to be compossible, then, it must come with some rights to external property attached. Self-ownership combined with unlimited acquisition turned out to be incompossible, so self-ownership must be revised in such a way that it comes with built-in restrictions to acquisition, and therefore comes with some guaranteed share of external property. Unlike Spencer, Steiner does not argue this means that there can be *no* private ownership of land (or natural resources) but rather that everyone must have an equal amount of natural resources in their private ownership. Given that this right to external property must be held by each person, the only way to render it coherently as a universal right is by making it an equal share of external property.[59] So self-ownership itself, as it turns out, must also include a right to an equal share of external property.[60]

The reductio that Steiner identifies does not, however, apply to the theory of acquisition defended here. From the very outset, individuals are taken to have rights not merely to their own body but rather a right that presupposes that they are spatio-temporally embodied and therefore necessarily occupy some space at some time in which they act. The claim against interference means that whatever acquisitions a person or group of persons make, action space and therefore juridical space are automatically left for all other persons. Steiner's proviso is an over-correction for an insufficient prima facie account of original rights.[61] We do not need full private ownership of an equal share of resources; we need a claim-right against interference.

Contra Spencer, the rights that persons have to live and move around will not be at the "sufferance" of property owners, because the right of necessity is a natural right, and property rights are acquired rights; therefore, the latter gives way to the former.

Internal Accounts of the Provisos

Mack articulates a version of the Lockean proviso as a "self-ownership proviso." This proviso is not concerned with patterns of distribution but rather in how persons use their property. He argues that self-ownership presupposes that we can acquire rights to extra-personal resources,[62] and that it also means we cannot use those extra-personal resources in ways that frustrate other self-owners' ability to exercise their self-ownership.

> To be a self-owner is to be an owner of the world-interactive agent who one is. To have rights over one's world-interactive powers is to have some sort of claim against being blocked from bringing those powers to bear on the extra-personal world.[63]

Mack's self-ownership proviso has two important applications. The first is that self-ownership can be violated without any physical contact being made with one's body. For example, if one were to have a cage dropped over one's head such that it did not touch one's body, this would still violate one's self-ownership. Self-ownership, on Mack's view, does not merely protect one as a physical object but as an *actor* (1995, 195; 2002, 246). The second application is what makes this principle, in Mack's eyes, count as a proviso: one is not permitted to use one's property in ways which are disabling to others' world-interactive powers. Whatever property one acquires, then, one is prohibited from using it in ways which make it impossible for others to exercise their self-ownership. Imagine *A* acquires all the property on a small remote island. *B* finds herself shipwrecked nearby. *A* is not permitted to stop *B* from coming ashore.[64] It is not that *A* has acquired too much property that the injustice consists in but rather that she uses her property to nullify *B*'s right to bring her powers to bear on the world.

Mack takes this proviso to simply be an application of self-ownership, and not an independent principle that moderates a prior principle about property acquisition. In Mack's words, it is part of a part of a broader set of constraints that describe how persons "may not deploy themselves or their . . . holdings."[65]

However, the content of the self-ownership proviso does not extend any further than a right of necessity. Therefore, the argumentative force of the idea does not motivate any need for a proviso. Indeed, the substantive content of this principle is more obviously entailed by a claim to non-interference, since stopping someone from landing on one's remote island when they are shipwrecked is obviously an interference in their activities. Whereas, as Mack notes, it only violates self-ownership in a "non-invasive way."[66] So, while the content of Mack's proviso is, I think, correct, I do not take it to count as a proviso as such.

Van der Vossen offers a view of the proviso similar to Mack.[67] It is both internal to the justification of property acquisition generally and deontological in nature without being egalitarian in a distributive sense. What the proviso is for, according to van der Vossen, is to ensure that private property continues to serve freedom, where freedom is understood to be a state of non-subjection in the exercise of one's rights; or when one may exercise one's rights without asking leave. I take this proviso to be internal to the principle of acquisition because the unilateral acquisition of private property is justified on the same grounds. One must be guaranteed permission to acquire property so that one can have a sphere in which one does not need to ask leave before acting and that one can create this sphere itself without asking leave. The proviso, on this view then, is an ex-post check to ensure that private property is fulfilling its rightful function: protecting freedom.

Substantively, I think that this is taken care of where acquisition of property rights is strictly an application of the right to non-interference. First, one cannot acquire private ownership over a resource where others are already using it in a way that fails to give rise to private ownership. They get to maintain their ongoing use without the permission of the appropriator – the appropriator's property rights automatically have a hole carved out of them in the shape of the initial user's actions. Second, even where non-appropriators have not already initiated any particular use of resources that are now largely under another person's control, they maintain a right against interference in any action they do initiate without needing to check with any owners. Everyone is duty-bound from stopping one another from accessing resources that are necessary for the preconditions of their activity. So, one may always unilaterally make use of property one needs to, without the say of its putative "owner." In this regard, one's right to non-interference can never be subjected to the power of another.[68] The right of necessity trumps any acquired rights.

Provisos such as Mack's and van der Vossen's are compatible with and demanded by the account of rights defended here. However, their substantive constraints are built into the justification for acquisition in the first instance. Once one moves away from the idea that one has a bare power to appropriate private property and pays attention to the specific kind of property rights required to protect liberty, the need for an ex-post check to make sure the property system remains faithful to liberty is unnecessary.

Conclusion

The proviso is often invoked as a necessary principle to clear up the moral remainders left by an insufficient positive principle of acquisition. This was the case in Nozick and was largely inherited by the left-Lockeans. A principle that grants a right or a power to acquire private ownership of external objects at will that is untethered to individual freedom – that is everyone's individual freedom – is obviously going to be too permissive and requires an ex-post check. However, when original acquisition is itself only ever possible as an application of one's right to non-interference, it is not possible for acquired rights to entrench upon the freedom-based interests of anyone else, and no ex-post check is required. Indeed, part of the rationale for Nozick's proviso is explicitly to stop people from being made worse off by being deprived of property that the principle defended here would recognise their *right* to. Not only do provisos, such as Nozick's, become superfluous, but also any further proviso, such as the egalitarian ones of the left-Lockeans, become unsustainable. In a properly derived principle of original acquisition, everyone's freedom rights are already properly accounted for. Where property really is freedom, property can do no injustice.

Notes

1. Christmas (2020a).
2. Nozick (1974, 175).
3. Schmidtz (1990, 1991, chap. 2, 1994, 42–50).
4. Nozick (1974, 175;177).
5. Nozick (1974, 175).
6. Hicks (1939); Kaldor (1939) Kaldor–Hicks optimality is sometimes parsed as *potential* Pareto optimality because Pareto optimality is achieved only *after* compensation is transferred. It should be underlined that, for Nozick, it was not the potential for sufficient compensation that justifies an acquisition, but its actuality (cf. Sen 1987, 33).
7. Nozick (1974, 174–82).
8. For example he notes that end-state principles and most patterned principles of distributive justice imply that persons are partial owners of one another, and this is taken to be a demerit of those principles. Nozick goes on to note that end-state and most patterned principles of distributive justice (which presume partial other-ownership) have to violate moral side-constraints, so it may be that he understood the content of moral side-constraints to be identical or near-identical to that of self-ownership (Nozick 1974, 172).
9. Nozick (1974, 174–75).
10. Simmons (1992, 268); Mautner (1982, 261); Flanigan (2019).
11. Nozick (1974, 174).
12. Gibbard (1976, 83) In Attas's terms, Nozick has only a negative principle of acquisition and no positive one (2003).
13. Nozick (1974, 176).
14. This is also the reading taken by Will Kymlicka (2002, 115–17).
15. One might object that by "no longer able to use freely" Nozick merely meant that they are now unable to use the property *if* they so desired to, and therefore does not imply that property that is in use by others is up for appropriation. However, this statement is supposed to describe an *additional* way in which a person can be made worse off by an appropriation by another to the potentially trivial loss of liberty in the form of an opportunity to appropriate something. He clearly thinks that use and appropriation come apart when he says, "to freely use (without appropriation)." (Nozick 1974, 176).
16. Perhaps there is an argument for the idea that self-ownership entails a bare moral power to acquire ownership over resources, but this argument is nowhere to be found.
17. It is plausible to suggest that Nozick was less interested in spelling out the connection between self-ownership or liberty and ownership of any

particular set of resources because his conception of liberty just presumed that one owned *some* such bundle (Long 2002; Brennan and van der Vossen 2018).
18. Nozick (1974, 176 italics in original).
19. Nozick (1974, 176).
20. Nozick (1974, 175).
21. Nozick (1974, 177).
22. It may be inconsistent to apply the stringent proviso to the *practice* of appropriation and the weaker one to *acts* of appropriation (Wolff 1991, 112), but I will not dwell on that here. On the distinction between an act-theoretic and a practice-theoretic justifications of acquisition, see Mack (1990).
23. Kymlicka (2002, 115).
24. Kymlicka imagines Amy also being made better off, due to the expanded product they derive from the land due to the division of labour (Kymlicka 2002, 115). Presumably, Kymlicka is imagining Amy's acquisition introducing hierarchy that was needed to expand productivity.
25. In this regard, property protects us from Pareto. Where the values we associate with our own property are incommensurable with any compensation, property rights protect us from being subjected to cost–benefit analyses that use standards of value that are alien to our own (Christmas 2017).
26. The controversy over which baseline of welfare ought to be selected for calculating the compensation required by the proviso (Francis and Francis 1976; Exdell 1977; Cohen 1986, 108–35, 1995, 79–91; Wolff 1991, 113; Otsuka 1998, 78, 2003, 23; Wündisch 2013; Hunt 2015, 184–92) is therefore altogether avoided by the theory of acquisition defended here as it does not invoke any claims about welfare.
27. De Jasay (1997, 176).
28. De Jasay (1997, 178).
29. De Jasay (1997, 176–77).
30. De Jasay (1997, 176).
31. As van der Vossen argues, the introduction of welfarist considerations is alien to the framework of rights as side-constraints that Nozick constructs hitherto (van der Vossen 2020, 5–7).
32. Harvey (2003, 137–82).
33. I give this date because Nozick's post-*Anarchy, State, and Utopia* work indicates a significant move away from libertarianism (1989, 286–92), though he himself denied such a shift in his thinking (2011).
34. Nozick (1974, 178–79 notes).
35. De Jasay (1997, 178).
36. Argenton and Rossi (2021).
37. Scott *(1995, 1996, 1998, 2017, chaps 2, 4); Carson (2011).
38. Locke (1764, sec. II.V.36–II.V.37; II.V.42) However, as noted in Chapter 3, he did regard uncultivated, but frequently used commons in England as common property that could not be privately appropriated (1764, sec. II.XXXV).
39. Arneil (1996, chap. 6).
40. Tully (1994, 168).
41. Tully (1994, 160).
42. However, it ought not to be overstated that Native Americans used land in wholly different ways as compared to Western Europeans. They did in fact practice private property along the lines of private ownership, as well as various commons systems. See Anderson (1997, 2016) for an overview of these systems.
43. Stromberg (1995); Carson (2011).

44. Carson (2007, 118–28, 2011).
45. Holcombe (2005, 12–13).
46. Wolff (1991, 141).
47. Steiner (1977b, 1987, 1994, chap. 8, 1999, 2017).
48. Steiner (1987, 1994, chap. 8, 2017, 220–27).
49. Henry George argued that labour was entitled to its product. Yet all production included some value added by the natural resources (land) one appropriates in order to produce. That portion of one's product, then, is rightly owned equally by all, and the producer must therefore pay a tax equal or proportionate to the value of the commonly owned natural resources she used as inputs. George advocated a tax on the value of land in order to compensate those with access to less valuable natural resources (George 1929, sec. VIII.II). Left-Lockeanism is really neo-Georgism.
50. Cohen (1995, 15, 105).
51. Otsuka (1998, 65–66, 2003, 11).
52. For a critique of the idea that such premises can be coherently motivated, see Risse (2004).
53. At least, virgin or abandoned resources, since the proviso means that these resources are in fact already, in essence, the property of someone else.
54. Otsuka (1998, 4–88, 2003, 29–40).
55. Otsuka (2003, 32).
56. Inoue (2007).
57. (1851, sec. IX.II italics in original).
58. Steiner (1977a, 1977b, 1987, 1994, 86–101, 2009, 241, 2011, n. 3).
59. Steiner (1994, 236).
60. Steiner also has another argument for original egalitarian ownership of external resources: it is the only way to explain why mixing one's labour with unowned resources does not simply dissipate one's labour into a state of non-ownership, rather than render the product owned by the labourer (1994, 233–36). So, equal original ownership fills a gap left in the system earlier; that is, how labour-mixing furnishes a positive principle of acquisition? This faces independent problems addressed in Chapter 3, section 3.
61. Cf. Long (2004, 2012b, 2012a).
62. Mack (1990).
63. Mack (2002, 246).
64. Mack (1995, 187–88).
65. Mack (1995, 187).
66. Mack (1995, 186–87).
67. van der Vossen (2020).
68. As Christopher Essert argues, not having any property rights whatsoever means that one is subjected to others since they can unilaterally determine whether or not you are able to act freely, which is to say you do not really have a *right* to freedom at all (Essert 2016).

7 Intentions and Conventions

Introduction

When one has a right to engage in a particular activity, one does not merely have a right to or over the objects and spaces that are involved in it per se; one only has rights over them so far as is necessary for the activity to not be interfered with. What is this other aspect of human action besides its physics, reference to which is essential to furnishing our acquired rights? It is intentionality. The nature of an action is, in part, cashed out for the purposes of rights in terms of its intention. Action is end-directed and purposive human behaviour. What counts as an interference in a particular activity then is whether it frustrates this end-direction. An interference might avert the attainment of the end it might otherwise reach, or it might avert the directedness with which it projects. Or, in the case of actions where means and ends are not separable, such as forms of cultural expression or ritual, both means and ends are simultaneously frustrated in the case of interference. In order then to know which action on the part of *A* would constitute interference in the actions of *B* we need to have some acquaintance with both actions not merely in terms of the time, place, and material at which and with which they occur, but also in terms of their intentionality. As I argued in Chapter 1, it is a necessary but insufficient condition for two actions being mutually frustrating that their extensional descriptions partially overlap. The sufficient conditions for two actions' mutual unperformability also include that plain fact that they frustrate one another as the kinds of actions they are. To ascertain this, we need to understand their intentionality.

This chapter will explicitly show the role of intentionality in furnishing rights with their content and overcome certain objections to such views as conflating two different kinds of intentionality. Moreover, it will explicitly show the role of social conventions in giving our acquired rights content. However, this does not mean that our acquired rights are merely conventional rather than natural. Since our intentional actions are defined by conventional constitutive rules, those constitutive rules determine the content of our rights. However, our natural rights still provide the normative criteria by which our regulative conventions ought to operate. While natural rights still give us guidance as to how to make our regulative social conventions just, there is also a part of those rights that we can only understand once we are acquainted with the constitution of the human practices.

Intentions: Public and Private

A person's actions can be truthfully described in terms of their intentionality in a number of ways, each of which will have a different degree of intentional extension, in terms of time and space. Some actions we perform by performing other actions, some actions we perform simpliciter. The latter are basic actions, and the former are non-basic or complex actions.[1] Ludwig von Mises writes:

> Human life is an unceasing sequence of single actions. But the single action is by no means isolated. It is a link in a chain of actions which together form an action on a higher level aiming at a more distant end. Every action has two aspects. It is on the one hand a partial action in the framework of a further-stretching action. The performance of a fraction of the aims set by a more far-reaching action. It is on the other hand itself a whole with regard to the actions aimed at by the performance of its own parts.

For example when one *flicks a light switch*, one might also be *turning on the light*, *illuminating the room*, and *scaring off a prowler*.[2] When one *lays a brick upon mortar*, one might also be *building a wall, a house, a city*.[3] I am going to assume that these different respective descriptions describe the same action, merely falling under different descriptors.[4] Yet, these actions have different spatio-temporal extensions when denoted by these different descriptions.[5] Therefore, which one of these descriptions we take as salient for vindicating a given property claim will have different implications for the content of the rights that are thereby acquired.

Where we take the relevant cut-off point to be for an act of acquisition – whether it be closer to the basic act-description or further along the continuum of non-basic act-descriptions of increasing complexity – has considerable moral import. If *A* initiates an action φ at t_1 that subsumes S_1, and *B* initiates ψ at t_2 that subsumes S_2, these respective performances of φ and ψ are mutually performable, non-frustrating, and hence no rights to non-interference are violated. However, if we were to take a more complex description of φ such that it also subsumes S_2, then this would not be the case, and *B* would in fact be initiating an interference in ψ-ing. Therefore, the description of *A*'s action that is operative in her claim to non-interference therein is of serious consequence, since under different levels of description her rights will envelope different objects and spaces.

What is needed, then, is a principled way to determine where that cut-off point should be. The answer I offer consists of two steps: first, and obviously, the description taken must fall short of making it count as an interference with anyone else. So, if there is a description of my action that makes it extend so far as to subsume objects that are subsumed into another person's actions in a way that interferes, then that obviously cannot be the description that we take to acquire rights. Second, the description taken must be one which is publicly ascertainable. It is the actor's intention in acting – so far as is consistent with others' rights – that is salient for acquisition. But it must be an intention which is embodied objectively in their action such that third parties can in principle know it. This brings us to an important distinction between two kinds of intention.

There are two senses of intentionality that are analytically distinct if not empirically separable in all cases. The first is intention as a kind of wish or desire that one might act upon but does not necessarily always act upon. This kind of intention is a private, psychological, or subjective state. The other sense of intentionality is something embodied in actual action itself, which other actors can ascertain from observing your action.

In the first, subjective sense, intentions are wishes, hopes, or desires *to* act, or beliefs about the actions one is in fact engaged in. For example, when one wants to go to a party but knows one might have to work late instead, one might say that one *intends* to go to the party, despite the fact that one has not taken any action towards this end. We can form intentions about ends at the purely psychological level outside of taking any actual action towards the end. Or imagine when a solder kills an innocent civilian while she was *intending* to kill an enemy combatant. In this case, she really had taken action towards the end she had formed a psychological intention to pursue, but it was just that she took the wrong action and failed to achieve her end. She was mistaken about what action she was actually taking. In both examples, the intention in question is subjective in the sense of being merely psychological and not embodied in any action taking place, either because the action did not get pursued (at least, not yet), or because the wrong action was pursued and there was a mismatch between intention and action. Psychological states do not necessarily manifest as actions that are publicly recognisable as embodying them.

In the second, objective sense, intentions are embodied in actions. They are the meaning of the action within the context of publicly defined and known rules. For example moving one's hand back and forth while making eye-contact with a person constitutes a greeting; it means "hello" and communicates an amicable acknowledgement of another person's presence and/or an attempt to alert them to one's own presence. What makes this motion of the arm an intentional action in the objective sense is not merely that the physical motion was purposefully or voluntarily brought about by the agent, but rather that it constitutes a socially meaningful act – it *does something* that has social meaning in a particular social context that partially furnishes such meaning. Anyone familiar with what waving is would not need to peer into one's mind in order to know that what one was doing was *greeting someone*. There are publicly available criteria which vindicate the meaning of the act; namely, that it was a particular combination of bodily motions within particular social circumstances. That this kind of action counts as waving is circumscribed by a social rule, it is not merely a fact of physics and not merely a fact about psychological states.

Taking an agent's subjective intention as indicative of the salient description of their action would raise serious problems, both epistemological and ontological. When it comes to subjective intentions, it is the agent herself who is the final authority on what intention she in fact has. The ontological privacy of such psychological states means that in any given case, it is down to the agent's judgement as to which state she was in. For such states to be the determinants of a person's acquired rights would mean that there were not any reliable public criteria by which to vindicate any given acquisition claim. This means that rights could be acquired by one person without there being any way, even in principle, for third parties to know that their duties are now directed in this way. This would be at odds with higher-order considerations about justice and rights. The point of justice is to provide normative guidance on how to manage the conflicts that arise specifically in a socio-economic context. Without that guidance being something that is in principle publicly ascertainable, it cannot perform this function. If it cannot perform this function, then it cannot be normative for us. This is an epistemological problem because it renders part of the content of justice a private matter that those who are meant to be subject to it do not have sufficiently reliable or direct epistemic access to.

The problem is exacerbated however because the epistemological problem becomes an ontological problem. The intending agent herself is the final epistemic authority on what subjective intentions she has due to their ontological privacy. She has privileged epistemic access to them, and any indirect access to them by others must go through her. However, her judgement about what subjective state she is in is also to a significant extent *up to her* in addition to being epistemologically accessible only to her. Not only is it up to her to identify what subjective intention she forms, it is also up to her to *determine* what subjective intention she forms. She may, at will, form whatever subjective intention she wants. The ontological privacy of her subjective intentions means that which intentions count is determined by her own discretionary judgement. There is no external check by which she can determine how to categorise her subjective states other than that which she creates herself. The states are subjective, so it is up to her to determine what they are to count as.[6] This means that how rights are assigned is down to not merely something that the public has unreliable and indirect epistemic access to, but down to something that that individual rights bearer herself can determine by an act of will. For rights to be assigned by mere act of private willing and be beholden to such private acts of willing mean acquired rights become radically indeterminate.

Why is that? Well, the criterion for whether a person has acquired a particular right or not, on the view under consideration, is whether or not that person has a particular subjective state. Not only is this person the only one who really knows, but they are also the one who has ontological *power* to determine that the subjective intention they have counts as the one that would acquire her the relevant rights or not. Criteria cannot be criteria if to think one has fulfilled them and actually fulfilling them are the same thing. Criteria, as standards by which we judge the correctness of the application of a rule of justice, must be in principle subject to an external check. As Ludwig Wittgenstein put it, "[T]o *think* one is obeying a rule is not to obey a rule. Hence it is not possible to obey a rule "privately": otherwise thinking one was obeying a rule would be the same thing as obeying it."[7]

To make the rule for vindicating an acquisition claim something that the very existence of which is subject to the claimants' will is to have no rule for such vindication.

It is crucial to note that the problem with taking subjective intentions as the basis for furnishing acquired rights with content is *not* that this would empower individuals to impose duties upon the world at will. Many Kantians raise this as a problem with unilateral acquisition per se: because it involves the imposition of new moral duties upon third parties simply because one chose to. Unilateral determination of the conditions under which duties can be imposed, they argue, undermines freedom, independence, and/or equality, because part of each person's moral status is subject to others' discretionary power.[8] If this was the problem with submitting subjective intentions as the basis for furnishing the content of acquired rights, it would also be a problem with submitting objective intentions in their stead, as I propose. Since, taking their objective intention as the basis for furnishing acquired rights involves a similar unilateral exercise of the will. The only difference is that the action they take is subject to their unilateral will, rather than the intentionality imputed to it. This is not what the problem is because there is no imposition of new duties on a third party.

This problem is not real for two reasons. First, acquiring property rights does not occur through the exercise of a power to create new obligations. Rather, property rights are acquired simply as an application of a pre-existing claim which has different content depending upon the actions the rightholder takes. It is therefore not the imposition of a new duty but the filling with content of a pre-existing duty, or as Bas van der Vossen puts it, duty-alteration rather than duty-activation.[9] The same kind of duty-alteration that takes place when I grow an additional hair, thereby adding to the list of actions you are duty bound to abstain from, namely, from pulling out this new hair. As detailed in Chapter 3, it is central to my account of property rights that they do not and need not involve an independent right of exclusion over and above one's original rights to not be interfered with; hence, it does not face this calamity.

Second, even if it were framed as an imposition of a new duty due to the exercise of a power, the fact that it is imposed in virtue of a unilateral action on the part of the acquirer does not arrogate them with the moral authority to determine how rights are acquired: natural justice tells us how rights are acquired – through actions. So long as the acquisition was made in the way specified by justice, the acquirer would be acting within her rights and therefore not in an unjust way. Justice assigns us discrete spheres of free action, so that we may have delineated spheres of discretionary power. Justice tells us how our respective exercises of discretionary power may and may not affect others through ascribing us with individual rights. So long as we act within these rights, though our actions are bound to affect one another's material and moral landscape, we do not thereby commit injustice.

The problem with taking subjective intentions as the basis for the content of the rights thereby acquired is that it removes any objective basis for vindicating rights claims and adjudicating between conflicting ones. This runs against the basic nature and function of rights as publicly knowable constraints on our actions in time and space in a socio-economic context. As noted in Chapter 2, as a set of normative constraints, the content of rights must in principle be knowable to those subject to them. In order to provide the necessary normative guidance that moral agents need in a socio-economic context, the constraints of justice must be objective so that they are in principle knowable to all in like manner. For the content of rights to not only be once removed epistemologically, but also subject to falsification or vindication by an individual determining *at will* whether or not she was in a particular subjective state or not turns this entirely on its head. Without a publicly knowable standard for what counts as an acquisition, there is no principled way to end any given dispute that may arise. Justice is an *interpersonal* virtue and therefore the criteria for when a change has occurred in its juridical elements must be something that is *intersubjectively* ascertainable.[10] Grounding the content of rights in the intentionality that is objectively embodied in human action achieves this.

The intentionality of our actions, and hence the manner in which they subsume time-indexed objects and spaces can be intelligible through publicly available criteria. That publicly available criteria are the informal, often unarticulated social rules that define human activities.

Understanding an action as embodying a particular intention involves identifying it as following the rules that constitute particular intentional activities. It is not reducible to knowing with certainty what kind of psychological state the actor might be it, nor is it reducible to her physical behaviour, bodily motions and sounds, and so forth. However, both these pieces of data may *contribute* to an identification of the intentionality there embodied. Social, often informal and unarticulated, rules constitute our intentional activities. It is understanding through a comprehension of these rules that we can identify actions as constituting instances of following them. Such rules are publicly known, and hence when the content of rights is determined by the intentionality of the action taken, the content of the rights is publicly knowable.

In virtue of one's knowledge of what it means to have a home, to farm land, and go fishing, one can observe the intentionality of those who engage in the activities of home-making, of farming, of fishing, because their activities follow the, albeit informal and unarticulated, rules of those activities as we understand their ends, means, and meanings. When someone starts to fence off land and till the soil, we know that they have initiated use of the water table, so if we were to immediately drill down on a plot adjacent to this land and drain the water table, we would be interfering. We know this to be the case without it needing to be true that this individual was necessarily in *any* particular psychological state or held any particular propositional attitude about what they were doing. We know that farming land is not interfered with by walking onto it (without disturbing the crops) to ask the farmer some innocuous question, and hence doing so does not violate her rights. For the farmer to engage in a speech-act which indicates that her activity is a private one (e.g. by uttering "please leave me alone right now") means that our remaining in her presence talking to her does interfere with the type of activity, and therefore does violate her rights (albeit to a relatively trivial extent).

If we fully comprehend what it means for a person to be engaging in the intentional action that they are, then we know what kinds of actions it would take on our part to interfere. However, interpretation of the intentionality is not automatic, nor is it necessarily always correct. For activities one is well acquainted with, one can very quickly see the intention embodied therein. For activities with which one is less acquainted, some hermeneutical work must be done where one observes resemblance with similar activities and decipher the intentionality by analogy. A certain amount of social embeddedness is presumed by successful hermeneutic interpretation. Socialisation into the rules that constitute particular activities makes it easier for one to recognise instances of it. However, the overlapping similarities or "family resemblances"[11] between different activities means agents can successfully comprehend intentions in actions they have yet not experienced by analogy with the ones they have. The description obtained is one not borne out of an understanding of the physics of the behaviour, nor the underlying private psychology that occurs with it but; rather, a thick description that is necessarily loaded with content imported from the social context that renders this action the kind of action that it is.[12]

One might be sceptical that comprehension of another's intentional actions so as to infer the precise content of her rights must really be so culturally loaded. Many of our activities constitute instances of rule-following in terms of social, informal, and unarticulated rules that give them meaning. But so much of our activity is not particularly social, nor particularly meaningful, but rather materially instrumental. With these activities, surely we can understand them purely as physical events and thereby know the content of the rights acquired. Indeed, many human activities are commonly defined simply in terms of their "natural effect"[13] – by their physical outcomes. For example, *planting seeds* might be defined by its natural effect: the physical placement of seeds within soil. From this definition, we can say that any action whose natural effect physically hinders or blockades the outcome of the seeds ending up remaining buried in the topsoil constitutes an interference in *planting seeds*. Therefore, anyone who plants seeds in unowned land acquires rights against third parties engaging in those actions, defined by their physical outcomes. Imagine a person standing on a patch of fertile land; we observe her till the soil, push in seeds, and then burry them. We know from a basic "natural effect" understanding of what she is doing that if someone else came along and dug them up, this would interfere with her action and violate her rights. It would be wrong however to define her intentional action as the physical process of burying seeds. In order to understand the actions of others and what it would take to interfere with them, we must hermeneutically interpret them within a social context.

Observing that a person is burying seeds is enough to tell us that digging them up would interfere; however, what if someone built a well nearby and drained the water table, resulting in the soil having an unsuitable composition for the seeds that were planted? The natural effect of the seeds being buried is not interfered with, but when we understand her action to be one of *planting seeds*, and not merely *burying* them, we can see that draining the water table *would* interfere. We did not watch her body go through the physical motions of "accessing the water table," we only know that draining the water table would interfere if we understand her action in the wider context of agricultural activities. In order then to have a full account of the rights acquired, we need to have a full account of the relevant activity qua intentional, purposeful, end-directed human activity.

There is a strong element of socially contextual interpretation in allocating acquired rights. First, in order to know what natural effect a given instance of action is aimed at, we need to know that under certain circumstances the physical event of burying seeds counts as *planting seeds* and is therefore directed at *cultivating crops* or that threading a worm onto a hook counts as *baiting a hook* and is therefore directed at *fishing*. If someone were simply burying seeds to *hide* them or *dispose of* them, then the matter would be different: they would not acquire rights to exclude others from depleting the water table or eroding the surrounding soil, etc. Likewise, if someone was actually not baiting a hook, but *culling worms* or *decorating a hook*,[14] they would not acquire rights over the river. Telling these activities apart requires contextual knowledge about the way in which these natural effects are sought. Second, in order to know what would interfere with the attainment of the relevant natural effect, we still need to know the way in which it is being sought; through which technique or customary practice it is being done, so that we can know what would interfere with it. If my action interferes with your action, it is no defence on my part that there are other ways of reaching your intended natural effect; what matters is that I interfered in the actual action you took.[15] Interference is not merely the undermining of one's ultimate ends but of one's particular chosen means of obtaining them.

The way in which we understand the constituent parts of activities as such is analogous the way in which we understand the rules that constitute games. We understand the relationship between the rules and the game, as with lower-level activities and the more complex activities they make up, conceptually. Moreover, there are public standards of correctness for what rules constitute what games and what constitute certain activities. These public standards, subsisting in the practices of the community, serve as an objective basis for judging what the intentional activity in question is and hence the contours of the property rights thereby acquired.

Recognising that someone is engaged in some ongoing activity by observing them engaging in only a small part of it is much like recognising a game being played, having only seen one move being made. As Wittgenstein said,

> Just as a move in chess doesn't consist simply in moving a piece in such-and-such a way on the board – nor yet in one's thoughts and feelings as one makes the move: *but in the circumstances that we call* "playing a game of chess", "solving a chess problem", and so on.[16]

One might object to the basic distinction I have made between public and private intentions. It might be thought that the connection between private, subjective psychological states and the public, objective behaviour that go along with them are *conceptually* connected – that the truth of their connection is analytic. If this were the case, it might mean that taking the public intentionality as salient for rights acquisition is simply a proxy for taking the private intention as salient, which may still lead to the problems noted earlier.

It is true that there is *some* conceptual relationship between private and public intentions. But the nature of that entanglement is not that it is analytically true that private intentions *just are* the mental states that (even dispositionally) give rise to particular kinds of intentional actions. To understand why it has to be the case that there is some conceptual relationship between private and public intentionality, consider the following from Wittgenstein.

> I cannot know what he's planning in his heart. But suppose he always wrote out his plans; of what importance would they be? If, for example, he never acted according to them. – Perhaps someone will say: Well, then they really aren't plans. But then neither would they be plans if they were *inside* him, and looking into him would do us no good.[17]

Wittgenstein's point is that *part* of what it means to be in the subjective state of planning something is that disposition to actually act on those plans. If someone insisted that they were making all sorts of plans in their head and *never* acted upon them, it would be reasonable to suggest they were in fact mistaken about what "planning" really is, and perhaps what they were really doing in their head was a form of wishing or speculating. So, there is a conceptual relationship between types of private intentions and the types of actions that objectively embody the concomitant intentionality.

However, the existence of the one token of that type does not analytically tell us about the existence of a token of the other. It is perfectly conceivable that people make plans and do not act on them. It is just that if we consistently called the psychological state that *never* led to action "planning," then planning would take on a different meaning and no longer be conceptually connected with the kind of action it is.[18] Anscombe is instructive here.

> [I]f I say: 'No, I quite agree, there is no way for a person at the top of the house to get the camera; but still I am going upstairs to get it' I begin to be unintelligible. In order to make sense of 'I do P with a view to Q', we must see how the future state of affairs Q is supposed to be a possible later stage in proceedings of which the action P is an earlier stage. . . . Thus there are many descriptions of happenings which are directly dependent on our possessing the *form* of description on intentional actions. It is easy not to notice this, because it is perfectly possible for some of these descriptions to be of what is done unintentionally. For example 'offending someone'; one can do this unintentionally, but there would be no such thing if it were never the description of an intentional action. And 'putting up an advertisement upside down', which would perhaps mostly be unintentional, is a description referring to advertisements, which are essentially

intentional; again, the kind of action done in 'putting up' intentional if not somnambulistic. . . . Surprising as it may seem, the failure to execute intention is necessarily the rare exception.[19]

The point is that it is not an imperfect way of getting at the subjective intention, rather it is seeking a public basis for determining what they are doing that all actors can in principle understand. Interpretation of action is not merely a process of deducing the private psychological states of the actor, even if it may involve that. It is a process of fitting their action within a set of social rules that make sense to us, given the social context, their physical behaviour, and the psychological state we think they might be in. The point is to get at that part of human actions which is ontologically public and that can therefore serve the basis for normative coordination of our action in a socio-economic context. Discovering the content of justice does not require getting inside one another's heads, but it does require us, to some extent, to understand what one another's actions mean.

Conventions: Constitutive and Regulative

There is a sense, then, in which the content of our rights is fixed by social convention – namely, those rules that tell us which actions count as which kinds of intentional activity. This needs clarification.

Natural rights are very often framed as rights that we have *not* in virtue of any social convention but by our very nature. It is simply due to our humanity, and all that that entails, which includes that fact that our moral conduct takes place in a socio-economic context. So, for the content of our rights to end up depending upon conventions that happen to exist for their content seems to make them rather more artificial and contrived then perhaps we were led to think at the outset. However, the sense in which the content of our natural rights depends upon actually existing conventions is very strictly delineated in such a way as to maintain their status as natural rather than conventional. In order to see how, I invoke the distinction between constitutive and regulative rules.[20]

Both constitutive and regulative rules are conventional in nature, meaning that they exist in virtue of converging regularity in the actions of social groups. Constitutive rules are conventional rules that define the conduct that they apply to. Activities are not existentially independent of their constitutive rules, because one cannot engage in those activities unless one complies with the constitutive rules. One has to conform one's conduct with the relevant constitutive rules for it to even count as the relevant conduct. Regulative rules on the other hand are conventional rules that merely regulate conduct that is existentially independent from them. Activities can be said to proceed as the kinds of activity they are even when they defy the regulative rules that conventionally apply to them. Social norms and positive law are both examples of regulative rules.

For example if one were to go down to the river in waders with a fishing rod, and when one got there, one just drunkenly waved the rod round in their air until the sun went down – this would not count as fly fishing. One's actions down at the river would not be identifiable as *fly fishing*, even if a third party might be able to tell that that may have been one's initial intention (subjectively speaking); it was not embodied in one's actions because one did not cohere with the constitutive rules of that activity. Fly fishing is an activity that is defined by certain constitutive rules, namely, that one use a hook decorated with an imitation of natural fly as opposed to a baited hook; that one use a partially weighted line; most importantly, that one actually pursue trout, rather than just going down to the river to swing one's rod around in a drunken frenzy. Fly fishing is subject to certain regulative rules as well as constitutive ones (at least, in England). For example you are not permitted to fly fish in natural waterways during spawning season. Fly fishing may not be permitted in certain private lakes that are designated for course fishing.

Sometimes constitutive and regulative rules come together. For example one is not permitted to fly fish with dynamite in any public river. But then again, the use of dynamite defies the defining technique of fly fishing, so does not really count as fly fishing in the first instance.[21] In these cases, it makes sense to speak of constitutive rules as supplying the function of regulative rules and vice versa.

The commonplace example of this is games. In football, for example, the rules regulate the game inasmuch as if you break them you are told to correct your conduct and often sanctioned (in accordance with rules) for defying the rules. However, they also define the game inasmuch as if you bend, break, or alter them *systematically*, you are no longer playing football. At a certain point, breaking the rules in a regulative sense becomes breaking them in a constitutive sense, and suddenly one is complying with the regulative rules of a new game with different constitutive rules – perhaps Gaelic football or Aussie Rules football. When playing chess, moving the king two places one would be breaking the rules, but if one did it consistently and neither player sanctioned it, one would in fact be playing chmess.[22] Or, if one moved each piece diagonally only and took opponent pieces by jumping them, one would be playing draughts, just with chess pieces.

The concrete content of our acquired rights presupposes only constitutive rules, not regulative rules. The basic structure of all acquired rights is a claim to not be interfered with in a particular activity vis-à-vis a particular set of time-indexed objects and spaces. In order to know what it amounts to – to know how others must constrain their action in order to comply with their correlative duty – we need to know what the rules are that constitutive the activity they are engaged in. We do not need to know (nor is there even need to *be*) any conventional rules that regulate that activity in question. In order to know what it would take to interfere with someone's making use of a river, we do not need to know what constraints the community *actually* imposes upon the users' behaviour. We only need to know what this use consists in.

It is natural justice that tells us what regulative social conventions we ought to have. It may turn out to endorse or indict actually existing regulative rules. But filling in the content of the constraints it imposes upon us does not require reference to any regulative constraints in fact adopted by any actually existing social group.

The application of our natural rights to the real social world is in part a conceptual matter. That is insofar as it is a matter of holding up our respective claim against interference to the regulative rules we find at work in the real social world and simply establishing where there is agreement or disagreement. If we know that *A* started φ-ing at t_1, and *B* started ψ-ing at t_2, and these two actions subsume some of the same time-indexed objects or spaces in a way that renders them mutual unperformable, then we know that *B* has violated *A*'s rights. However, in order for this judgement to amount to any indictment or vindication of the justice of anyone's action in the real world, other than a statement of the a priori content of justice, we need to successfully interpret individuals' respective actions as constituting particulars that fall under these types – namely, that the motions and sounds of *A*'s body counted as φ-ing at t_1 and so forth. This requires practical anthropology. As Kant says, "a metaphysics of morals cannot dispense with application."[23] When what our rights are rights *to* is particular kinds of activity with regard to particular time-indexed objects, it is necessary that we come to know what constitutes those activities not merely as subsumptions of objects in space–time, but as human, intentional activities. Understanding the rules that constitute the activities we pursue, therefore, is essential to applying our natural rights. However, the normative concepts do not come from the regulative conventions present in the actually existing social world. We do not need any acquaintance with any actually existing regulative conventions because natural justice tells us how we ought to regulate conduct itself. Kant goes on:

> [W]e shall often have to take as our object the particular *nature* of human beings, which is cognized only by experience, in order to *show* in it what can be inferred from universal moral principles. But this will in no way detract from the purity of these principles or cast doubt in their *a priori* source. – This is to say, in effect, that a metaphysics of morals cannot be based on anthropology but can be applied to it.[24]

The content of justice needs to be filled in with actually existing constitutive rules, and the constitutive rules cannot tell us anything normative (at least, not normative in the sense of justice) without placing it within a theory of justice.

Theories of natural rights that, in their enumeration of what are rights are rights to, make reference to actually existing regulative conventions, therefore face a serious calamity that does not befall the theory defended here. If it were that each person has a natural right "to private property," in order to furnish that right with content we will need to refer to certain regulative conventions, namely, those of property that we find either in the real world or in the mind of a legal scholar or in folk imagination. There will, no doubt, be *many possible versions* of this regulative type. Loren Lomasky considers this issue:

> Suppose that A views from a mountaintop a vast expanse of virgin territory, rides around half of it, places boundary markers to set off a quarter of it, grazes his cattle over an eighth of it, fences in a sixteenth, clears a thirty-second, and plants a sixty-forth. How much of land that A first saw does he "have"? When the morally minded B comes by, how much of the land should he feel obliged to acknowledge as belonging to A? If B eventually settles downstream from A, and A damns up the stream to create a pleasant lake for himself, have B's property rights been invaded?
>
> There are no clear answers to these questions. Or, rather, there is no one best answer that can be deduced from the theory of basic rights. Persons will be unable to know and act on property rights that are ill-specified, and therefore it is requisite for the success of an order of rights that some determination be made. Social conventions are necessary to give concrete form to concepts such as appropriation, sale, bequest, and externality.

In order to decide which version is authorised by justice, we cannot look back to justice, since it just says we have a right to private property and we cannot look at the regulative type "private property" since there are multiple realisations of it in the world and in the mind. The same goes for the idea that we have a right to "freedom of contract" or "freedom of conscience." Justice, when enumerated in this way, narrows down a range of regulative conventions that might be just but does not give final pronouncement on which one is uniquely just. We are therefore left wondering how to constrain our action: in line with *this* regulative rule or *that*?[25] Often, the fact that there are a variety of possible conventional realisations of natural rights (enumerated in this way) is noted but seemingly assumed not to raise a problem due to there only being one salient set of actually existing regulative conventions that fix natural rights' application.[26]

Theories formulated this way would have to do one of three things: deferring to a meta-principle that provides further normative guidance, deferring to actually existing regulative conventions (where there is a single coherent set in force),[27] or demoting justice to a different kind of moral status that can tolerate indeterminacy, if that exists.

The theory defended here does not face this calamity. Our rights are rights to non-interference in the activities that we in fact choose to pursue. We need only look to constitutive rules in order to know what this amounts to. The existence of regulative rules is only of interest insofar as they will tell us how just the real social world in fact is. Natural rights, enumerated thus, tell us what regulative conventions we should actually have.

When natural rights are specified as pertaining to particular activities, it is the constitutive rules of those activities that provide determinacy. When natural rights are specified as pertaining to particular regulative norms, there is a degree of indeterminacy to the extent that there are many different versions of the norms. Saying that there is a natural right to private property makes the question of what private property is rather urgent. Saying that one has a right to non-interference in one's activities tells us what private property ought to be (if anything).

At least, so long as the constitution of one another's actions can be established.

To make correct judgements about the rules that constitute actions, one needs *some* acquaintance with the form of life within which those actions are situated. Which is to say, one needs to know the rules constituting actions which bear some overlapping similarity.

These are judgements of identity between events which are not merely physicalistically constituted, nor merely psychologically constituted, but something that incorporates the two: intentional human action. Intentional human activity cannot be reductively understood in reference to some other sort of thing. Judging that a particular kind of intentional activity took place involves understanding it as an instance of rule-following vis-à-vis the relevant constitutive rules. Identifying something as an instance of a particular kind of rule-following involves an application of rules, much as actually *doing* the rule-following does. Judgements that a particular kind of activity took place, then, require a kind of internal acquaintance with the activity itself.

Peter Winch writes:

> The concepts and criteria according to which the sociologist judges that, in two situations, the same thing has happened, or the same action performed, must be understood *in relation to the rules governing . . . what the sociologist is studying. . . .* And it is these rules,

> rather than those which govern the sociologist's investigation, which specify what is to count as 'doing the same kind of thing' in relation to that kind of activity.[28]

Judging that someone has initiated an act of fishing in a river (and therefore, subsumed the surrounding resources in a particular way) rather than merely culling worms on a hook (which would involve different and more minimal subsumption of the surrounding resources) is not something that can necessarily be read off of the physical behaviour, nor is it something that could necessarily be known by peering into the actor's subjective states. Rather, it is something one knows because it fits into a pattern of rule-following that one is acquainted with, as a social practice.

When one is deeply acquainted with a range of intentional activities, one does not even need to consult with the constitutive rules as a set of criteria to hold the activity up against to check what it is.[29] To a farmer, or anyone well-acquainted with farming, one only has to see that wheat is growing to know that the land is being used in a very particular kind of way and therefore know what it would take to interfere with this. We do not need to see the farmer sweating, we do not need to see the field progress from fallow to harvested over the course of a year to know its use shifts, we know just by seeing the wheat in a particular kind of circumstance and context. As Searle puts it,

> [w]e live in a sea of human institutional facts. Much of this is invisible to us. . . . One of the advantages of living in other cultures is that one can become more acutely conscious of the different and unfamiliar institutional structures. But at home one is less aware of the sea of institutionality.[30]

Wittgenstein goes so far as to say that, when we have fully internalised rules that define activities, we apply them and follow them "*blindly*." But this is not always going to be the case. We cannot take such an internal point of view of every conceivable human activity: there are always going to be new ones emerging and ones that are simply novel to us. In these cases, the intentionality of them will be more opaque because we are not as well-acquainted with how its constitutive rules are applied. However, even to someone who has never heard of fishing, they would only need to observe someone cast their line, pull in a fish, and unhook it a few times to gain a pretty good understanding of the intentionality involved – particularly, if one had any other background understanding of what rivers are, what hunting is, that fish are edible, that humans need food, etc. The intentionality of our activities is something that is publicly ascertainable and not reducible to any private mental state, so it is always in principle something that another person can understand, by analogy with elements of our activities. As Hayek writes,

> [a]s long as I move among my own kind of people, it is probably the physical properties of a bank note or a revolver from which I conclude that they are money or a weapon to the person holding them. When I see a savage holding cowrie shells or a long, thin tube, the physical properties of the thing will probably tell me nothing. But the observations which suggest to me that the cowrie shells are money to him and the blowpipe a weapon will throw much light on the object – much more light that these same observations could possibly give if I were not familiar with the conception of money or a weapon. In recognizing the things as such, I begin to understand the people's behaviour. I am able to fit into a scheme of actions which "makes sense".[31]

There is a form of agreement of judgement that is necessary for constitutive rules to emerge, as with any other kinds of convention. But this is not a form of agreement akin to deliberate endorsement or consent. It is merely a convergence or regularity in our understandings of socially salient activities. As Wittgenstein put is, "not agreement in opinions but in form of life."[32]

Is it not possible for there to be fundamental failures of understanding? Where two communities with different constitutive rules for similar activities fail to converge on agreement in their form of life, and hence what activities they are respectively engaged is no longer public and objective, but only relative to the particular community, what happens then? We might call this *hermeneutical conflict*: a situation wherein there is an integration failure in the constitutive rules of a community (of communities). To some, fencing off an acre of land and planting seeds is agriculture, and it is interfered with when others trample on the cultivated earth or block out the sun light. To others, this might be an invitation to communal worship – not interfered with by others pulling up the seed and throwing them in the air in glorification of the Creator – but rather an act of consent to such actions in one's presence. One community just cannot understand the other's intentionality when they engage in the same behaviour. Does the logical possibility of this kind of case not mean that the content of our rights might often be ontologically indeterminate after all? It would not raise a problem for different and *separated* communities to apply the principles of justice differently as befits their different activities. But when such communities overlap or interact, it is important that at least insofar as they interact with each other, there is a common understanding of one another's actions.

Indeed, justice just presupposes that we are able to understand one another's actions. We cannot hope to live in relations of justice until we can actually understand what we are doing. Where *A* cannot tell the difference between when *B* is attacking her, worshipping her God, or gathering food, then the socio-economic conditions which give rise to the possibility and need for justice simply are not there. Coordination over the use of the external world cannot take place unless there is agreement of what *constitutes* different kinds of uses of the external world. For radically different kinds of forms of life to coexist in relations of justice, they must converge on some common means of telling apart their visually or physically similar behaviours, which nonetheless constitute very different forms of intentional activity. Indeed, this is something language has proven useful for.

When two communities do not interact, their hermeneutical incompatibility does not matter. Once they are interacting, the groundwork for their hermeneutical integration has already been laid.[33]

Many forms of social contract theory require that society take the form of a pre-constituted *people* who are capable of agreement (whether acquiescence or consent) before justice or the institutions for its enforcement can be put in place. Natural rights theory does not require anything this strong – society can be an open-ended, mutually disinterested entity. All that is required is that there be publicly available criteria upon which we can converge in taking to be constitutive of what it means to act in one way rather than another. It is our capability of understanding one another's actions that is required for relations of justice to apply. I take it that this is an essentially human capability.

Natural Rights and Social Change

The concrete content of justice varies not only with the actions that persons freely choose to initiate, but also social understandings of actions over time, as well as the technological capabilities of society at any given time. All accounts of the historical entitlement theory render the content of justice at any given time partially determined by the historical choices made by persons. Moreover, having the technical ability to engage in an activity in a way that does not interfere with others naturally alters the range of actions that can be pursued.[34] Social change – in terms of the gradual (or not so gradual) changes in the constitutive rules that define our activities – will alter what actions are permitted, prohibited, and required.

Change in the constitutive rules that define our activities mean that, given the change in the way we understand what the activity actually is, will often naturally covary with a change in what counts as interfering with it. Over time, or at the same time among different communities, there are changes in the nature and constitutions of activities such that φ-ing really did not constitute an interference in ψ-ing at t_1 but it does at t_2. For example the stench of horse faeces in the street and the physical obstacle they presented to pedestrians did not interfere with the use of streets as market places or as thoroughfares prior to the advent of motor vehicles in urban areas. The social understanding of *running a grocery stall* or *walking down the street* did not include being free from the smell of animal excrement. Cultural and technological changes no doubt made it possible for us to engage in activities in public places that did not include exposure to such scents. Yet, at a certain point, the horse is out of the barn, so to speak, and such activities became constituted, in part, by excluding exposure to what are now considered nuisances and sensory invasions.

Sometimes judicial opinion implicitly invokes constitutive rules – and how they change over time and vary across space – in determining whether nuisances are actionable or not. For example, in the landmark English case *Bamford v. Turnley*, the appellant was seeking damages for the purported nuisance caused by the odour of the smoke from the respondent's kiln that he used for firing bricks to build a house on his land. Baron Bramwell made the judgement that the respondent's use of his land for brickmaking was part-and-parcel of the *ordinary use* of his land and, as such, does not constitute a nuisance to surrounding landowners, because the ordinary use of their land is not socially understood to be interfered with by such ordinary activities. Judge wrote the following:

> There must be, then, some principle on which such cases must be excepted. It seems to me that that principle may be deduced from the character of these cases, and is this, viz., that those acts necessary for the common and ordinary use and occupation of land and houses may be done, if conveniently done, without submitting those who do them to an action. . . . It is as much for the advantage of one owner as of another, for the very nuisance the one complains of, as the results of the ordinary use of his neighbour's land, he himself will create in the ordinary use of his own, and the reciprocal nuisances are of a comparatively trifling character. The convenience of such a rule may be indicated by calling it a rule of give and take, live and let live.[35]

Bramwell is often taken to be making the case that the prima facie content of our property rights can be reciprocally attenuated where this is beneficial to the welfare of all affected parties.[36] I do not intend to claim that this instance of case law somehow vindicates my own claim; I only intend to illustrate a way in which the constitutive rules of intentional activities such as the "ordinary use and occupation of land and houses" is something that is clearly relative to time, place, and community and therefore something which can change. There is no doubt that my ordinary use of my home does not include emission of fumes from a brick kiln, even though it might had I occupied the land it is built on 150 years ago. A similar illustration is evident in the US case of *Hinman vs. Pacific*

Air Transport. Hinman sought damages for the flight of commercial air traffic over his land. Indeed, the *ad coelum* doctrine of the time made Hinman qua owner of his land also owner of a pillar of space reaching upward and outward to the heavens and reaching downward and inward toward the core of the Earth. Judge Haney argued that Hinman's right to the space above his land could not be construed so as to prohibit aeroplanes from flying over. The doctrine comes from a time where air flight did not exist, therefore understanding one's use of a field as extending up to the heavens was perfectly understandable given that it was costless to third parties. However, as soon as airspace could now be used in this other way, farming could not be deemed to be constituted by an *exclusive* use of the skies above:

> This formula "from the center of the earth to the sky" was invented at some remote time in the past when the use of space above land actual or conceivable was confined to narrow limits, and simply meant that the owner of the land could use the overlying space to such an extent as he was able, and that no one could ever interfere with that use.
>
> This formula was never taken literally, but was a figurative phrase to express the full and complete ownership of land and the right to whatever superjacent airspace was necessary or convenient to the enjoyment of the land.
>
> Title to the airspace unconnected with the use of land is inconceivable.[37]

Changes in the constitution of activities often come with other cultural and technological changes.

Such genuine – ontological – changes in the constitution of activities as they are publicly understood by the community of actors must be distinguished from mere epistemic changes regarding the nature of activities. There are two kinds of epistemic changes. Sometimes we may just be unaware that φ-ing interferes with ψ-ing, and upon discovery that it does, our regulative conventions may be altered so as to prohibit φ-ing to the extent that it interferes with ψ-ing. For example carbon dioxide emissions were interfering with activities that depend upon a certain disposition of ecosystem services before it was discovered that they were. Passive smoking interfered with the health of people before they were aware that it was. These interferences were always going on, it was just not known. In these cases, it is technological changes that generated these epistemic shifts that *reveal* that we were wrong about the compatibility of our different activities. We were wrong about the nature of the subsumption of objects that were involved in things like fossil fuel burning and social smoking. It might be that we were wrong about the *nature* of the subsumption, or we were wrong about which spatio-temporal objects were in fact subsumed at all.

Conclusion

We have a right to non-interference in our intentional activities, not as we necessarily think they are, but as the kinds of action they actually are, the standard of which is provided by publicly knowable constitutive rules. It should come as no surprise that we should have to have some basic understanding of the actions of one another before we can know concretely how to treat one another justly. Yet this in no way renders the content of our natural rights dependent on pre-existing regulative conventions such as social norms or the positive law. Since the content of regulative conventions is altogether orthogonal to specifying the constitution of our actions; their existence is ontologically and epistemology separable to specifying the content of justice. Natural justice therefore remains the supreme virtue against which our regulative conventions must be held accountable. While the formal content of justice is unchanging, its concrete content changes with our constitutive rules, therefore just societies will all look very different across cultural contexts. The acquaintance with constitutive rules that is necessary to fully determine the content of rights means that for those with less acquaintance with a culture, it will be relatively more difficult for them to make judgements of justice.

Notes

1. Danto and Morgenbesser (1963); Danto (1965); Martin (1972); Annas (1978).
2. Davidson (1963, 686–87).
3. Mises (2007, 45–46); Steiner (1994, 50–51).
4. Anscombe (1963); Davidson (1963); Richards (1976); Hornsby (1979) This is the predominant, if not consensus view. For dissent, see (Goldman 1970, 24–28).
5. Carter (1999, 179).
6. As G.E.M. Anscombe puts it, in this sense of intention, the individual is the "sole authority" on what her intentions are Anscombe (1963, sec. 4).
7. Wittgenstein (1986, sec. 202).
8. For various forms of the worry about the unilateral imposition of duties with regard to original acquisition, see Gibbard (1976); Waldron (1988a, 265–67, 1996, 1999, chap. 3); Wenar (1998); Flikschuh (1999, 2000, chap. 4, 2008); Varden (2008, 2010); Ripstein (2004, 2006, 2009, chap. 6); Stilz (2009, chap. 2, 2011, 2012, 2014, 2018); Hodgson (2010a); Pallikkathayil (2010); Hasan (2018); Sinclair (2018); Spafford (2000).
9. van der Vossen (2015).
10. This is also a Kantian idea, elements of which can be found in Kant (1991, sec. I.I.VI.VI); Fressola (1981, 321); Barnett (1986, 302); Long (1999); Hoppe (2004, 87, 2006, 320–27, 2010, 23–55); Ripstein (2009, 105); Stilz (2009, 52, 2019, 70).
11. Wittgenstein (1986, secs 67–68); Suter (1989, chap. 2).
12. Geertz (1973).
13. Searle (1969, 39).
14. Granted, this would be exceptionally eccentric way of doing both those activities.

15. Conventions are "practical" in the sense of being directed towards certain outcomes in the material world (Lewis 1969, 36–42; Bicchieri 2006, 34–42). Yet we must understand the convention in order to know what would interfere in the particular *way* of achieving that outcome where done so through a particular conventional means since that is how the action in question takes concrete shape.
16. Wittgenstein (1986, sec. 33 emphasis added).
17. Wittgenstein (1982, secs 234–35), similarly, Wittgenstein asks rhetorically whether it would make sense to say that one could intend to play chess in a world in which no such game ever existed, since chess is defined by its rules. It is not possible to intend, psychologically speaking, to engage in a social custom that does not exist, in Wittgenstein's view Wittgenstein (1986, sec. 205).
18. For a very helpful exposition of this view and how it relates to logical behaviourism, see Long (Unpublished manuscript, chap. 5).
19. Anscombe (1963, secs 22, 47–48).
20. I draw this distinction from John Searle (1969, 33–42, 1995, chap. 2). However, it bears direct analogy to Kant's distinction between constitutive and regulative use of our faculties of judgement (Kant 1998; Friedman 1991).
21. I am grateful to Oliver Banks for this example.
22. Dennet (2006).
23. Kant (1991, sec. 6:217).
24. Kant (1991, sec. 6:217).
25. Ben Bryan calls this the "problem of authority" (Bryan 2017).
26. Lomasky (1987, 578–79).
27. There are two prominent approaches that combine both of these strategies. Kantian statists invoke a "natural duty of justice" that obliges us to establish and maintain a state that coerces us all into aligning with a particular set of regulative rules (Christmas 2020b, 2021). The meta-principle is the natural duty to the state, and it selects the positive law of the state as the set of regulative rules among competitors that should be privileged. Thomists such as John Finnis invoke the meta-value of the common good to our individual rights. The common good is served, so Finnis argues, in part, through convergence on rules, and that we should therefore defer to whatever the most socially salient regulative conventions are, since these are most likely to garner widespread convergence (Finnis 2011, chaps 9–11).
28. Winch (1990, 86–87).
29. Wittgenstein (1986, sec. 219).
30. Searle (2010, 90).
31. Hayek (1948, 65–66).
32. Wittgenstein (1986, secs 241–42).
33. Bernard Williams remark on moral relativism may be useful here:

    > For standard relativism, one may say, it is always too early or too late. It is too early, when the parties have no contact with each other, and the neither can think of itself as "we" and the other as "they." It is too late, when they have encountered one another: the moment that they have done so, there is a new "we" to be negotiated.
    >
    > (2005, 69).

34. Technological change make it possible for persons to engage in actions $\varphi_1, \ldots \varphi_n$ in a way that is non-interfering at t_2 that would have been interfering at t_2, ceteris paribus. For example the possibility of safe and high-altitude aeroplane travel opens up action space previously closed off, both physically and normatively. When aeroplanes flew lower and were far less safe – perhaps at the most experimental stage – it would have been an interference with land

owners below from them to fly over them. A change in technological capacity means not only that they can fly higher (creating less of a noise and particulate nuisance), but also that they are less likely to crash and therefore mean that same action (at least as long as it is not described in a way that includes predicates making direct reference to safety) is now normatively open where it previously was not.

35. Bramwell (1862).
36. For example see Epstein (1979, 2009); Russell (2018).
37. Haney (1936), again, some take a slightly more welfarist reading of the justificatory argument here, for example see (Schmidtz 2009, 2010, 2011b, 2011a, 2017; Russell 2018).

Conclusion

Natural Rights and Liberal Politics

I have argued that the content of justice is a set of individual rights to engage in the activities we choose to pursue, which do not interfere with the activities of others. Most of these pages have been occupied with trying to show that this view of justice can meaningfully, determinately, and fruitfully be understood as property. I believe I have provided exhaustive answers (or, at least, provided the resources for exhaustive answers) to questions over the structure and content of natural rights in all socio-economic contexts. In this sense, I believe I have shown how natural rights apply to the real world in a plausible way, and that they do not delegate questions about the hard cases of property rights to other fields. This book therefore gives a detailed evaluative standard for socio-economic institutions that relate to the use of, access to, and exchange of things.

I believe the ground I have treaded is between moral and political philosophy. My claims here occupy a restricted subset of questions of moral philosophy in that they are concerned only with those parts of morality that liberals typically think are relevant to politics: the ethics of liberty and coercion or, in the language I have more often employed here, interference and non-interference. However, they are on the moral side of political philosophy because they do not directly concern the status of political institutions and organisations themselves.

While it might be clear that I have made normative propositions about law (and other regulative conventions) as pertains to the economic sphere, I have not said anything about how that law should be created or enforced nor anything about how any institution that does the creating and enforcing ought to be structured itself. I take the latter to be questions of political and economic science.

Aside from remarks in the introduction, the reader may notice that I have not discussed the status of my theory as *libertarian*, despite its obvious closer attachment to the theories of Nozick, Rothbard, Steiner, and Mack, all of whom are uncontroversially regarded as libertarian theorists, than other contemporary liberals such as Rawls, Arneson, Waldron, and Wolff who are all liberals but not libertarians.[1] I am hesitant to – at least uncritically – label this book's contribution as proposing some take on *libertarian political philosophy*. Though what I say about natural rights is similar to what libertarians (who defend natural rights) have to say about them, I do not believe that they imply a great deal of what libertarians often *also* say about politics.

Within the realm of politics, libertarian defenders of natural rights typically argue that either no state or only a "minimal state" is justifiable; that taxation (beyond what is absolutely necessary to fund the protection of rights, if that) is illegitimate. The idea, then, is that what we ought to do in the realm of politics – that is as activists, voters, citizens, or as persons with the capacity to affect public discourse – is to oppose all violations of rights and therefore to oppose the state, almost tout court. Of course, if we are minarchists, we should not oppose its very existence, but in the context of the way the state actually exists, we should fight it on almost every front. I think this presupposes that knowledge about the content of rights gives us knowledge about politics that it does not. For example Nozick tells us what it is legitimate for a state to do and not to do. Assuming he is right, this does not tell us how a state should be constituted in order to ensure it sticks to this remit. It does even tell us whether a state with this remit is itself even a stable equilibrium. What kind of constitution would be best for safeguarding it? What is the appropriate combination of election, selection, and hereditary appointment when it comes to the offices of the state? What kinds of deviations from the remit are legitimate, assuming the central functions are faithfully executed? Should taxes be raised on assets or transfers? Indeed, there is nothing in or about the content and structure of our rights that could yield such knowledge. It is a question of political and economic *science*, not a question of the nature of justice.

Our natural rights provide an evaluative standard by which we judge political institutions and organisations as *just* and *unjust*, but if any justice whatsoever means tolerating – even perpetuating – some injustices, I do not take myself to have provided any guidance on how that should be done, even if I have provided an articulation of the basic currency at stake. An evaluative standard for institutions is not the same as a theory of ideal institutions.[2]

Individuals pursuing justice on their own (even if perfectly morally informed) do not necessarily thereby promote a just society. Given that others may not act justly, just persons must act together so as to best mitigate the injustice of others. As soon as they act with others, compromise is inevitable and essential, Decisions as to what to sacrifice for what is a *political* one – even in a stateless society. Even if we are anarchists, a stateless society will not always or necessarily ever be perfectly just, and we will always have to decide whether or not to tolerate or even perpetuate some injustice in order to avoid or remedy some other injustice.

Because this involves considering how our actions shape the environment in which others act, these actions are political and therefore our agency matters beyond our moral responsibility. Sure, we are not morally responsible for the actions of others, but if the goal is a *just society*, we must consider the causal relationship between our own actions and those of others.

I think that libertarian politics is mistaken in thinking that answers to these questions follow readily from an account of what freedom consists in. However, I also think liberal–egalitarians are mistaken in thinking that because libertarian politics might be mistaken, their claims about what freedom consists in must be too. Redistribution of wealth and the state provision of certain goods might be good for solidarity and nation-building, and these factors might have a positive feedback effect on the stability and/or scope of freedom, but that does not mean that freedom partially consists in receipt of goods from the state. Democracy might be good for limiting rent-creation and generating long-term stability and therefore have a positive feedback effect on liberty, but that does not mean that freedom partially consists in democracy.[3] The centralised power to tax may avert the need for unpredictable periodic plunder by political actors or for the need for political actors to appeal to oppressive and supernatural sources of legitimation,[4] but that does not mean that natural justice must include a duty of obedience to the fiscal state. We should be frank in admitting that our best chance in securing freedom will often involve denying ourselves and one another's freedom in other areas. Just because trade-offs are necessary and possible does not mean that the initial conflict is illusory.

Liberal–egalitarians tend to think that if a theory of justice says that *xyz* is a demand of justice, then there is some public policy or state institution or obvious and established political avenue for action *XYZ* that is therefore demanded.[5] I think this is a mistake. There need be no such visual parity between justice and government. However, it is also a mistake when libertarians think that since the content of justice is property rights, any political institution, organisation, or policy not directly and exclusively concerned with the protection of property is to be resisted. It is a mistake to think that conceptual truths about justice should mirror empirical truths about political economy. The content of justice is quite simple because its content is determined by that which all humans have in common; that is an abstraction. Politics is complex because it is determined not by abstractions but by real contingencies. Again, this does not mean that justice cannot provide an evaluative standard, but it cannot provide a road map to optimising that standard, certainly not alone. And when libertarians say "individuals have natural property rights, therefore taxation should be abolished," they are presuming that justice does provide such a road map.

It is quite clear what an individual needs to do to be just. We could write a list of actions they must abstain from and they could very feasible comply with it, simply through acting on the will to do so. However, it is *not* clear what a society must do in order for it to be just. Of course, we could write the same list and give it to everyone, and they could individually comply. But the difference is that for the individual, they can be just in their own actions regardless of whether other people are – they have that kind of control over themselves that they can keep their hands clean. On the presumption that some, even *many* members of society will engage in those actions that justice demands they abstain from, what should we do to get in their way or mitigate the damage? Even if we knew and agreed on what form those efforts should take, how should we organise the efforts themselves? For the individual to only be concerned with the justice of her own actions, she can think very simply – almost solipsistically, but for her to be concerned with justice everywhere, she must think strategically and politically.[6] And ultimately, research in political and economic science will tell us which of these strategies are likely to be successful and why, because it is well placed to identify causal mechanisms at the social level. The content of justice determines what the ends are, but political economy tells us the most strategically prudent means to those ends. Some of these means will be more just than others, but they will seldom involve merely conforming one's own actions with justice.

"[S]eek ye first the kingdom of God"[7] might seem to provide grounds for the Christian anarchist to divest herself of concern about worldly matters and simply order her own conduct so that she does not wrong other persons. At least then her soul is in order even if her society is not. I cannot see anything ethically wrong with the Christian anarchist, but I do not see them as liberal in any political sense, or tangibly pursuing justice in any meaningful sense. Liberalism is something that should be achieved on Earth, not merely within one's soul, and that means it must be achieved as far as possible among sinners.[8] Obviously, if everyone were perfectly just we would not need politics, least of all a state, but this is never going to be the case. So, if we want to establish justice, we must consider the political question of how our actions interact with those of the unjust. Questions of what positive steps must be taken to take up the slack of those who do not honour their negative obligations is not a question that can be answered by appealing to the structure or content of natural justice. Rather, the latter is presumed in order for the former to even be a question with any moral content and urgency at all.

Natural rights can tell us a lot about how property ought to be ordered. They tell us very precisely what right individuals have to particular resources when used in certain ways; which, given what we might know about how resources are actually used, is a great deal. It does not delegate difficult work to the cost–benefit calculations of law-and-economics researchers nor to bureau executives under a democratic mandate. Justice itself provides a final and determinate voice on how to deal with questions over river pollutants, spectrum allocation, airway easements, urban and rural public roads, etc. But the overarching account of rights does not in any obvious and straightforward way tell us how best to make sure those rights – or something as close to them as possible – are in fact safeguarded in our world.[9] That is not something that I believe a philosopher *as such* is best placed to know.

Notes

1. Of course, Steiner is in both these camps.
2. Christopher Freiman identifies the problems of "ideal institutional theory" at play in liberal–egalitarian theories (and even social contract theory much more broadly) (Freiman 2017, chap. 1), but I think it applies to the kind of institutional and policy prescriptions often made by libertarians as well.
3. On the relationship between modern redistribution and democracy with economic freedom, see North, Wallis, and Weingast (2009, esp. chap. 4).
4. On the relationship between fiscal consolidation and religious and economic freedom, see Johnson and Koyama (2019).
5. Byas and Christmas (2021).
6. Schmidtz (2017).
7. *The Bible* (Matthew 6: 33).
8. Saint Augustine (1984).
9. Levy (2018b, 2018a).

Bibliography

Alchian, Armen A. 1965. 'Some Economics of Property Rights'. *Il Politico* 30 (4): 816–29.

Anderson, Terry L. 1997. 'Conservation Native American Style'. *The Quarterly Review of Economics and Finance* 37: 769–85.

———. 2016. 'Native American Loved Private Property'. *Foundation for Economic Education* (blog). https://fee.org/articles/native-americans-loved-private-property/.

Annas, Julia. 1978. 'How Basic Are Basic Actions?'. *Proceedings of the Aristotelian Society* 78: 195–213.

Anscombe, G. E. M. 1963. *Intention.* 2nd ed. Cambridge: Harvard University Press.

Aquinas, Thomas. 1947. *Summa Theologica.* Translated by Fathers of the English Dominican Province. New York: Benziger.

Argenton, Carlo, and Enzo Rossi. Forthcoming. 'Property, Legitimacy, Ideology: A Reality Check'. *The Journal of Politics.*

Aristotle. 1981. *The Politics.* Translated by T. A. Sinclair. Revised. London: Penguin.

———. 2009. *Nichomachean Ethics.* Translated by W. D. Ross. Oxford: Oxford University Press.

Arneil, Barbara. 1996. *John Locke and America: The Defence of English Colonialism.* Oxford: Oxford University Press.

Arneson, Richard J. 1991. 'Lockean Self-Ownership: Towards a Demolition'. *Political Studies* 39 (1): 36–54.

Attas, Daniel. 2003. 'The Negative Principle of Just Appropriation'. *Canadian Journal of Philosophy* 33: 343–71.

———. 2006. 'Fragmenting Property'. *Law and Philosophy* 25 (1): 119–49.

———. 2008. 'Lockean Justifications of Intellectual Property'. In *Intellectual Property and Theories of Justice*, edited by Axel Gosseries, Alain Marciano, and Alain Strowel. Basingstoke: Palgrave Macmillan.

Bader, Ralf M. 2013. *Robert Nozick.* London: Bloomsbury Academic.

———. 2018. 'Moralizing Liberty'. In *Oxford Studies in Political Philosophy*, edited by David Sobel, Peter Vallentyne, and Steven Wall. Vol. 4. Oxford: Oxford University Press.

———. n.d. 'Liberty, Threats, and Ineligibility'. *Unpublished Draft.*

Barnett, Randy E. 1986. 'A Consent Theory of Contract'. *Columbia Law Review* 86: 269–321.

Becker, Lawrence C. 1977. *Property Rights: Philosophic Foundations*. London: Routledge.

Bell, Tom W. 2002. 'Indelicate Imbalancing in Copyright and Patent Law'. In *Copy Fights: The Future of Intellectual Property in the Information Age*, edited by Adam D. Thierer and Clyde Wayne Jr. Crews. Washington, DC: The Cato Institute.

Benson, Peter. 2019. *Justice in Transactions: A Theory of Contract Law*. Cambridge: The Belknap Press of Harvard University Press.

Berlin, Isaiah. 2002. 'Two Concepts of Liberty'. In *Four Essays on Liberty*, edited by Henry Hardy. Oxford: Oxford University Press.

Biasetti, Pierfrancesco. 2015. 'Infinite Regress and Hohfeld: A Comment on Hillel Steiner's "Directed Duties and Inalienable Rights"'. *Ethics* 126 (1): 139–52.

The Bible. 1611. King James.

Bicchieri, Cristina. 2006. *The Grammar of Society: The Nature and Dynamics of Social Norms*. Cambridge: Cambridge University Press.

Blackstone, William. 1893. *Commentaries on the Laws of England in Four Books*. Vol. 1. Philadelphia, PA: J. B. Lippincott.

Block, Matthew, and Walter E. Block. 1996. 'Roads, Bridges, Sunlight, and Private Property Rights'. *Journal Des Économistes et Des Études Humaines* 7: 351–62.

Block, Walter E. 1977. 'A Comment on "The Extraordinary Claim of Praxeology" by Professor Gutiérrez'. *Theory and Decision* 3: 377–87.

———. 2009. *The Privatization of Roads and Highways: Human and Economic Factors*. Auburn: The Ludwig von Mises Institute.

———. 2011. 'Review of Governing the Commons by Elinor Ostrom'. *Libertarian Papers* 3 (35).

Boétie, Etienne de la. 1942. *The Discourse of Voluntary Servitude*. Translated by Harry Kurz. New York: Columbia University Press.

Bradshaw, Karen, Billy Christmas, and Dean Lueck. 2020. 'Special Issue: Overlapping Resources and Mismatched Property Rights'. *International Journal of the Commons* 14 (1).

Bradshaw, Karen, and Dean Lueck. 2015. 'Contracting for Control of Landscape-Level Resources'. *Iowa Law Review* 100: 2507–49.

Bramwell, George. 1862. Bamford v. Turnley, 122 27. Court of the Exchequer.

Breakey, Hugh. 2011. 'Two Concepts of Property: Ownership of Things and Property in Activities'. *The Philosophical Forum* 42 (3): 239–65.

Brennan, Geoffrey, and James M. Buchanan. 2000. *The Reason of Rules: Constitutional Political Economy*. Vol. 10. The Collected Works of James M. Buchanan. Indianapolis: Liberty Fund.

Brennan, Jason. 2015. 'Elinor Ostrom, Governing the Commons'. In *The Oxford Handbook of Classics in Contemporary Political Theory*, edited by Jacob T. Levy, np. Online: Oxford University Press. www.oxfordhandbooks.com/view/10.1093/oxfordhb/9780198717133.001.0001/oxfordhb-9780198717133-e-61.

Brennan, Jason, and David Schmidtz. 2010. *A Brief History of Liberty*. Oxford: Wiley-Blackwell.

Brennan, Jason, and Bas van der Vossen. 2018. 'The Myths of the Self-Ownership Thesis'. In *The Routledge Handbook of Libertarianism*, edited by Jason Brennan, Bas van der Vossen, and David Schmidtz. New York: Routledge.

Bryan, Ben. 2017. 'The Conventionalist Challenge to Natural Rights Theory'. *Social Theory and Practice* 43 (3): 569–87.

Byas, Jason Lee, and Billy Christmas. 2021. 'Methodological Anarchism'. In *The Routledge Handbook of Anarchy and Anarchist Thought*, edited by Gary Chartier and Chad Van Shoelandt. New York: Routledge.

Cardozo, Benjamin N. 1928. *The Paradoxes of Legal Science*. New York: Columbia University Press.

Carnegy-Arbuthnott, Hannah. 2019. 'My Body and Other Objects: The Internal Limits of Self-Ownership'. *European Journal of Philosophy* 27 (3): 723–40.

Carson, Kevin A. 2006. 'Contract Feudalism'. *Libertarian Alliance, Economic Notes* (105).

———. 2007. *Studies in Mutualist Political Economy*. Fayetteville: Self-published.

———. 2011. 'Communal Property: A Libertarian Analysis'. 13. Center for a Stateless Society. http://c4ss.org/wp-content/uploads/2012/02/Communal-Property.pdf.

Carter, Ian. 1999. *A Measure of Freedom*. New York: Oxford University Press.

Christmas, Billy. 2017. 'Incommensurability and Property Rights in the Natural Environment'. *Environmental Politics* 26 (3): 502–20.

———. 2018a. 'Rescuing the Libertarian Non-Aggression Principle'. *Moral Philosophy and Politics* 5 (2): 305–22.

———. 2018b. 'Responsibility, Respect, and Justice: Skepticism About Metanorms'. *Reason Papers* 39 (2): 48–59.

———. 2019a. 'Hugo Grotius and Private Property'. *Raisons Politiques* 73: 21–38.

———. 2019b. 'Social Equality and Liberty'. In *The Dialectics of Liberty: Exploring the Context of Human Freedom*, edited by Chris Matthew Sciabarra, Edward W. Younkins, and Roger E. Bissel. Lanham: Rowman and Littlefield.

———. 2019c. 'A Reformulation of the Structure of a Set of Compossible Rights'. *The Philosophical Quarterly* 69 (275): 221–34.

———. 2020a. 'Ambidextrous Lockeanism'. *Economics and Philosophy* 36: 193–215.

———. 2020b. 'Answering the Conventionalist Challenge to Natural Rights Theory', *Res Publica*.

———. 2021. 'Against Kantian Statism'. *The Journal of Politics*.

Claeys, Eric R. 2009. 'Property 101: Is Property a Thing or a Bundle?' *Seattle University Law Review* 32: 617–31.

———. 2013a. 'Intellectual Usufructs: Trade Secrets, Hote News, and the Usufructuary Paradigm at Common Law'. In *Intellectual Property and the Common Law*, edited by Shyam Balganesh. Cambridge: Cambridge University Press.

———. 2013b. 'Productive Use in Acquisition, Accession, and Labour Theory'. In *Philosophical Foundations of Property Law*, edited by James E. Penner and Henry E. Smith. Oxford: Oxford University Press.

———. 2017. 'Labor, Exclusion, and Flourishing in Property Law'. *North Carolina Law Review* 95: 413–91.

———. 2018. 'Intellectual Property and Practical Reason'. *Jurisprudence* 9 (2): 251–75.

Coase, Ronald H. 1937. 'The Nature of the Firm'. *Economica* 4: 386–405.

Cohen, G. A. 1979. 'The Labour Theory of Value and the Concept of Exploitation'. *Philosophy and Public Affairs* 8: 338–60.

———. 1982. 'Freedom, Justice, and Capitalism'. *New Left Review* 126: 3–16.

———. 1983. 'The Structure of Proletarian Unfreedom'. *Philosophy and Public Affairs* 14: 3–33.

———. 1985a. 'Are Workers Forced to Sell Their Labour Power?'. *Philosophy and Public Affairs* 14 (1): 99–105.

———. 1985b. 'Self-Ownership, World-Ownership, and Equality'. In *Justice and Equality Here and Now*, edited by Frank Lucash. Ithaca: Cornell University Press.

———. 1986. 'Self-Ownership, World Ownership, and Equality: Part II'. *Social Philosophy and Policy* 3 (2): 77–96.

———. 1989. *History, Labour, and Freedom*. Oxford: Oxford University Press.

———. 1995. *Self-Ownership, Freedom, and Equality*. Cambridge: Cambridge University Press.

———. 2009. *Why Not Socialism?* Princeton, NJ: Princeton University Press.

Cox, Gary W., Douglass C. North, and Barry R. Weingast. Unpublished manuscript. 'The Violence Trap: A Political-Economic Approach to the Problems of Development'. https://papers.ssrn.com/sol3/papers.cfm?abstract_id=2370622.

Cwik, Bryan. 2016. 'Property Rights in Non-Rival Goods'. *The Journal of Political Philosophy* 24: 470–86.

Danto, Arthur C. 1965. 'Basic Actions'. *American Philosophical Quarterly* 2 (2): 141–48.

Danto, Arthur C., and Sidney Morgenbesser. 1963. 'What We Can Do'. *The Journal of Philosophy* 60 (15): 435–45.

Davidson, Donald. 1963. 'Actions, Reasons, and Causes'. *The Journal of Philosophy* 60: 685–700.

Day, J. P. 1966. 'Locke on Property'. *The Philosophical Quarterly* 16 (64): 207–20.

de Araujo, Marcelo. 2009. 'Hugo Grotius, Contractualism, and the Concept of Private Property: An Institutionalist Perspective'. *History of Philosophy Quarterly* 26: 353–71.

De Jasay, Anthony. 1997. *Against Politics: On Government, Anarchy, and Order*. London: Routledge.

DeLong, James V. 2002. 'Defending Intellectual Property'. In *Copy Fights: The Future of Intellectual Property in the Information Age*, edited by Adam D. Thierer and Clyde Wayne Jr. Crews. Washington, DC: The Cato Institute.

Dennet, Daniel C. 2006. 'Higher-Order Truths About Chmess'. *Topoi* 25: 39–41.

Den Uyl, Douglas J., and Douglas B. Rasmussen. 1991. *Liberty and Nature: An Aristotelian Defense of Liberal Order*. LaSalle: Open Court Publishing Company.

———. 2005. *Norms of Liberty: A Perfectionist Basis for Non-Perfectionist Politics*. University Park: Pennsylvania State University Press.

———. 2006. 'The Myth of Atomism'. *The Review of Metaphysics* 59 (4): 841–68.

———. 2016. *The Perfectionist Turn: From Metanorms to Metaethics*. Edinburgh: Edinburgh University Press.

———. 2018. 'The Need for Metanormativity: A Response to Christmas'. *Reason Papers* 39 (2): 60–68.
———. 2020. *The Realist Turn: Beyond Constructivism*. Basingstoke: Palgrave Macmillan.
Douglas, Simon, and Ben McFarlane. 2013. 'Defining Property Rights'. In *Philosophical Foundations of Property Law*, edited by James E. Penner and Henry E. Smith. Oxford: Oxford University Press.
Dowding, Keith. 2011. 'Republican Freedom, Rights, and the Coalition Problem'. *Politics, Philosophy and Economics* 10 (3): 301–22.
Duarte d'Almeida, Luís. 2016. 'Fundamental Legal Concepts: The Hohfeldian Framework'. *Philosophy Compass* 11 (20): 554–69.
Dworkin, Ronald. 1984. 'Rights as Trumps'. In *Theories of Rights*, edited by Jeremy Waldron. Oxford: Oxford University Press.
———. 2000. *Sovereign Virtue: The Theory and Practice of Equality*. Cambridge: Harvard University Press.
Eleftheriadis, Pavlos. 2008. *Legal Rights*. Oxford: Oxford University Press.
Ellickson, Robert C. 1993. 'Property in Land'. *The Yale Law Journal* 102: 1315–400.
Enoch, David. 2002. 'A Right to Violate One's Duty'. *Law and Philosophy* 21: 355–84.
Epstein, Richard A. 1979a. 'Possession as the Root of Title'. *Georgia Law Review* 13: 1221–43.
———. 1979b. 'Nuisance Law: Corrective Justice and Its Utilitarian Constraints'. *Journal of Legal Studies* 8 (1): 49–102.
———. 1985. *Takings: Private Property and the Power of Eminent Domain*. Cambridge: Harvard University Press.
———. 1990. 'Property and Necessity'. *Harvard Journal of Law and Public Policy* 13 (2): 2–9.
———. 1994. 'The Optimal Mix of Private and Common Property'. *Social Philosophy and Policy* 11: 17–41.
———. 1997. *Simple Rules for a Complex World*. Cambridge: Harvard University Press.
———. 1998. *Principles for a Free Society: Reconciling Individual Liberty with the Common Good*. Cambridge: Basic Books.
———. 2005a. 'Liberty versus Property – Cracks in the Foundations of Copyright Law'. *San Diego Law Review* 42: 1–28.
———. 2005b. 'The Not So Minimum Content of Natural Law'. *Oxford Journal of Legal Studies* 25 (2): 219–55.
———. 2009. 'Property Rights, State of Nature Theory, and Environmental Protection'. *New York University Journal of Law and Liberty* 4: 1–35.
———. 2015. 'From Natural Law to Social Welfare: Theoretical Principles and Practical Applications'. *Iowa Law Review* 100: 1743–72.
———. Forthcoming. 'Property Rights: Long and Skinny'. *International Journal of the Commons* 14 (1).
Essert, Christopher. 2013. 'The Office of Ownership'. *University of Toronto Law Journal* 63: 418–61.
———. 2016. 'Property and Homelessness'. *Philosophy and Public Affairs* 44 (4): 266–95.

Exdell, John. 1977. 'Distributive Justice: Nozick on Property Rights'. *Ethics* 87: 142–49.Haakonssen, Knud. 1985. 'Hugo Grotius and the History of Political Thought'. *Political Theory* 13 (2): 239–65.

Halpin, Andrew. 1991. 'More Comments on Rights and Claims'. *Law and Philosophy* 10: 271–310.

Haney, Bert E. 1936. Hinman v. Pacific Air Transport, 755 84. Circuit Court of Appeals, Ninth Circuit.

Hardin, Garret. 1968. 'The Tragedy of the Commons'. *Science* 162: 1243–48.

Harris, James W. 1986. 'Ownership of Land in English Law'. In *The Legal Mind: Essays for Tony Honoré*, edited by Neil MacCormick and Peter Birks. Oxford: Clarendon Press.

Hart, H. L. A. 1982. *Essays on Bentham*. Oxford: Oxford University Press.

———. 1985. *Essays in Jurisprudence and Philosophy*. Oxford: Oxford University Press.

———. 1994. *The Concept of Law*. 2nd ed. Oxford: Clarendon Press.

Harvey, David. 2003. *The New Imperialism*. New York: Oxford University Press.

Hasan, Rafeeq. 2018. 'The Provisionality of Property Rights in Kant's Doctrine of Right'. *Canadian Journal of Philosophy* 48: 850–76.

Hayek, F. A. 1948. *Individualism and Economic Order*. Chicago: The University of Chicago Press.

———. 1982. *Law, Legislation, and Liberty: A New Statement of the Liberal Principles of Justice and Political Economy*. London: Routledge.

———. *The Constitution of Liberty*. Edited by Ronald Hamowy. The Definitive Edition. Chicago: The University of Chicago Press.

Heller, Michael A., and Hanoch Dagan. 2001. 'The Liberal Commons'. *The Yale Law Journal* 110 (4): 549–623.

Herstein, Ori J. 2012. 'Defending the Right to Do Wrong'. *Law and Philosophy* 31: 343–65.

Hettinger, Edwin C. 1989. 'Justifying Intellectual Property'. *Philosophy and Public Affairs* 18 (1): 31–52.

Hicks, John R. 1939. 'The Foundations of Welfare Economics'. *The Economic Journal* 49: 696–712.

Hobbes, Thomas. 1983. *De Cive*. Edited by Howard Warrender. Oxford: Clarendon Press.

———. 2012. *Leviathan*. Edited by Malcolm Norman. Oxford: Oxford University Press.

Hodgson, Louis-Philippe. 2010a. 'Kant on Property Rights and the State'. *Kantian Review* 15 (1): 57–87.

———. 2010b. 'Kant on the Right to Freedom: A Defence'. *Ethics* 120 (4): 791–819.

Hohfeld, Wesley Newcomb. 1913. 'Some Fundamental Legal Conceptions as Applied in Judicial Reasoning'. *The Yale Law Review* 23: 16–59.

———. 1917. 'Fundamental Legal Conceptions as Applied in Judicial Reasoning'. *The Yale Law Review* 26: 710–70.

Holcombe, Randall G. 2005. 'Common Property in Anarcho-Capitalism'. *Journal of Libertarian Studies* 19: 3–29.

Holmes, Stephen, and Cass R. Sunstein. 2013. *The Cost of Rights: Why Liberty Depends on Taxes*. New York: W. W. Norton.

Honoré, Anthony M. 1961. 'Ownership'. In *Oxford Essays in Jurisprudence*, edited by A. G. Guest. London: Oxford University Press.

Hoppe, Hans-Hermann. 2004. 'Property, Causality, and Liability'. *The Quarterly Journal of Austrian Economics* 7: 87–95.

———. 2006. *The Economics and Ethics of Private Property*. 2nd ed. Auburn: The Ludwig von Mises Institute.

———. 2010. *A Theory of Socialism and Capitalism*. Auburn: The Ludwig von Mises Institute.

———. 2011. 'Of Private, Common, and Public Property and the Rationale for Total Privatization'. *Libertarian Papers* 3: 1–13.

———. 2018. *Getting Libertarianism Right*. Auburn: The Ludwig von Mises Institute.

Hornsby, Jennifer. 1979. 'Actions and Identities'. *Analysis* 39 (4): 195–201.

Horwitz, Morton J. 1979. *The Transformation of American Law, 1780–1860*. Cambridge: Harvard University Press.

Huber, Jakob. 2020. 'Putting Proximity in Its Place'. *Contemporary Political Theory*.

Hume, David. 1739. *A Treatise of Human Nature*. Edited by Lewis Amherst Selby-Brigge. 3 vols. Oxford: The Clarendon Press.

———. 1987. *Essays Moral, Political, Literary,* edited by Eugene F. Miller, Revised ed. Indianapolis: Liberty Fund.

———. 1902. *Enquiries Concerning the Human Understanding and Concerning the Principles of Morals*, edited by L. A. Selby-Bigge, 2nd ed. Oxford: Clarendon Press.

Hunt, Lester H. 2015. *Anarchy, State, and Utopia: An Advanced Guide*. Chichester: Wiley-Blackwell.

Inoue, Akira. 2007. 'Can a Right of Self-Ownership Be Robust?'. *Law and Philosophy* 26 (6): 575–87.

Jefferson, Thomas. 1950. *The Papers of Thomas Jefferson*. Edited by James P. McClure. Princeton, NJ: Princeton University Press.

Johnson, Noel D., and Mark Koyama. 2019. *Persecution and Toleration: The Long Road to Religious Freedom*. Cambridge: Cambridge University Press.

Kaldor, Nicholas. 1939. 'Welfare Propositions of Economics and Interpersonal Comparisons of Utility'. *The Economic Journal* 49: 549–52.

Kamm, F. M. 2013. 'Nonconsequentialism'. In *The Blackwell Guide to Ethical Theory*, edited by H. Lafollette and I. Persson. Oxford: Wiley-Blackwell.

Kant, Immanuel. 1991. *The Metaphysics of Morals*. Edited by Mary Gregor. Cambridge: Cambridge University Press.

———. 1998. *Critique of Pure Reason*. Translated by Paul Guyer and Allen W. Wood. Cambridge: Cambridge University Press.

Katz, Larissa. 2008. 'Exclusion and Exclusivity in Property Law'. *University of Toronto Law Journal* 58: 275–315.

Kinsella, N. Stephan. 2008. *Against Intellectual Property*. Auburn: The Ludwig von Mises Institute.

Klein, Benjamin, Robert G. Crawford, and Armen A. Alchian. 1978. 'Vertical Integration, Appropriable Rents, and the Competitive Contracting Process'. *Journal of Law and Economics* 21: 297–326.

Klimchuk, Dennis. 2013. 'Property and Necessity'. In *Philosophical Foundations of Property Law*, edited by James E. Penner and Henry E. Smith. Oxford: Oxford University Press.

———. 2018. 'Grotius on Property and the Right of Necessity'. *Journal of the History of Philosophy* 56 (2): 239–60.

Kogelmann, Brian, and Benjamin G. Ogden. 2018. 'Enough and as Good: A Formal Model of Lockean First Appropriation'. *American Journal of Political Science* 62: 682–94.

Korsgaard, Christine. 1996. *The Sources of Normativity*. Cambridge: Cambridge University Press.

Kramer, Matthew H. 1998. 'Rights Without Trimmings'. In *A Debate Over Rights: Philosophical Enquiries*, edited by Matthew H. Kramer, Nigel E. Simmonds, and Hillel Steiner. Oxford: Oxford University Press.

———. 2010. 'Refining the Interest Theory of Rights'. *American Journal of Jurisprudence* 55 (1): 31–39.

———. 2017. 'In Defence of the Interest Theory of Right-Holding: Rejoinders to Leif Wenar on Rights'. In *New Essays on the Nature of Rights*, edited by Mark McBride. Oxford: Hart Publishing.

Kramer, Matthew H., and Hillel Steiner. 2005. 'Theories of Rights: Is There a Third Way?'. *Oxford Journal of Legal Studies* 55 (2): 281–310.

Kurki, Visa A. J. 2017. 'Hohfeldian Infinites: Why Not to Worry'. *Res Publica* 23: 137–46.

Kymlicka, Will. 2002. *Contemporary Political Philosophy: An Introduction*. 2nd ed. Oxford: Oxford University Press.

Layman, Daniel. Forthcoming. 'Republican Liberty as Liberty within Rights'. In *Oxford Studies in Political Philosophy*, edited by Peter Vallentyne, Steven Wall, and David Sobel. Vol. 8.

Levine, Bruce L. 1986. 'The Tragedy of the Commons and the Comedy of Community: The Commons in History'. *Journal of Community Psychology* 14: 18–99.

Levy, Jacob T. 2017a. 'Against Fraternity: Democracy Without Solidarity'. In *The Strains of Commitment: The Political Sources of Solidarity in Diverse Societies*, edited by Keith Banting and Will Kymlicka. Oxford: Oxford University Press.

———. 2017b. 'Contra Politanism'. *European Journal of Political Theory* Online first.

———. 2018a. 'Political Libertarianism'. In *The Cambridge Handbook of Classical Liberal Thought*, edited by M. Todd Henderson. Cambridge: Cambridge University Press.

———. 2018b. 'Toward a Non-Lockean Libertarianism'. In *The Routledge Handbook of Libertarianism*, edited by Jason Brennan, Bas van der Vossen, and David Schmidtz. New York: Routledge.

Lewis, David. 1969. *Convention: A Philosophical Study*. Oxford: Blackwell.

Lewis, John. 1900. A Treatise on the Law of Eminent Domain in the United States. 2nd ed. Chicago: Callaghan & Co.

Lifshitz, Yael. n.d. 'Horizontal Property'. *Unpublished Draft*.

Lippert-Rasmussen, Kasper. 2008. 'Against Self-Ownership: There Are No Fact-Insensitive Ownership Rights over One's Body'. *Philosophy and Public Affairs* 36 (1): 86–118.

Lloyd, William Forster. 1833. 'Two Lectures on the Checks to Population'. *Population and Development Review* 6: 473–96.

Locke, John. 1764. *Two Treatises of Civil Government.* Edited by Thomas Hollis. London: A. Millar.

Lomasky, Loren E. 1987. *Persons, Rights, and the Moral Community.* Oxford: Oxford University Press.

Long, Roderick T. 1993. 'Abortion, Abandonment, and Positive Rights: The Limits of Compulsory Altruism'. *Social Philosophy and Policy* 10 (1): 166–91.

———. 1995. 'The Libertarian Case Against Intellectual Property'. *Formulations* 3 (1). http://freenation.org/a/f31l1.html.

———. 1999. 'The Irrelevance of Responsibility'. *Social Philosophy and Policy* 16 (2): 118–45.

———. 2000. *Reason and Value: Aristotle Versus Rand.* Washington, DC: The Objectivist Center.

———. 2001. 'Equality: The Unknown Ideal'. *Mises Daily* (blog). https://mises.org/library/equality-unknown-ideal.

———. 2002. 'Robert Nozick, Philosopher of Liberty'. *The Freeman: Ideas on Liberty* 52: 30–33.

———. 2004. 'This Land Is Mine'. *Austro-Athenian Empire* (blog). http://praxeology.net/unblog03-04.htm#23.

———. 2005. 'Liberty: The Other Equality'. *Foundation for Economic Education* (blog). http://fee.org/articles/liberty-the-other equality/.

———. 2012a. 'Self-Ownership and External Property'. *Bleeding Heart Libertarians* (blog). https://bleedingheartlibertarians.com/2012/04/self-ownership-and-external-property/.

———. 2012b. 'Spencer, Hodgskin, and Land Rights'. *Austro-Athenian Empire* (blog). https://aaeblog.com/2012/05/18/spencer- hodgskin-and-land-rights/.

———. 2014. 'Why Libertarians Believe There Is Only One Right'. *Center for a Stateless Society* (blog). https://c4ss.org/content/25648.

———. 2015. 'Review of Rationalism, Pluralism, and Freedom by Jacob T. Levy'. *Reason.* https://reason.com/2015/09/23/two-liberalisms/.

———. Unpublished manuscript. *Wittgenstein, Austrian Economics, and the Logic of Action: Praxeological Investigations.* http://praxeology.net/wiggy-draft.pdf.

Lueck, Dean. 1995. 'The Rule of First Possession and the Design of the Law'. *The Journal of Law and Economics* 38 (2): 393–436.

Machan, Tibor R. 2001. 'The Perils of Positive Rights'. *Foundation for Economic Education* (blog). https://fee.org/articles/the-perils-of- positive-rights/.

———. 2006. *Libertarianism Defended.* Aldershot: Ashgate Publishing.

MacCallum, Gerald C., Jr. 1967. 'Negative and Positive Freedom'. *The Philosophical Review* 76 (3): 312–34.

MacCormick, Neil. 2008. *Institutions of Law: An Essay in Legal Theory.* Oxford: Oxford University Press.

Mack, Eric. 1989. 'Moral Individualism: Agent-Relativity and Deontic Restraints'. *Social Philosophy and Policy* 7 (1): 81–111.

———. 1990. 'Self-Ownership and the Right of Property'. *The Monist* 79: 519–43.

———. 1995. 'The Self-Ownership Proviso: A New and Improved Lockean Proviso'. *Social Philosophy and Policy* 12: 186–218.
———. 1998. 'Deontic Restrictions Are Not Agent-Relative Restrictions'. *Social Philosophy and Policy* 15 (2): 61–83.
———. 2002. 'Self-Ownership, Marxism, and Egalitarianism Part II: Challenges to the Self-Ownership Thesis'. *Politics, Philosophy and Economics* 1: 237–76.
———. 2006. 'Hayek on Justice and the Order of Actions'. In *The Cambridge Companion to Hayek*. Cambridge: Cambridge University Press.
———. 2010. 'The Natural Right of Property'. *Social Philosophy and Policy* 27: 53–78.
———. 2013. 'John Locke on Property'. *Liberty Matters* (blog). https://oll.libertyfund.org/pages/lm-locke#leadessay.
———. 2015. 'Elbow Room for Rights'. In *Oxford Studies in Political Philosophy*, edited by David Sobel, Peter Vallentyne, and Steven Wall. Vol. 1. Oxford: Oxford University Press.
———. 2018. *Libertarianism*. Cambridge: Polity Press.
Mandeville, Bernard. 1988. *The Fable of the Bees: Or, Private Vices, Public Benefits*. Edited by F. B. Kaye. Oxford: Oxford University Press.
Martin, Jane R. 1972. 'Basic Actions and Simple Actions'. *American Philosophical Quarterly* 9 (1): 59–68.
Marx, Karl. 1970. 'Critique of the Gotha Programme'. In *Marx/Engels Selected Works*. Vol. 3. Moscow: Progress Publishers.
———. 1994. 'On the Jewish Question'. In *Marx: Early Political Writings*, edited by Joseph J. O'Malley. Cambridge: Cambridge University Press.
Mautner, Thomas. 1982. 'Locke on Original Appropriation'. *American Philosophical Quarterly* 19: 259–70.
McCall, Grant S., and Karl Widerquist. 2015. 'Myths about the State of Nature and the Reality of Stateless Societies'. *Analyse und Kritik* 37: 233–57.
———. 2017. *Prehistoric Myths in Modern Political Philosophy*. Edinburgh: Edinburgh University Press.
———. Forthcoming. *The Prehistory of Private Property: Implications for Modern Political Theory*. Edinburgh University Press.
McKean, Margaret, and Elinor Ostrom. 1995. 'Common Property Regimes in the Forest: Just a Relic From the Past?'. *Unasylva* 46: 3–5.
Menger, Carl. 2007. *Principles of Economics*. Translated by James Dingwall and Bert F. Hoselitz. Auburn: The Ludwig von Mises Institute.
Merrill, Thomas W. 1998. 'Property and the Right to Exclude'. *Nebraska Law Review* 77 (4): 730–55.
Merrill, Thomas W., and Henry E. Smith. 2017. *Property: Principles and Policies*. 3rd ed. New York: Foundation Press.
Messina, J. P. 2019. 'Kant's Provisionality Thesis'. *Kantian Review* 24: 439–46.
Mildenberger, Carl David. 2020. *Commutative Justice: A Liberal Theory of Just Exchange*. London: Routledge.
Mills, Charles. 1997. *The Racial Contract*. Ithaca: Cornell University Press.
Mises, Ludwig von. 2007. *Human Action: A Treatise on Economics*. Edited by Bettina Bien Greaves. 4 vols. Indianapolis: Liberty Fund.
Moller, Dan. 2017. 'Property and the Creation of Value'. *Economics and Philosophy* 33: 1–23.

Mossoff, Adam. 2002. 'Locke's Labor Lost'. *University of Chicago Law School Roundtable* 9: 155–64.

———. 2003. 'What Is Property? Putting the Pieces Back Together'. *Arizona Law Review* 45: 371–443.

———. 2009. 'Exclusion and Exclusive Use in Patent Law'. *Harvard Journal of Law and Technology* 22 (2): 321–79.

———. 2011. 'The False Promise of the Right to Exclude'. *Econ Journal Watch* 8 (3): 255–64.

———. 2012. 'Saving Locke from Marx: The Labor Theory of Value in Intellectual Property Theory'. *Social Philosophy and Policy* 29 (2): 283–317.

———. 2019. 'Institutional Design in Patent Law: Private Property Rights or Regulatory Entitlements'. *Southern California Law Review* 92: 921–47.

Mossoff, Adam, and Eric R. Claeys. 2019. 'Patent Injunctions, Economics, and Rights'. *Journal of Legal Studies* 49: 51–71.

Mulkeen, Nicola. 2019. 'Rescuing Self-Ownership: Tackling the Pollution Problem'. *Critical Review of International Social and Political Philosophy* 22 (6): 660–80.

Nagel, Thomas. 1975. 'Libertarianism Without Foundations: Review of Anarchy, State, and Utopia by Robert Nozick'. *The Yale Law Journal* 85 (1): 136–49.

Narveson, Jan. 2006. 'Libertarianism: A Philosophical Introduction'. *Against Politics* (blog). http://againstpolitics.com/jan-narveson-libertarianism-a-philosophical-introduction/.

Newman, Chirstopher M. 2018. 'Using Things, Defining Property'. In *Property Theory: Legal and Political Perspectives*, edited by James E. Penner and Michael Otsuka. Cambridge: Cambridge University Press.

Nieswandt, Katharina. 2019. 'Beyond Frontier Town: Do Early Modern Theories of Property Apply to Capitalist Economies?'. *Ethical Theory and Moral Practice* 22 (4): 909–23.

North, Douglas C. 1991. 'Institutions'. *Journal of Economic Perspectives* 5 (1): 97–112.

North, Douglass C., John Joseph Wallis, and Barry R. Weingast. 2009. *Violence and Social Orders: A Conceptual Framework for Interpreting Recorded Human History*. Cambridge: Cambridge University Press.

Nozick, Robert. 1969. 'Coercion'. In *Philosophy, Science, and Method: Essays in Honor of Ernest Nagel*, edited by Sidney Morgenbesser, Morton White, and Patrick Suppes. New York: St. Martin's Press.

———. 1974. *Anarchy, State, and Utopia*. New York: Basic Books.

———. July 26, 2011. *An Interview with Julian Sanchez*. http://www.juliansanchez.com/an-interview-with-robert-nozick-july-26-2001/12/5/17.

Olsaretti, Serena. 1998. 'Freedom, Force and Choice: Against the Rights-Based Definition of Voluntariness'. *The Journal of Political Philosophy* 6 (1): 53–78.

———. 2004. *Liberty, Desert and the Market: A Philosophical Study*. Cambridge: Cambridge University Press.

———. 2007. 'Debate: The Concept of Voluntariness – A Reply'. *The Journal of Political Philosophy* 16 (1): 112–21.

———. 2013. 'Coercion and Libertarianism: A Reply to Gordon Barnes'. *Analysis* 73 (2): 295–99.

Olsen, Mancur. 1965. *The Logic of Collective Action: Public Goods and the Theory of Groups*. Cambridge: Harvard University Press.

O'Neill, Onora. 1976. 'Robert Nozick's Entitlements'. *Theoria* 19: 468–81.

Ostrom, Elinor. 1990. *Governing the Commons: The Evolution of Institutions for Collective Action*. Cambridge: Cambridge University Press.

Otsuka, Michael. 1998. 'Self-Ownership and Equality: A Lockean Reconciliation'. *Philosophy and Public Affairs* 27: 65–92.

———. 2003. *Libertarianism Without Inequality*. Oxford: Clarendon Press.

———. 2006. 'Comment Être Libertarian Sans Être Inégalitaire'. *Raisons Politiques* 23: 9–22.

Otsuka, Michael, Hillel Steiner, and Peter Vallentyne. 2005. 'Why Left-Libertarianism Is Not Incoherent, Indeterminate, or Irrelevant: A Reply to Fried'. *Philosophy and Public Affairs* 33: 201–15.

Øverland, Gerhard. 2007. 'The Right to Do Wrong'. *Law and Philosophy* 26: 47–66.

Overton, Richard. 2014. *An Arrow Against All Tyrants and Tyranny*. Edited by David M. Hart and Ross Kenyon. Vol. 3. Tracts on Liberty by the Levellers and Their Critics. Indianapolis: Liberty Fund.

Pallikkathayil, Japa. 2010. 'Deriving Morality from Politics: Rethinking the Formula of Humanity'. *Ethics* 121 (1): 116–47.

———. 2011. 'The Possibility of Choice: Three Accounts of the Problem with Coercion'. *Philosophers' Imprint* 11 (16): 1–20.

Palmer, Tom G. 1990. 'Are Patents and Copyrights Morally Justified? The Philosophy of Property Rights and Ideal Objects'. *Harvard Journal of Law and Public Policy* 13: 817–65.

Parry, Geraint. 1978. *John Locke*. London: George Allen & Unwin.

Penner, James E. 1996. 'The "Bundle of Rights" Picture of Property'. *UCLA Law Review* 43: 711–820.

———. 1997. *The Idea of Property in Law*. Oxford: Clarendon Press.

Pettit, Philip. 1999. *Republicanism: A Theory of Freedom and Government*. Oxford: Oxford University Press.

———. 2012. *On the People's Terms: A Republican Theory and Model of Democracy*. Cambridge: Cambridge University Press.

Piano, Ennio, and Alexander William Salter. 2020. 'The Fundamental Coase of Development: Property Rights Foundation of the Effective State'. *Journal of Institutional Economics* Online first.

Quong, Jonathan. 2015. 'Proportionality, Liability, and Defensive Harm'. *Philosophy and Public Affairs* 43: 144–73.

———. 2017. 'A Comment on Ripstein's Reclamation'. *Journal of Applied Philosophy* 34 (1): 31–37.

———. 2018. 'Consequentialism, Deontology, Contractualism, and Equality'. In *The Oxford Handbook of Distributive Justice*, edited by Serena Olsaretti. Oxford: Oxford University Press.

Radin, Max. 1929. 'Correlation'. *Columbia Law Review* 29: 901–5.

———. 1938. 'A Restatement of Hohfeld'. *Harvard Law Review* 51: 1141–64.

Railton, Peter. 1985. 'Locke, Stock, and Peril: Natural Property Right, Pollution and Risk'. In *To Breathe Freely: Risk, Consent, and Air*, edited by Mary Gibson. Totowa: Rowman and Allanheld.

Rainbolt, George W. 2006. *The Concept of Rights*. Dordrecht: Springer.

Rand, Ayn. 1964. 'The Ethics of Emergencies'. In *The Virtue of Selfishness*. New York: Signet.
———. 1967. 'Patents and Copyrights'. In *Capitalism: The Unknown Ideal*. New York: Signet.
Rawls, John. 1955. 'Two Concepts of Rules'. *The Philosophical Review* 64: 3–32.
———. 1980. 'Kantian Constructivism in Moral Theory'. *Journal of Philosophy* 77 (9): 515–72.
———. 1999. *A Theory of Justice*. Revised. Cambridge: The Belknap Press of Harvard University Press.
Raz, Joseph. 1986. *The Morality of Freedom*. Oxford: Oxford University Press.
———. 1994. *Ethics in the Public Domain*. Revised. Oxford: Oxford University Press.
Richards, Norvin. 1976. 'E Pluribus Unum: A Defense of Davidson's Individuation of Action'. *Philosophical Studies* 29: 191–98.
Ripstein, Arthur. 2004. 'Authority and Coercion'. *Philosophy and Public Affairs* 32: 2–25.
———. 2006. 'Private Order and Public Justice: Kant and Rawls'. *Virginia Law Review* 92: 1391–1438.
———. 2008. 'Hindering a Hindrance to Freedom'. *Jahrbuch Für Recht Und Ethik* 16: 227–50.
———. 2009. *Force and Freedom: Kant's Legal and Political Philosophy*. Cambridge: Harvard University Press.
———. 2013. 'Possession and Use'. In *Philosophical Foundations of Property Law*, edited by James E. Penner and Henry E. Smith. New York: Oxford University Press.
———. 2012. 'Kant and the Circumstances of Justice'. In *Kant's Political Theory: Interpretations and Applications*, edited by Elisabeth Ellis. University Park: Pennsylvania State University Press.
———. 2017. 'Reclaiming Proportionality'. *Journal of Applied Philosophy* 34 (1): 1–18.
Risse, Mathias. 2004. 'Does Left-Libertarianism Have Coherent Foundations?'. *Politics, Philosophy and Economics* 3 (3): 337–64.
Rose, Carol M. 1985. 'Possession as the Origin of Property'. *University of Chicago Law Review* 52: 73–88.
———. 1986. 'The Comedy of the Commons: Commerce, Custom, and Inherently Public Property'. *University of Chicago Law Review* 53: 711–81.
———. 1998. 'The Several Futures of Property: Of Cyberspace and Folk Tales, Emission Trades and Ecosystems'. *Minnesota Law Review* 83: 129–82.
Rosenblatt, Helena. 2018. *The Lost History of Liberalism: From Ancient Rome to the Twenty-First Century*. Princeton, NJ: Princeton University Press.
Rothbard, Murray N. 1976. 'Praxeology: The Methodology of Austrian Economics'. In *The Foundations of Modern Austrian Economics*, edited by Edwin G. Dolan. Kansas City: Sheed and Ward.
———. 1997. 'Law, Property Rights, and Air Pollution'. In *The Logic of Action Two: Applications and Criticism from the Austrian School*. Cheltenham: Edward Elgar Publishing.
———. 1998. *The Ethics of Liberty*. New York: New York University Press.

———. 2006. *For a New Liberty: The Libertarian Manifesto*. 2nd ed. Auburn: The Ludwig von Mises Institute.

———. 2009. *Man Economy and State with Power and Market*. Scholar's 2nd ed. Auburn: The Ludwig von Mises Institute.

Rozumalski, Jason Ross. 2017. 'Lords of All They Survey: The Social and Economic Origins of the English State, c. 1520–1620'. University of California, Berkeley.

Russell, Daniel C. 2010. 'Embodiment and Self-Ownership'. *Social Philosophy and Policy* 27 (1): 135–65.

———. 2018. 'Self-Ownership as a Form of Ownership'. In *The Oxford Handbook of Freedom*, edited by David Schmidtz and Carmen E. Pavel. Oxford: Oxford University Press.

Ryan, Cheyney C. 1977. 'Yours, Mine, and Ours: Property Rights and Individual Liberty'. *Ethics* 87 (2): 126–241.

Saint Augustine. 1984. *Concerning the City of God Against the Pagans*. Edited by Henry Bettenson. London: Penguin.

Salter, Alexander William. 2015a. 'Rights to the Realm: Reconsidering Western Political Development'. *American Political Science Review* 109 (4): 725–34.

———. 2015b. 'Sovereignty as Exchange of Political Property Rights'. *Public Choice* 165: 79–96.

———. 2016a. 'Political Property Rights and Governance Outcomes: A Theory of the Corporate Polity'. *Journal of Private Enterprise* 31 (4): 1–20.

———. 2016b. 'Post-Cameralist Governance: Towards a Robust Political Economy of Bureaucracy'. *Economic Affairs* 36 (3): 294–308.

———. Forthcoming. 'Political Property Rights and Entangled Political Economy'. In *Emergence, Entanglement, and Political Economy*, edited by David Herbert and Diana Thomas. Springer.

Salter, Alexander William, and Andrew Young. 2019. 'Polycentric Sovereignty: The Medieval Constitution, Governance Quality, and the Wealth of Nations'. *Social Science Quarterly* 100 (4): 1241–53.

Salter, John. 2001. 'Hugo Grotius: Property and Consent'. *Political Theory* 29 (4): 537–55.

Salmond, John W. 1902. *Jurisprudence or the Theory of the Law*. London: Stevens and Haynes.

Sayre-McCord, Geoffrey. 2016. 'Hume on the Artificial Virtues'. In *The Oxford Handbook of Hume*, edited by Paul Russell. New York: Oxford University Press.

Scanlon, Thomas. 1976. 'Nozick on Rights, Liberty, and Property'. *Philosophy and Public Affairs* 6: 3–25.

Schlatter, Richard. 1951. *Private Property: The History of an Idea*. London: Allen and Unwin.

Schmidtz, David. 1990. 'When Is Original Appropriation Required?' *The Monist* 3: 504–18.

———. 1991. *The Limits of Government: An Essay on the Public Goods Argument*. Boulder: Westview Press.

———. 1994. 'The Institution of Property'. *Social Philosophy and Policy* 11: 42–62.

———. 1996. 'Critical Notice: An Essay on Rights by Hillel Steiner'. *Canadian Journal of Philosophy* 26 (2): 283–302.

———. 2005. 'History and Pattern'. *Social Philosophy and Policy* 2 (1): 148–77.

———. 2006. *The Elements of Justice*. Cambridge: Cambridge University Press.

———. 2009. 'Functional Property, Real Justice'. In *European Liberal Forum*. Berlin.

———. 2010. 'Property and Justice'. *Social Philosophy and Policy* 27 (1): 79–100.

———. 2011a. 'Nonideal Theory: What It Is and What It Needs to Be'. *Ethics* 121 (4): 772–96.

———. 2011b. 'Property'. In *The Oxford Handbook of the History of Political Philosophy*, edited by George Klosko. Oxford: Oxford University Press.

———. 2017a. 'Realistic Idealism'. In *Methods in Analytical Political Theory*, edited by Adrian Blau. Cambridge: Cambridge University Press.

———. 2017b. 'After Solipsism'. In *Oxford Studies in Normative Ethics*, edited by Mark Timmons. Vol. 6. Oxford: Oxford University Press.

Schmitt, Carl. 1996. *The Concept of the Political*. Chicago: University of Chicago Press.

Scott, James C. 1995. 'State Simplifications: Nature, Space and People'. *The Journal of Political Philosophy* 3 (3): 191–223.

———. 1996. 'State Simplifications: Nature, Space, and People'. *Noûs* 38: 42–85.

———. 1998. *Seeing Like a State: How Certain Schemes to Improve the Human Condition Have Failed*. New Haven, CT: Yale University Press.

———. 2017. *Against the Grain: A Deep History of the Earliest States*. New Haven, CT: Yale University Press.

Searle, John R. 1969. *Speech Acts: An Essay in the Philosophy of Language*. Cambridge: Cambridge University Press.

———. 1995. *The Construction of Social Reality*. New York: Simon & Schuster.

———. 2010. *Making the Social World*. Oxford: Oxford University Press.

Seipp, David J. 1994. 'The Concept of Property in the Early Common Law'. *Law and History Review* 12 (1): 29–91.

Sen, Amartya. 1987. *On Ethics and Economics*. Oxford: Blackwell.

Sinclair, Thomas. 2018. 'The Power of Public Positions: Official Roles in Kantian Legitimacy'. In *Oxford Studies in Political Philosophy*, edited by David Sobel, Peter Vallentyne, and Steven Wall. Vol. 4. Oxford: Oxford University Press.

Simmonds, Nigel. 1998. 'Rights at the Cutting Edge'. In *A Debate Over Rights: Philosophical Enquiries*, edited by Matthew H. Kramer, Nigel E. Simmonds, and Hillel Steiner. Oxford: Oxford University Press.

Simmons, A. John. 1992. *The Lockean Theory of Rights*. Princeton, NJ: Princeton University Press.

———. 2001. *Justification and Legitimacy: Essays on Rights and Obligations*. Cambridge: Cambridge University Press.

Simpson, Thomas W. 2017. 'The Impossibility of Republican Freedom'. *Philosophy and Public Affairs* 45 (1): 27–53.

Singer, Joseph William. 1982. 'The Legal Rights Debate in Analytical Jurisprudence From Bentham to Hohfeld'. *Wisconsin Law Review* 1982 (6): 975–1060.

Smith, G. W. 1976. 'Review of Anarchy, State, and Utopia by Robert Nozick'. *Philosophical Books* 17 (2): 87–90.

Smith, Henry E. 2007. 'Intellectual Property as Property: Delineating Entitlements in Information'. *The Yale Law Journal* 116 (8): 1742–822.

———. 2012. 'Property as the Law of Things'. *Harvard Law Review* 125: 1691–726.

Sobel, David. 2012. 'Backing Away from Libertarian Self-Ownership'. *Ethics* 123: 32–60.

———. 2013. 'Self-Ownership and the Conflation Problem'. In *Oxford Studies in Normative Ethics*, edited by Mark Timmons. Vol. 3. Oxford: Oxford University Press.

———. 2016. 'The Point of Self-Ownership'. In *The Oxford Handbook of Freedom*, edited by David Schmidtz and Carmen E. Pavel. Oxford: Oxford University Press.

Spafford, Jesse. 2000. 'Does Initial Appropriation Create New Obligations?' *Journal of Ethics and Social Philosophy* 17 (2): 228–38.

Spector, Horacio. 1992. *Autonomy and Rights*. Oxford: Clarendon Press.

Spencer, Herbert. 1851. *Social Statics*. London: John Chapman.

Spooner, Lysander. 1855. *The Law of Intellectual Property; or an Essay on the Right of Authors and Inventors to a Perpetual Property in Their Ideas*. Boston, MA: Bela Marsh.

Sreenivasan, Gopal. 2005. 'A Hybrid Theory of Claim Rights'. *Oxford Journal of Legal Studies* 25 (2): 257–74.

———. 2010. 'Duties and Their Direction'. *Ethics* 120 (3): 465–94.

Steiner, Hillel. 1974a. 'Individual Liberty'. *Proceedings of the Aristotelian Society* 75: 33–50.

———. 1974b. 'The Natural Right to Equal Freedom'. *Mind* 83 (330): 194–210.

———. 1977a. 'Justice and Entitlement'. *Ethics* 87 (2): 150–52.

———. 1977b. 'The Natural Right to the Means of Production'. *The Philosophical Quarterly* 27 (10): 41–49.

———. 1977c. 'The Structure of a Set of Compossible Rights'. *The Journal of Philosophy* 74 (12): 767–75.

———. 1987. 'Capitalism, Justice and Equal Starts'. *Social Philosophy and Policy* 5 (1): 49–71.

———. 1994. *An Essay on Rights*. Oxford: Blackwell.

———. 1998a. 'Critical Notices: A Reply'. *International Journal of Philosophical Studies* 6 (1): 128–37.

———. 1998b. 'Working Rights'. In *A Debate Over Rights: Philosophical Enquiries*, edited by Matthew H. Kramer, Nigel E. Simmonds, and Hillel Steiner. Oxford: Oxford University Press.

———. 1999. 'Just Taxation and International Redistribution'. *Nomos* 41: 171–91.

———. 2009. 'Responses'. In *Hillel Steiner and the Anatomy of Justice: Themes and Challenges*, edited by Stephen de Wijze and Ian Carter. Oxford: Routledge.

———. 2013. 'Directed Duties and Inalienable Rights'. *Ethics* 123 (2): 230–44.

———. 2011. 'Sharing Mother Nature's Gifts: A Reply to Quong and Miller'. *The Journal of Political Philosophy* 19 (1): 110–23.

———. 2017. 'Corrective Rights'. In *New Essays on the Nature of Rights*. Oxford: Hart Publishing.

Stern, James Y. 2017. 'The Essential Structure of Property Law'. *Michigan Law Review* 115: 1167–212.

Stevenson, Glenn G. 1991. *Common Property Economics: A General Theory and Land Use Applications*. Cambridge: Cambridge University Press.

Stilz, Anna. 2009. *Liberal Loyalty: Freedom, Obligation, and the State*. Princeton: Princeton University Press.

———. 2011. 'Nations, States, and Territory'. *Ethics* 121: 572–601.

———. 2012. 'Why Does the State Matter Morally? Political Obligation and Particularity'. In *Varieties of Sovereignty and Citizenship*, edited by Sigal R. Ben-Porath and Roger M. Smith. Philadelphia: University of Pennsylvania Press.

———. 2014. 'Provisional Right and Non-State Peoples'. In *Kant and Colonialism: Historical and Critical Perspectives*, edited by Katrin Flikschuh and Lea Ypi. Oxford: Oxford University Press.

———. 2018. 'Property Rights: Natural or Conventional?' In *The Routledge Handbook of Libertarianism*, edited by Jason Brennan, Bas van der Vossen, and David Schmidtz. New York: Routledge.

———. 2019. *Territorial Sovereignty: A Philosophical Exploration*. Oxford: Oxford University Press.

Stromberg, Joseph R. 1995. 'English Enclosures and Soviet Collectivisation: Two Instances of an Anti-Peasant Mode of Development'. *Agorist Quarterly* 1.

Suter, Ronald. 1989. *Interpreting Wittgenstein: A Cloud of Philosophy, and a Drop of Grammar*. Philadelphia, PA: Temple University Press.

Tebble, Adam J. 2016. 'On the Circumstances of Justice'. *European Journal of Political Theory* Online first.

Thomson, Judith Jarvis. 1971. 'A Defense of Abortion'. *Philosophy and Public Affairs* 1: 47–66.

———. 1986. *Rights, Restitution and Risk*. Cambridge: Harvard University Press.

———. 1990. *The Realm of Rights*. Cambridge: Harvard University Press.

Tomasi, John. 1991. 'Individual Rights and Community Virtues'. *Ethics* 101 (3): 521–36.

Tomasi, John, and Matt Zwolinski. 2012. 'A Bleeding Heart History of Libertarianism'. *Cato Unbound* (blog). www.cato-unbound.org/2012/04/02/matt-zwolinski-john-tomasi/bleeding-heart-history-libertarianism.

———. Forthcoming. *A Brief History of Libertarianism*. Princeton, NJ: Princeton University Press.

Tuck, Richard. 1979. *Natural Rights Theories: Their Origin and Development*. Cambridge: Cambridge University Press.

Tully, James. 1994. 'Aboriginal Property and Western Theory: Recovering A Middle Ground'. *Social Philosophy and Policy* 11: 153–80.

Valentini, Laura. 2011. 'Coercion and (Global) Justice'. *American Political Science Review* 105 (1): 205–20.

———. 2012. 'Kant, Ripstein and the Circle of Freedom: A Critical Note'. *European Journal of Philosophy* 20 (3): 450–59.

Vallentyne, Peter. 2000. 'Introduction: Left-Libertarianism – A Primer'. In *Left-Libertarianism and Its Critics: The Contemporary Debate*, edited by Peter Vallentyne and Hillel Steiner. New York: Palgrave Macmillan.

———. 2006. 'Against Maximizing Act Consequentialism'. In *Contemporary Debates in Moral Theory*, edited by James Dreier. New York: Blackwell.

van der Vossen, Bas. 2009. 'What Counts as Original Appropriation?' *Politics, Philosophy and Economics* 8: 355–73.

———. 2015a. 'Imposing Duties and Original Appropriation'. *The Journal of Political Philosophy* 23: 64–85.

———. 2015b. 'Locke on Territorial Rights'. *Political Studies* 63: 712–28.

———. 2020. 'As Good as "Enough and as Good"'. *The Philosophical Quarterly* Online first.
Varden, Helga. 2008. 'Kant's Non-Voluntarist Conception of Political Obligations: Why Justice Is Impossible in the State of Nature'. *Kantian Review* 13: 1–45.
———. 2010. 'Kant's Non Absolutist Conception of Political Legitimacy – How Private Rights "Concludes" Private Right in the "Doctrine of Right"'. *Kant-Studien* 101 (3): 331–51.
von Pufendorf, Samuel. 1934. *De Jure Naturae et Gentium, Libri Octo*. Translated by Charles Henry Oldfather and William Abbott Oldfather. Oxford: Clarendon Press.
Waldron, Jeremy. 1981. 'A Right to Do Wrong'. *Ethics* 92 (1): 21–39.
———. 1983. 'Two Worries About Mixing One's Labour'. *The Philosophical Quarterly* 33: 37–44.
———. 1988a. *The Right to Private Property*. New York: Oxford University Press.
———. 1988b. 'When Justice Replaces Affection: The Need for Rights'. *Harvard Journal of Law and Public Policy* 11 (3): 625–47.
———. 1991. 'Homelessness and the Issue of Freedom'. *UCLA Law Review* 39: 295–324.
———. 1992. 'Superseding Historic Injustice'. *Ethics* 103 (1): 4–28.
———. 1993. 'Special Ties and Natural Duties'. *Philosophy and Public Affairs* 22 (1): 3–30.
———. 1996. 'Kant's Legal Positivism'. *Harvard Law Review* 109 (7): 1535–66.
———. 1999. *The Dignity of Legislation*. Cambridge: Cambridge University Press.
———. 2011. 'The Principle of Proximity'. In *Public Law and Legal Theory Research Paper Series*. http://ssrn.com/abstract=1742413.
Walras, Léon Walrus. 1954. *Elements of Pure Economics: Or the Theory of Social Wealth*. Translated by William Jaffé. London: Routledge.
Wellman, Carl. 1985. *A Theory of Rights: Persons Under Law, Institutions, and Morals*. Lanham: Rowman and Allanheld.
———. 1995. *Real Rights*. Oxford: Oxford University Press.
———. 2000. 'Review of a Debate Over Rights by Matthew H. Kramer, Nigel E. Simmonds, and Hillel Steiner'. *Mind* 106 (436): 954–56.
Wenar, Leif. 1998. 'Original Acquisition of Private Property'. *Mind* 107: 799–819.
———. 2005. 'The Nature of Rights'. *Philosophy and Public Affairs* 33 (3): 223–52.
———. 2013. 'The Nature of Claim-Rights'. *Ethics* 123 (2): 202–29.
Wendt, Fabian. 2018. 'The Sufficiency Proviso: A Case for Moderate Libertarianism'. In *The Routledge Handbook of Libertarianism*, edited by Jason Brennan, Bas van der Vossen, and David Schmidtz. New York: Routledge.
Wheeler, Samuel C. III. 1980. 'Natural Body Rights and Body Rights'. *Noûs* 14: 171–93.
Wilson, Bart J. 2020. *The Property Species: Mine, Yours, and the Human Mind*. New York: Oxford University Press.
Williams, Bernard. 2005. *In the Beginning Was the Deed: Realism and Moralism in Political Argument*. Edited by Geoffrey Hawthorne. Princeton, NJ: Princeton University Press.

Williams, Glanville. 1956. 'The Concept of Legal Liberty'. *Columbia Law Review* 56: 1129–50.

Williams, Roger John. 1953. *Free and Unequal: The Biological Basis of Individual Liberty*. Austin: University of Texas Press.

Winch, Peter. 1990. *The Idea of a Social Science and Its Relation to Philosophy*. 2nd ed. London: Routledge.

Wittgenstein, Ludwig. 1982. *Last Writings on the Philosophy of Psychology, Vol. 1: Preliminary Studies for Part 2 of Philosophical Investigations*. Edited by Georg Henrik von Wright and Heikki Nyman. Translated by C. G. Luckhardt and Maximillian A. E. Aue. Chicago: University of Chicago Press.

———. 1986. *Philosophical Investigations*. Translated by G. E. M. Anscombe. 3rd ed. Oxford: Blackwell.

Wolff, Jonathan. 1991. *Robert Nozick: Property, Justice and the Minimal State*. Oxford: Polity.

Wündisch, Jaochim. 2013. 'Nozick's Proviso: Misunderstood and Misappropriated'. *Rationality, Markets and Morals* 4: 205–20.

Zwolinski, Matt. 2008. 'The Separateness of Persons and Liberal Theory'. *The Journal of Value Inquiry* 42: 147–65.

———. 2014. 'Libertarianism and Pollution'. *Philosophy and Public Policy Quarterly* 32: 9–21.

———. 2016. 'The Libertarian Nonaggression Principle'. *Social Philosophy and Policy* 32 (2): 62–90.

Index

FSC
www.fsc.org
MIX
Papier | Fördert
gute Waldnutzung
FSC® C083411

Kolibri 360 GmbH
Ferdinand-Jühlke-Straße 7
99095 Erfurt, Deutschland
produktsicherheit@kolibri360.de